Tomasz Stępniewski, George Soroka (eds.)

UKRAINE AFTER MAIDAN

Revisiting Domestic and Regional Security

ibidem-Verlag
Stuttgart

Bibliografische Information der Deutschen Nationalbibliothek
Die Deutsche Nationalbibliothek verzeichnet diese Publikation in der Deutschen Nationalbibliografie; detaillierte bibliografische Daten sind im Internet über http://dnb.d-nb.de abrufbar.

Bibliographic information published by the Deutsche Nationalbibliothek
Die Deutsche Nationalbibliothek lists this publication in the Deutsche Nationalbibliografie; detailed bibliographic data are available in the Internet at http://dnb.d-nb.de.

∞

Gedruckt auf alterungsbeständigem, säurefreien Papier
Printed on acid-free paper

ISSN: 1614-3515

ISBN-13: 978-3-8382-1075-9

© *ibidem*-Verlag
Stuttgart 2018

Alle Rechte vorbehalten

Das Werk einschließlich aller seiner Teile ist urheberrechtlich geschützt. Jede Verwertung außerhalb der engen Grenzen des Urheberrechtsgesetzes ist ohne Zustimmung des Verlages unzulässig und strafbar. Dies gilt insbesondere für Vervielfältigungen, Übersetzungen, Mikroverfilmungen und elektronische Speicherformen sowie die Einspeicherung und Verarbeitung in elektronischen Systemen.

All rights part of this publication may be reproduced, stored in or introduced into a retrieval system, or transmitted, in any form, or by any means (electronic, mechanical, photocopying, recording or otherwise) without the prior written permission of the publisher. Any person who does any unauthorized act in relation to this publication may be liable to criminal prosecution and civil claims for damages.

Printed in the EU

Contents

Tomasz Stępniewski and George Soroka
Introduction: Ukraine in Fragile Security Contexts 7

Yuval Weber
The Juiciest Fruit Left on the Vine:
Ukraine as a Bargaining Failure 13

Tomasz Stępniewski
The Ukraine Crisis, NATO, and Eastern Europe's
Grey Zone of Security 45

Jussi Laine
The Ukraine Crisis and Ontological (In)Security:
Implications from a Finnish Perspective 63

George Soroka
Assessing Domestic Security Challenges in
Post-Maidan Ukraine: Two Critical Dimensions 93

Yuriy Matsiyevsky
Western Leverage, Russia's Resistance and the Breakdown
of the Yanukovych Regime 135

Joanna Fomina
On Ukraine's Geopolitical Identity:
Public Opinion Dynamics on NATO Accession in
the Aftermath of the War with Russia 167

Andrzej Szabaciuk
**Demography and Migration as Determinants of
Ukrainian Policy in the Context of State Security....................... 191**

Notes on Contributors 211

Soviet and Post-Soviet Politics and Society (SPPS) Vol. 188
ISSN 1614-3515

General Editor: Andreas Umland,
Institute for Euro-Atlantic Cooperation, Kyiv, umland@stanfordalumni.org

Commissioning Editor: Max Jakob Horstmann,
London, mjh@ibidem.eu

EDITORIAL COMMITTEE*

DOMESTIC & COMPARATIVE POLITICS
Prof. **Ellen Bos**, *Andrássy University of Budapest*
Dr. **Ingmar Bredies**, *FH Bund, Brühl*
Dr. **Andrey Kazantsev**, *MGIMO (U) MID RF, Moscow*
Prof. **Heiko Pleines**, *University of Bremen*
Prof. **Richard Sakwa**, *University of Kent at Canterbury*
Dr. **Sarah Whitmore**, *Oxford Brookes University*
Dr. **Harald Wydra**, *University of Cambridge*
SOCIETY, CLASS & ETHNICITY
Col. **David Glantz**, *"Journal of Slavic Military Studies"*
Dr. **Marlène Laruelle**, *George Washington University*
Dr. **Stephen Shulman**, *Southern Illinois University*
Prof. **Stefan Troebst**, *University of Leipzig*
POLITICAL ECONOMY & PUBLIC POLICY
Prof. em. **Marshall Goldman**, *Wellesley College, Mass.*
Dr. **Andreas Goldthau**, *Central European University*
Dr. **Robert Kravchuk**, *University of North Carolina*
Dr. **David Lane**, *University of Cambridge*
Dr. **Carol Leonard**, *Higher School of Economics, Moscow*
Dr. **Maria Popova**, *McGill University, Montreal*

FOREIGN POLICY & INTERNATIONAL AFFAIRS
Dr. **Peter Duncan**, *University College London*
Prof. **Andreas Heinemann-Grüder**, *University of Bonn*
Dr. **Taras Kuzio**, *Johns Hopkins University*
Prof. **Gerhard Mangott**, *University of Innsbruck*
Dr. **Diana Schmidt-Pfister**, *University of Konstanz*
Dr. **Lisbeth Tarlow**, *Harvard University, Cambridge*
Dr. **Christian Wipperfürth**, *N-Ost Network, Berlin*
Dr. **William Zimmerman**, *University of Michigan*
HISTORY, CULTURE & THOUGHT
Dr. **Catherine Andreyev**, *University of Oxford*
Prof. **Mark Bassin**, *Södertörn University*
Prof. **Karsten Brüggemann**, *Tallinn University*
Dr. **Alexander Etkind**, *University of Cambridge*
Dr. **Gasan Gusejnov**, *Moscow State University*
Prof. em. **Walter Laqueur**, *Georgetown University*
Prof. **Leonid Luks**, *Catholic University of Eichstaett*
Dr. **Olga Malinova**, *Russian Academy of Sciences*
Prof. **Andrei Rogatchevski**, *University of Tromsø*
Dr. **Mark Tauger**, *West Virginia University*

ADVISORY BOARD*

Prof. **Dominique Arel**, *University of Ottawa*
Prof. **Jörg Baberowski**, *Humboldt University of Berlin*
Prof. **Margarita Balmaceda**, *Seton Hall University*
Dr. **John Barber**, *University of Cambridge*
Prof. **Timm Beichelt**, *European University Viadrina*
Dr. **Katrin Boeckh**, *University of Munich*
Prof. em. **Archie Brown**, *University of Oxford*
Dr. **Vyacheslav Bryukhovetsky**, *Kyiv-Mohyla Academy*
Prof. **Timothy Colton**, *Harvard University, Cambridge*
Prof. **Paul D'Anieri**, *University of Florida*
Dr. **Heike Dörrenbächer**, *Friedrich Naumann Foundation*
Dr. **John Dunlop**, *Hoover Institution, Stanford, California*
Dr. **Sabine Fischer**, *SWP, Berlin*
Dr. **Geir Flikke**, *NUPI, Oslo*
Prof. **David Galbreath**, *University of Aberdeen*
Prof. **Alexander Galkin**, *Russian Academy of Sciences*
Prof. **Frank Golczewski**, *University of Hamburg*
Dr. **Nikolas Gvosdev**, *Naval War College, Newport, RI*
Prof. **Mark von Hagen**, *Arizona State University*
Dr. **Guido Hausmann**, *University of Munich*
Prof. **Dale Herspring**, *Kansas State University*
Dr. **Stefani Hoffman**, *Hebrew University of Jerusalem*
Prof. **Mikhail Ilyin**, *MGIMO (U) MID RF, Moscow*
Prof. **Vladimir Kantor**, *Higher School of Economics*
Dr. **Ivan Katchanovski**, *University of Ottawa*
Prof. em. **Andrzej Korbonski**, *University of California*
Dr. **Iris Kempe**, *"Caucasus Analytical Digest"*
Prof. **Herbert Küpper**, *Institut für Ostrecht Regensburg*
Dr. **Rainer Lindner**, *CEEER, Berlin*
Dr. **Vladimir Malakhov**, *Russian Academy of Sciences*

Dr. **Luke March**, *University of Edinburgh*
Prof. **Michael McFaul**, *Stanford University, Palo Alto*
Prof. **Birgit Menzel**, *University of Mainz-Germersheim*
Prof. **Valery Mikhailenko**, *The Urals State University*
Prof. **Emil Pain**, *Higher School of Economics, Moscow*
Dr. **Oleg Podvintsev**, *Russian Academy of Sciences*
Prof. **Olga Popova**, *St. Petersburg State University*
Dr. **Alex Pravda**, *University of Oxford*
Dr. **Erik van Ree**, *University of Amsterdam*
Dr. **Joachim Rogall**, *Robert Bosch Foundation Stuttgart*
Prof. **Peter Rutland**, *Wesleyan University, Middletown*
Prof. **Marat Salikov**, *The Urals State Law Academy*
Dr. **Gwendolyn Sasse**, *University of Oxford*
Prof. **Jutta Scherrer**, *EHESS, Paris*
Prof. **Robert Service**, *University of Oxford*
Mr. **James Sherr**, *RIIA Chatham House London*
Dr. **Oxana Shevel**, *Tufts University, Medford*
Prof. **Eberhard Schneider**, *University of Siegen*
Prof. **Olexander Shnyrkov**, *Shevchenko University, Kyiv*
Prof. **Hans-Henning Schröder**, *SWP, Berlin*
Prof. **Yuri Shapoval**, *Ukrainian Academy of Sciences*
Prof. **Viktor Shnirelman**, *Russian Academy of Sciences*
Dr. **Lisa Sundstrom**, *University of British Columbia*
Dr. **Philip Walters**, *"Religion, State and Society"*, *Oxford*
Prof. **Zenon Wasyliw**, *Ithaca College, New York State*
Dr. **Lucan Way**, *University of Toronto*
Dr. **Markus Wehner**, *"Frankfurter Allgemeine Zeitung"*
Dr. **Andrew Wilson**, *University College London*
Prof. **Jan Zielonka**, *University of Oxford*
Prof. **Andrei Zorin**, *University of Oxford*

* While the Editorial Committee and Advisory Board support the General Editor in the choice and improvement of manuscripts for publication, responsibility for remaining errors and misinterpretations in the series' volumes lies with the books' authors.

Soviet and Post-Soviet Politics and Society (SPPS)
ISSN 1614-3515

Founded in 2004 and refereed since 2007, SPPS makes available affordable English-, German-, and Russian-language studies on the history of the countries of the former Soviet bloc from the late Tsarist period to today. It publishes between 5 and 20 volumes per year and focuses on issues in transitions to and from democracy such as economic crisis, identity formation, civil society development, and constitutional reform in CEE and the NIS. SPPS also aims to highlight so far understudied themes in East European studies such as right-wing radicalism, religious life, higher education, or human rights protection. The authors and titles of all previously published volumes are listed at the end of this book. For a full description of the series and reviews of its books, see www.ibidem-verlag.de/red/spps.	**Recent Volumes**
	187 *Marina Lebedeva* Russian Studies of International Relations From the Soviet Past to the Post-Cold-War Present With a foreword by Andrei P. Tsygankov ISBN 978-3-8382-0851-0
	188 *Tomasz Stępniewski, George Soroka (eds.)* Ukraine after Maidan Revisiting Domestic and Regional Security ISBN 978-3-8382-1075-9
	189 *Petar Cholakov* Ethnic Entrepreneurs Unmasked Political Institutions and Ethnic Conflicts in Contemporary Bulgaria ISBN 978-3-8382-1189-3
	190 *A. Salem, G. Hazeldine, D. Morgan (eds.)* Higher Education in Post-Communist States Comparative and Sociological Perspectives ISBN 978-3-8382-1183-1
Editorial correspondence & manuscripts should be sent to: Dr. Andreas Umland, Institute for Euro-Atlantic Cooperation, vul. Volodymyrska 42, off. 21, UA-01030 Kyiv, Ukraine	*191* *Igor Torbakov* After Empire Nationalist Imagination and Symbolic Politics in Russia and Eurasia in the Twentieth and Twenty-First Century With a foreword by Serhii Plokhy ISBN 978-3-8382-1217-3
	192 *Aleksandr Burakovskiy* Jewish-Ukrainian Relations in Late and Post-Soviet Ukraine Articles, Lectures and Essays from 1986 to 2016 ISBN 978-3-8382-1210-4
Business correspondence & review copy requests should be sent to: *ibidem* Press, Leuschnerstr. 40, 30457 Hannover, Germany; tel.: +49 511 2622200; fax: +49 511 2622201; spps@ibidem.eu.	*193* *Olga Burlyuk, Natalia Shapovalova (eds.)* Civil Society in Post-Euromaidan Ukraine From Revolution to Consolidation With a foreword by Richard Youngs ISBN 978-3-8382-1216-6
Authors, reviewers, referees, and editors for (as well as all other persons sympathetic to) SPPS are invited to join its networks at www.facebook.com/group.php?gid=52638198614 www.linkedin.com/groups?about=&gid=103012 www.xing.com/net/spps-ibidem-verlag/	*194* *Franz Preissler* Positionsverteidigung, Imperialismus oder Irredentismus? Russland und die „Russischsprachigen", 1991–2015 ISBN 978-3-8382-1262-3
	196 *Anke Giesen* „Wie kann denn der Sieger ein Verbrecher sein?" Eine diskursanalytische Untersuchung der russlandweiten Debatte über Konzept und Verstaatlichungsprozess der Lagergedenkstätte „Perm'-36" im Ural ISBN 978-3-8382-1284-5

Introduction:
Ukraine in Fragile Security Contexts

For nearly three decades now, we have been witnessing the gradual demise of the bi-polar international order first established in a world dominated by the Cold War. This outcome was inevitable; after the collapse of the Soviet Union the global environment, along with its attendant geopolitical realities, changed markedly. But the slow-motion disintegration of this security system has ushered in the advent of a still-inchoate replacement, the parameters and meaning of which continue to be vigorously contested. Consequently, it is proving difficult to characterize the new system that is emerging, one wherein ascendant powers that do not share the values of the West are attempting to construct a multi-polar and ideologically diverse world. Illustrative of this are Russia's efforts to sway Ukraine back into its orbit. Proceeding through political and military means as well as various "hybrid" tactics, they exemplify what Poland's former Foreign Minister, Adam Rotfield, has labelled a "new game without rules."[1]

Indeed, the conflict in—and over—Ukraine dramatically illustrates the extent to which the post-Cold War international order, along with regional- and state-level dynamics in the post-communist space, have evolved since the 1990s. The essential nature of this change, as well as its practical implications, requires careful study and analysis. To this end the Ukrainian crisis provides a useful lens into wider processes, as it is not merely a domestic issue but also an international crisis, bracketed by the rivalry between two external powers—the so-called "Western world," as represented by the US and EU (though these entities do not agree with one another in many important respects) and a Russian Federation eager to restore and defend a privileged sphere of influence in what Russian officials refer to as its "near abroad." As a result, while the internal impact of events such as the annexation of Crimea by Russia in March 2014 and the outbreak of separatist violence in the Donbas region soon thereafter has been profound for Ukraine, the external ramifications have been no less significant. Broadly speaking, the unwillingness of Russia, the US and the UK to uphold the assurances of Ukraine's territorial integrity that were agreed to in the 1994 Budapest Memorandum (in exchange for Kyiv relinquishing its nuclear arsenal and signing on to the Treaty on the Non-Proliferation of Nuclear Weapons) has devalued international security cooperation and thwarted efforts to prevent the proliferation of weapons of mass destruction. Concomitantly, the imposition of sanctions resulting from Moscow's actions in Ukraine has also had a negative impact on Russia's economy, postponing its integration with Europe and hindering the implementation of the Wider Europe concept, which seeks the development of a free trade and security zone spanning from Lisbon to Vladivostok.[2]

As exemplified by its involvement in the Ukrainian conflict, the Russian Federation's policies over the course of the past few years suggest that Moscow is attempting to develop a security paradigm based on being able to project military power while simultaneously limiting its dependence on the international system as it is presently configured, which the Kremlin perceives as being hypocritical (e.g., insisting others adopt liberal democratic values while countries like the US pursue a *realpolitik* foreign policy, violating state sovereignty with pre-emptive military interventions, and so forth) and fundamentally antagonistic towards its interests. This has forced international and supranational organizations such as NATO and the EU to alter how they understand and approach international security, both in regard to Ukraine and the world more generally. The geopolitical tensions that have arisen from this development have had far-reaching consequences. Attesting to this is the ongoing war in Syria, which, in pitting Russian interests against those of Western states, has highlighted the global relevance of instability in Europe's immediate neighborhood. Moreover, the consequences of such distant conflicts have proven capable of turning back on Europe, with issues like the EU's migrant fiasco and the continuing threat of Islamist terrorism on European soil only emphasizing this inherent interconnectedness.

What has happened in Ukraine also calls into question the EU's eastern policy as it currently stands, as well as Russia's emerging approach towards the post-Soviet space. Effectively, the country has become an arena of contention for two rival integration projects: that of Europe, represented by the EU and normatively envisaged as liberal-democratic politically and market-driven economically, and that of Eurasia, conceived of as an alternative, Russia-led union. But this geopolitical rivalry, today frequently cast in civilizational terms, is not confined to Ukraine; the whole of Eastern Europe is in some fashion or another embroiled in it. On the one hand, this is evident in EU projects such as the European Neighborhood Policy and the Eastern Partnership, although both initiatives have so far failed to meaningfully bolster relations between the Union and its Eastern partners. On the other hand, it is also apparent in the steps the Russian Federation has taken to undermine the independence of the erstwhile Soviet states, regarding their sovereignty as permeable and subject to Moscow's influence. As a result of these actions, systemic insecurity and regional instability have increased, developments reflected in the "frozen conflicts" that currently exist in such places as Transnistria, Abkhazia, and South Ossetia.

Unsurprisingly, in post-Maidan Ukraine Russia's policy has followed a similar script, with the Kremlin backing separatist militias in the east of the country (officially, Russia is not involved in the Ukrainian conflict, though it openly supports the breakaway regions of Luhansk and Donetsk). However, while Russia managed to successfully annex Crimea, sporadic fighting continues in the Donbas and Ukrainian public opinion has notably soured on its larger and increasingly assertive neighbor, with a December 2017 survey by the Kyiv International Institute of Sociology not only finding that the steep decline in the number of Ukrainians who exhibit a positive attitude towards Russia initially evinced in early 2014 continues to hold, but also that a plurality now support their country joining both the EU (49% for, 28% against) and NATO (41% for, 32% against).[3] This represents the geopolitical byproduct of a Ukrainian socio-political identity that appears to be coalescing around a civic conception of nationhood.[4] Meanwhile, bilateral and multi-lateral relations between the Western states and Russia, catalyzed by events in Ukraine, have reached a post-Soviet nadir.

Obviously, there is much to scrutinize in this context. However, the effects of the Maidan protests have previously been analyzed mainly in terms of Ukraine's domestic politics or relative to various dyadic relationships (e.g., Ukraine/EU, Ukraine/Russia, or even Russia/EU, with Ukraine serving as a proxy). But although these are undoubtedly important categories of inquiry (and ones that our contributing authors evaluate as well), what has not taken place thus far is any sort of sustained and meaningful analysis of how the Maidan has reverberated politically through the post-communist region, and what this means for observers in Europe and throughout the world. Consequently, the goals of this book are to provide insight into the impact the crisis is having on Ukraine's internal security and the global resonances that proceed from it, as well as to shed light on how it affects proximate countries. In this respect, our project possesses an important temporal advantage, having come together at a time when we are far enough removed from the events of late 2013 and early 2014 to have achieved some measure of objectivity in analyzing them, but yet close enough that their meaning and salience has not been eroded from the minds of participants and observers. In other words, we are still at the stage of assessing them as political scientists and international relations specialists rather than as historians.

Contributors to this volume purposely span an array of empirical and methodological approaches. Yuval Weber analyzes the ambiguous end of the Cold War and the resultant mismatch between Russia's ambitions and material capabilities, using the lens of the Ukrainian crisis to examine larger cross-sectional and longitudinal processes. Tomasz Stępniewski considers how events in Ukraine have altered the role of NATO in Eastern Europe and its relationship to what he terms the region's "grey zone" of security. Jussi Laine looks at the ontological security dilemma the Ukrainian crisis has produced in Finland and evaluates how Finnish leaders and publics have responded to it. George Soroka focuses on two critical dimensions of Ukraine's internal security, namely issues of nation-building and stateness and the degree and quality of governance, privileging their evaluation in terms of domestic dynamics but also examining how these factors relate to transnational and cross-border processes. Yuriy Matsiyevsky examines the role of external leverage over Ukraine not just from the side of the Western powers, but also from that of the Russian Federation, assessing the impact of Russian backing for the Yanukovych regime and the role played by Moscow in its subsequent breakdown. Joanna Fomina discusses the dynamics of public opinion formation in Ukraine relative to NATO accession, as well as what citizens in NATO member states think of Ukraine's potential inclusion in the defense alliance. Finally, Andrzej Szabaciuk writes about demographic factors and migration relative to domestic security and the evolving challenges Ukraine faces in this sphere.

This book is the result of an active collaboration between researchers from Finland, Poland, Russia, Ukraine and the United States. The editors would like to extend their special thanks to the contributors for the considerable time and effort they put into writing and revising these chapters. We also wish to express our gratitude to the editors and staff at ibidem-Verlag for their support (and forbearance, given how long this project took to complete!). Clearly, much more research is needed into Ukraine's security dynamics and their local, regional and global implications, particularly as the situation on the ground remains unresolved and fluid. As such, this book represents a starting point regarding what may be said about this topic. We therefore hope that readers will appreciate the authors' perspectives and come away feeling that the volume makes a positive contribution to the unfolding discussion concerning the future of Ukraine and the post-communist region, as well as the international order more generally.

Tomasz Stępniewski & George Soroka
Lublin (Poland) and Cambridge (USA), August 2018

NOTES

1. Adam Rotfeld (2014). "Porządek międzynarodowy. Parametry zmiany," *Sprawy Międzynarodowe 4*, 47: 46.
2. Andreas Umland (2015). "The Global Impact of the "Ukraine Crisis": Russia's Decline and Euro-Asiatic Security in the Early 21st Century," *Krytyka* (June), available: http://krytyka.com/en/articles/global-impact-ukraine-crisis-russias-decline-and-euro-asiatic-security-early-21st-century#sthash.ufEIB3S9.dpuf.
3. "Ukraïns'ke suspil'stvo za 25 rokiv: dinamika deiakikh sotsial'nikh pokaznikiv," available: http://www.kiis.com.ua/?lang=ukr&cat=reports&id=732&page=1. Crimea and separatist-held areas in eastern Ukraine were not surveyed.
4. See, for example, Grigore Pop-Elches and Graeme B. Robertson (2018). "Identity and Political Preferences in Ukraine—Before and After the Euromaidan," *Post-Soviet Affairs 34*, 2-3: 107–118, and Volodymyr Kulyk (2018). "Shedding Russianness, Recasting Ukrainianness: The Post-Euromaidan Dynamics of Ethnonational Identifications in Ukraine," *Post-Soviet Affairs 34*, 2-3: 119–138.

Yuval Weber

The Juiciest Fruit Left on the Vine: Ukraine as a Bargaining Failure

Russia's dissatisfaction with the current international order and the origins of its current policy towards Ukraine both stem from the ill-fated post-Cold War settlement. Mikhail Gorbachev and George H.W. Bush negotiated a peaceful denouement to the Cold War in 1989 at the Malta Summit. The USSR's collapse only two years later forced policymakers to concentrate on urgent domestic concerns, removing Russia from its traditional place at the heart of international politics. This mismatch between Russia's prestige as a great power and the meager benefits it enjoyed as a post-Soviet state generated dissatisfaction with the Euro-Atlantic alliance. I begin by evaluating the strategies Russian leaders used to raise their political standing, including accommodating the U.S.-led order, balancing with other European powers in the run-up to the Iraq War, and finally challenging that order through Eurasian integration. I argue that the final strategy sought to reduce the value of the Euro-Atlantic alliance by promoting multipolarity (BRICS), creating a Russia-led "Eurasia" bloc through tighter regional binding to compete with other blocs, and using energy windfalls to increase consumption and fund military modernization. I show that Ukraine was a linchpin of the strategy because of its industrial importance to the Russian economy and its potential as a bridge to Europe. The events of Euromaidan not only removed a friendly Ukrainian leader, but the "loss" of Ukraine meant that Russia's Eurasian integration strategy as a mechanism to revise the international order had reached its zenith. Facing a negative shift in bargaining power, Vladimir Putin selected the rational strategy: challenge Ukraine before European integration rendered any such challenge non-credible. I conclude by updating the Correlates of War Composite Index of National Capability (CINC) to evaluate in hard power terms whether Russia is able to sustain its challenge to the international order.

Introduction

Russia's dissatisfaction with the current international order and the origins of its current policy towards Ukraine both stem from the ambiguous and overlapping conclusions to the Cold War and the Soviet Union. Mikhail Gorbachev and George H.W. Bush negotiated a peaceful denouement to the Cold War in 1989 at the Malta Summit. The USSR's collapse only two years later forced Russian policymakers to concentrate on urgent domestic concerns, removing Russia from its traditional place at the heart of international politics. This mismatch between Russia's prestige as the inheritor of Soviet power and the meager benefits it enjoyed as a post-Soviet state generated dissatisfaction with the Euro-Atlantic alliance.

I begin by outlining the nature of systemic struggle, or "Cold War" as it was called in the period between 1947 and 1989, and comparing that to the current standoff between Russia and its adversaries. I demonstrate through analysis of National Material Capabilities data collected by the Correlates of War project that the level of potential conflict between Russia and its adversaries in the present standoff does not match what was possible in the first Cold War. In evaluating the hard power capabilities by which the Soviet Union and the United States maintained their challenges to each other, I show that the Soviet challenge to the U.S.-led bloc faltered by the early 1960s. In turn, I show that Russia's current attempted revisionism of the international order is similarly unsustainable on a global basis, but feasible on a regional basis should Ukraine join its Eurasian hierarchical order.

Accordingly, I evaluate Russia's Eurasian integration strategy — for which Ukraine was the linchpin — as a culmination of various strategies Russian leaders have used to raise their post-1991 political standing. Beginning with accommodating the U.S.-led order, Russian leaders also attempted to balance with other European powers in the run-up to the Iraq War and, finally, to challenge that order through Eurasian integration. I argue that the final strategy sought to reduce the value of the Euro-Atlantic alliance by promoting multi-polarity (BRICS),[1] creating a Russia-led "Eurasia" bloc through tighter regional binding to compete with other blocs, and using energy windfalls to increase consumption and fund military modernization.

Finally, I show that Ukraine's material importance to the Russian economy and its potential as a bridge to Europe made it a linchpin of this strategy whether its leaders liked it or not. The events of Euromaidan not only removed a friendly Ukrainian leader, but the "loss" of Ukraine meant that Russia's Eurasian integration strategy to revise the international order had reached its zenith in the zero-sum view of international politics that is practiced by Russia. Facing a negative shift in bargaining power, Vladimir Putin selected the rational strategy: challenge Ukraine before European integration rendered any such challenge non-credible.

Prime Minister Medvedev Raises the Issue

At the annual Munich Security Conference, the world's political and military leaders gather to discuss the most pressing global security issues. Speaking at the February 2016 iteration, Dmitri Medvedev, Prime Minister of Russia and one-time President, directly acknowledged the elephant in the room: "Speaking bluntly, we are rapidly rolling into a period of a new cold war. Russia has been presented as well-nigh the biggest threat to NATO, or to Europe, America and other countries. They show frightening films about Russians starting a nuclear war. I am sometimes confused: is this 2016 or 1962?" (Medvedev 2016).

While Mr. Medvedev was careful to note that the world is moving towards cold war but is not yet there, merely referencing the 1962 Cuban Missile Crisis and raising the specter of nuclear war raised the stakes of the ongoing struggle between Russia and its adversaries. What had started as disagreements over specific

---

[1] The "BRICS" multilateral grouping is comprised of Brazil, Russia, India, China, and South Africa and is a putative alternative source of international order beyond the Euro-Atlantic alliance led by the United States and its allies.

issues, such as conflicts in Ukraine and Syria, threatened to grow into a confrontation of two systems akin to the Cold War, that state of unremitting international hostility that lasted from roughly 1947 to 1989.

The dissatisfaction noted by the Russian prime minister, with the current international order generally and the Euro-Atlantic bloc's current policy towards Ukraine specifically, both stem from the Cold War's ill-fated settlement (Ikenberry 2001, Deudney and Ikenberry 2009). Mikhail S. Gorbachev and George H.W. Bush negotiated a peaceful denouement to the Cold War in December 1989 at the Malta Summit. Their prevailing sense of relief was on clear display with the General Secretary asserting, "I assured the President of the United States that I will never start a hot war against the USA. The world is leaving one epoch and entering another. We are at the beginning of a long road to a lasting, peaceful era. The threat of force, mistrust, psychological and ideological struggle should all be things of the past." President Bush replied, "We can realize a lasting peace and transform the East-West relationship to one of enduring co-operation. That is the future that Chairman Gorbachev and I began right here in Malta" (BBC 1989).

The resolution that was reached by the Soviet and American leaders reflected recognition of the events happening across Central Europe. Democratic activists and moderate insiders had brought down socialist governments over the preceding weeks (Garton Ash 1999), and Gorbachev deliberately declined to intervene on behalf of his ostensible allies to secure Western—especially American and German—support for his own embattled reform project at home (Reuters 1989).[2] From 1947 to 1989, systemic confrontation had produced a geopolitical contest across the globe (Westad 2005) and the threat of nuclear Armageddon (Hoffman 2009) that was easily one of the most dangerous periods in human history. Gorbachev

---

2   Then-Soviet Foreign Ministry spokesman Gennadi I. Gerasimov was memorably quoted as saying: "We now have the Frank Sinatra doctrine. He has a song, I Did It My Way. So every country decides on its own which road to take." When asked whether this would include Moscow accepting the rejection of communist parties in the Soviet bloc. He replied: "That's for sure... political structures must be decided by the people who live there."

traded the threat of annihilation for external financial and diplomatic support of internal goals (Sarotte 2014).

The Europe envisioned by Bush and especially Gorbachev following this momentous policy shift was one in which some new integrative framework that could balance American, European, and Soviet interests would replace systemic confrontation. Prior to any notion of NATO expansion or even the existence of an independent Russia, no contemporary observer doubted that the Soviet Union would retain a leading role in European security given its overwhelming size, traditional security interests, and military capabilities (Kramer 2009, Kornushov 2014, Goldgeier 2016, Shifrinson 2016).

The international order that Gorbachev agreed to at that time was still to be determined, but the contours were clear enough: a "common European home" (Roland 1990, Risse-Kappen 1994) and some version of great power condominium with the West (Garthoff 1994) that would permit a fully transformed and vibrant domestic economy and society (Brown 1997). Whereas Soviet leaders could live with an international order that began at the Malta Summit in 1989, Russian leaders had to live with the one that actually existed from 1991 onwards—a smaller, poorer, and more bewildered state. The Soviet Union's collapse forced Russian policymakers to concentrate on urgent domestic concerns, such as maintaining the food supply to the cities from the countryside and staving off urban starvation and civil war (Gaidar 2010), restoring markets and the currency itself (Leitzel 1995, Seabright 1999, Woodruff 2000), holding together a fracturing state with multiple claims on sovereignty (Slocum 1999), conducting a vicious and seemingly endless war in the North Caucasus (Politkovskaya 2009), and defending state capacity against increasing levels of sub-state violence and corruption (Varese 2001).

Under those conditions, Russia withdrew from active and consistent participation in international politics (Lynch 2002). From Gorbachev's purposeful retrenchment, such as removing a half-million troops from Eastern Europe and cutting off subsidies to marginal socialist clients (Gaidar 2010) to the foreign policy confusion of trying to determine national identity (Tishkov 1995, Shevel 2011) and interests in an uncertain international environment, this period of Russian retrenchment provided an explicit mismatch between Russia's prestige as a great power and the meager benefits it enjoyed as a post-Soviet state that has proved far more difficult to revise.[3] As Richard Sakwa (2017) put it:

> Two incompatible narratives came into conflict after the Eastern Bloc began to crumble in 1989. For the West, nothing needed to change. The Atlantic community had effectively won the Cold War, demonstrating the superiority of the Western order, and thus all that was required was for Russia to join the expanded Western community. The door was indeed opened, but the terms were not right… The West invited Russia to join an expanded Atlantic community, but Russia sought to join a transformed West and a reconfigured Europe [… where] Moscow could work with the Western powers to create a new political community as equal founding members. The historical West, with NATO and the European Union at its core, would, in the Russian idea, become a greater West, with Russia a founding member of a new political community. This was accompanied by various Gaullist ideas to establish some sort of pan-continental greater Europe, stretching from Lisbon to Vladivostok. But the Atlantic powers, fearing that Russia was trying to drive a wedge between its two wings in Europe and America, rejected these ideas.

These "incompatible narratives" have driven Russia's uneasy relationship with its Western neighbors, its inconsistent ability to shape its external environment, and a grand strategy that has cycled all the way from accommodation of the West to its current attempt to create an alternative hierarchical order to challenge the West on its own terms. This chapter is organized around the consequences of the incompatible narratives represented by the two worlds of 1989 and 1991: an undisputed Cold War has been replaced by a conflict that resembles key aspects of the earlier struggle but does not match the stakes or intensity of the first on a global level, except at the regional level.

---

3   The most famous example comes from the period following the conclusion of the Crimean War in the mid-19th century when Russian diplomat Alexander Gorchakov informed European powers that Russia would be taking a temporary breathing spell or *peredyshka* from diplomatic affairs ("*La Russie ne boude pas; elle se recueille*" or "Russia is not sulking; she is composing herself").

Russia's pursuit of external security, consistent with the world envisioned by Gorbachev at Malta in 1989, explains not only Russia's existential opposition to Ukraine's attempts to get on the path towards European Union accession but also the decision to annex Crimea and support a civil war in the eastern part of Ukraine. To make the world look more like 1989 than 1991, Russia needs Ukraine as the linchpin of its Eurasian hierarchical order to compete geopolitically with the states that its leaders consider to be their peer competitors, such as Germany, China, and the United States — undisputed great powers with regional spheres of influence. Its security, economic viability, and pathway to exist alongside Europe, China, and the United States as a co-equal great power collectively depend on Ukraine in ways unappreciated by Western observers and policymakers both now and at the time of the Euromaidan's culmination in early 2014. Then-President of Ukraine Viktor Yanukovych's abandonment of power, Kyiv, and finally Ukraine itself threatened Russia's grand strategy of securing Ukraine as the core element of its external Eurasian hierarchy. Euromaidan defined a negative shift in Russian bargaining power vis-à-vis its peer competitors and threatened Russia's ability to revise the international order.

I demonstrate the centrality of Ukraine to Russia's foreign policy aims via National Material Capabilities data collected by the Correlates of War project. These data, which are collated into a Composite Index of National Capabilities demonstrate several key insights in international relations and Russia's place within it. First, the Cold War as a systemic struggle was won and lost by the alliance networks that were built up by the United States and the Soviet Union. Second, restriction of Russia's external aims on the European continent to Eastern and Central Europe demonstrate the outsized importance of Ukraine to regional security. Finally, the loss of Ukraine as a core member of Russia's mooted Eurasian hierarchical network has pushed Russia into a high-risk, high-reward expansionist period to forestall another devastating retrenchment. The chapter concludes by evaluating Russia's ongoing challenge to the international order and the role played by

U.S. President Donald Trump, a leader providing an unprecedentedly benign external environment for Russia to pursue its external interests.

Cold War vs. "Cold War"

A central policy debate within international politics is whether Russia merits classification as a great power (Corbetta et al. 2009). Quantitative political scientists raise no objection (Danilovic 2002), and most observers would point to veto power at the United Nations Security Council, the number of men under arms, and a fearsome nuclear arsenal as confirmation of that status (SIPRI 2016). To Russian policymakers, however, the question revolves around a clear privilege accorded to undisputed great powers that it does not possess: the ability to set the agenda and rules of international political and economic interaction or to carve out exceptions for itself from the rules set by others. Russia's dissatisfaction with the post-1991 international order is that it seeks to conduct an independent foreign policy with agenda and rule-setting powers, but its prestige as a traditional great power and leading nuclear state has not been matched by actual abilities to influence international politics for a full generation (Krickovic and Weber 2017). As Gilpin (1983) and Blainey (1988) noted, where prestige does not match benefits in international politics, a state can be motivated to revise the international order. This section evaluates the key elements of "cold war"—all-encompassing systemic struggle, alliance warfare—to understand the current iteration, a "cold war" where Russia's current revisionist challenge to be considered a great power is aimed at the international order but prosecuted chiefly through regional policies (Korolev 2016). This mismatch between global ambitions and regional realities is a high-risk, high-reward proposition because it bets that Russian dissatisfaction over the Cold War settlement can be ameliorated through satisfactory resolutions of the crises in Ukraine and Syria beyond what pure hard-power measurements would merit.The controversy over Russia's current status and classification contrasts with the Cold War of 1947–1989, where no international controversy either did not have Russia as a protagonist or whose solution did not rely upon Russia in some way. That period was a systemic struggle over the institutions of international political and economic interaction, that is, the rules of the game (North 1990). Robert Legvold (2016) argues that as an historical event, the 1947–1989 Cold War can be defined most broadly as several fundamental disagreements that could not be resolved but which individually did not merit going to full (nuclear) conflict. Legvold specifically holds that five features defined the Cold War beyond mere great power rivalry:

1. Each side assumed that the confrontation was the fault of the other side, and specifically the essence of the other side caused the conflict;
2. Not simply conflict of interests but conflict of purpose;
3. The contest would not end until the other side collapsed or changed fundamentally;
4. Deals regarding specific issues would be at most transactional, not cumulative; and
5. Conflicts that occurred did not remain compartmentalized but would metastasize such that all issues were linked or linkable.

The all-encompassing ideological, developmental, and security rivalry between the United States and the Soviet Union thus becomes simpler to understand. The Soviet Union and the United States advocated compelling yet vastly different ideological and developmental visions. The Soviets offered a world in which the cruelty of free market capitalism would be ameliorated by common ownership of the means of production. The absence of the profit motive would alleviate the deprivation experienced by workers in the industrialized countries and native populations in colonized areas. The Americans countered with a world defined by the freedoms individuals possessed to choose their political and religious beliefs, occupations, and persons and organizations with whom they wished to interact. The stark differences in the two worlds meant that not only would each bloc seek to promote its own ideological and developmental vision, but they would each demonize the other: the Soviets accused the Americans of preventing liberation and progression towards higher levels of social organization and Americans routinely railed against submission to the will of a tiny, terroristic elite.

Beyond the qualitative differences between the two systems, the quantitative differences between the two states revealed the sustainability of each side's challenge to the other. The underlying motivation behind the Containment Doctrine was the belief that the Soviet Union was a powerful adversary and one that could quickly put itself on war footing should conflict between the two superpowers erupt (Gaddis 2005). U.S. policymakers during the early Cold War years believed that the Soviet Union possessed significant short-term advantages relative to the United States, whether it was a conventional conflict or the exchange of nuclear missiles (Kydd 2000). The containment strategy aimed to engage in extended deterrence, partially through military build-up and partially through the construction of an alliance network that would surround and contain the Soviet Union and its military assets and allies. By seeking to match and not explicitly overcome the Soviets, American policymakers believed that their liberal-capitalist system would prevail in a long-term conflict by being more productive (Thompson 2009).

The theory behind containment proved correct, and the strategy, expensive though it was, demonstrated its value by the 1970s and provides insight into the Russian challenge to the status quo today. The "National Material Capabilities" (NMC) dataset collected by the Correlates of War (COW) project (Singer et al. 1972, Singer 1987, Greig and Enterline 2017),[4] provides data encompassing the key components of latent military capabilities central to raising and maintaining the ability to deter and compel adversaries. For all state members of the international system, the NMC tallies annual values for total population, urban population, iron and steel

---

[4] A leading source of civil and international conflict data most well-known for its militarized interstate disputes (MIDs) datasets.

production, energy consumption, military personnel, and military expenditure.[5] Each state's share of each measure is then aggregated into an annual Composite Index of National Capabilities (CINC).

To provide an example, the following table 1 displays the United States from 1816, the first full year of NMC data. It shows that in 1816, the United States produced 80,000 tons of iron and steel, spent approximately 3.8 million nominal British pounds on defense, had 17,000 men under arms, consumed 254,000 coal-ton equivalents of energy, and had a total population of just under 8.7 million, and an urban population of just over one hundred thousand. As a share of international hard power capabilities per category, the aggregated composite index of national capabilities for the United States was 0.03970, that is, just under 4% of international material capabilities to exploit for purposes of compulsion or deterrence.

Table 1. National Material Capabilities, United States, 1816

State	Year	IRST	MILEX	MILPER	PEC	TPOP	UPOP	CINC
USA	1816	80	3823	17	254	8659	101	0.03970

As a measure of how the United States compared to the leading states of that era, the subsequent table shows that the United States, the United Kingdom, France, Prussia, Austria-Hungary, Russia, and the Ottoman Empire combined for a total of 85.75% of international hard power capabilities, reflecting European dominance of the state system. The United Kingdom's 33.66% share of national material capabilities reflects its victory in the Napoleonic Wars, displayed first in table 2 and then graphically in figure 1.

---

5   The values for the data include the following: total population (thousands), urban population (population living in cities with population greater than 100,000, in thousands), iron and steel production (thousands of tons), energy consumption (thousands of coal-ton equivalents), military personnel (thousands), and military expenditure (1816-1913: thousands of current year British pounds; 1914 and beyond: thousands of current year US dollars).

Table 2. National Material Capabilities, Great Powers, 1816

Country, 1816	USA	UK	FRA	GMY (Prussia)	AUH (Austria-Hungary)	RUS	TUR (Ottoman)	Total
CINC	0.03970	0.3366	0.1173	0.0522	0.086052	0.1643	0.0614	0.8575

Figure 1. National Material Capabilities, Great Powers, 1816

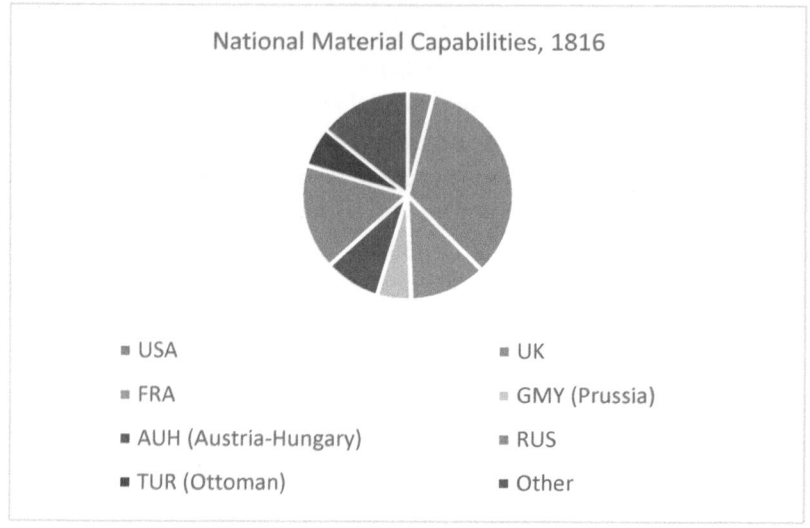

Turning to the 20th century, the CINC scores of the Soviet Union, the United States, and their respective blocs tell the story of how the Cold War settled in favor of the United States. Following the conclusion of World War II, the United States commanded just under one-third of international hard power capabilities through its victory, the exhaustion of its allies, and the defeat of its enemies. As the rest of Europe and Japan recovered from the war, and as the Soviet Union kept expanding its own economy, the United States fell in its relative share of material capabilities from the early 1950s onwards. Figure 2 shows the CINC scores for the United States and the Soviet Union from 1947 until 1993.

Figure 2. Composite Index of National Material Capabilities, USA and USSR, 1947–1993

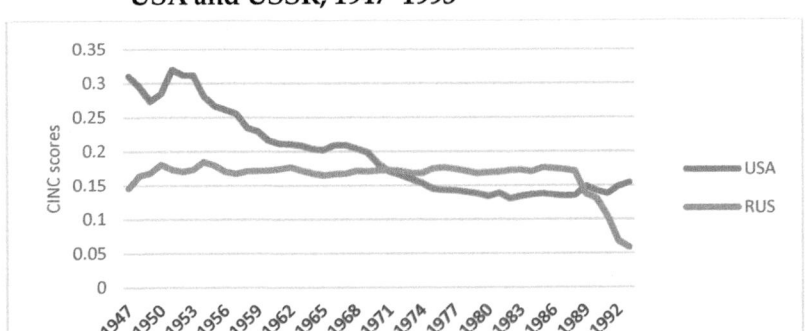

The data show that the decline of the United States from the 1950s through the beginning of the 1980s, falling from a high of 0.32 in 1951 to a low of 0.13 in 1982, was not matched by the Soviet Union, which kept a relatively consistent share of about 0.17-0.18. Even as the Soviet Union overtook the United States on a bilateral basis, a fear of Presidents Truman and Eisenhower and their senior staffs, the Soviet Union was unable to extract concessions from the United States on a bilateral basis, although détente followed in this era. The reason, of course, was that each side constructed an alliance network; tables 3a and 3b provide a list of the states and the years of their multilateral and bilateral defense commitments to and from the United States and the Soviet Union/Russia. Figure 3 follows and shows both American and Soviet-led blocs tracking each other until the late 1950s, after which economic troubles in the Soviet Union never allowed the Soviet bloc to come close again.

Table 3a. Treaty Commitments to and from the United States, 1947–2017

Rio Treaty from 1948 to the present (dates of exit in parentheses except where indicated): Argentina, Bahamas (joined 1982), Bolivia (2012), Brazil, Chile, Columbia, Costa Rica, Cuba (suspended 1962, withdrew 2012), Dominican Republic, Ecuador (2014), El Salvador, Guatemala, Haiti, Honduras, Mexico (2004), Nicaragua (2012), Panama, Paraguay, Peru, Trinidad (joined 1967), Uruguay, Venezuela (2012), Belize
NATO from 1947 to present (dates of entry in parentheses): Belgium, Canada, Denmark, France, Iceland, Italy, Luxembourg, Netherlands, Norway, Portugal, United Kingdom, Greece (1952), Turkey (1952), Germany (1955/1990), Spain (1982), Czech Republic (1999), Hungary (1999), Poland (1999), Bulgaria (2004), Estonia (2004), Latvia (2004), Lithuania (2004), Romania (2004), Slovakia (2004), Slovenia (2004), Albania (2009), Croatia (2009), Montenegro (2017)
Multilateral defense treaties (dates of entry in parentheses): Australia and New Zealand (1952)
Bilateral defense treaties (dates of entry in parentheses): Philippines (1951), Japan (1951), Spain (1953–1982, replaced by NATO membership), Republic of Korea (1953), Taiwan (1954–1979, some commitments remain), Liberia (1959), Pakistan (1959), Jamaica (1963), Barbados (1967), Grenada (1975), Suriname (1977), Saint Lucia (1979), Dominica (1979), Antigua and Barbuda (1981), Saint Vincent and Grenadine (1981), Belize (1991), Guyana (1991)

Table 3b. Treaty Commitments to and from the Soviet Union/Russia, 1947–2017

1947: Yugoslavia
1947–1990: East Germany
1947–1991: Bulgaria, Czechoslovakia, Finland, Hungary, Mongolia, Poland, Romania
1947–1995: Democratic People's Republic of Korea
1949–1959: People's Republic of China
1991–2017: Armenia, Belarus, Kazakhstan, Kyrgyzstan, Tajikistan
1991–1997: Azerbaijan, Georgia
1991–1998, 2006–2012: Uzbekistan

Figure 3. Composite Index of National Material Capabilities, USA-led and USSR-led Blocs, 1947–1993

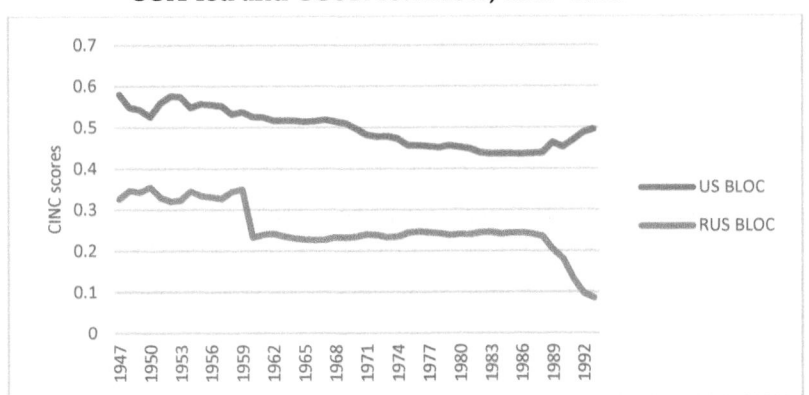

In the systemic struggle of the Cold War, time was on the side of the United States and its allies versus their adversaries. While both sides sought to avoid nuclear conflict at all costs, an underlying motivation on the Euro-Atlantic side was a clear quantitative advantage of aggregate material capabilities compared to their Soviet-led adversaries. Even if the Soviets could turn around their economies towards a war footing more quickly than Euro-Atlantic states, the arms race was more sustainable on the Euro-Atlantic side so long as war did not break out. The features identified by Legvold that made the Cold War so tense were thus fundamentally acceptable trade-offs compared to seeking peace with the Soviets on terms favorable to the Soviet Union because the status quo favored the Euro-Atlantic side.

When the Malta Summit brought the Soviet and American leaders together, they made peace but on American terms (Braumoeller 2013). In a counterfactual world in which the Soviet Union had not collapsed, we might expect that the West — particularly the United States — and a decidedly less imperial Soviet Union might have worked out a reasonable balance of power in Europe that left the Soviet Union intact while it attempted to undergo transition to a market-based economy. While counterfactual scenarios always become difficult to flesh out, then-

President Bush's attempts to support Gorbachev and specifically his speech in August 1991 to the Ukrainian parliament warning them in light of a disintegrating Yugoslavia not to expect support if they seek "independence in order to replace a far-off tyranny with a local despotism" or "promote a suicidal nationalism based upon ethnic hatred," implies what might have become U.S. policy had the Soviet Union survived (Goldgeier and McFaul 2003). In short, once the Cold War ended and the Euro-Atlantic side and Gorbachev had achieved overlapping security goals, the former had an interest in supporting Gorbachev's reforms and helping the Soviet Union become a market-oriented state to lock in those reforms. An economically vibrant and non-confrontational USSR could very well have served as the partner to the United States in co-governing international affairs in ways that Gorbachev sought then — and Putin seeks now.

Yet the Soviet Union did not survive to see 1992, and the political decisions taken in 1990 to allow the two Germanys to unify and then integrate the unified Germany into ready-made Western structures proved far more significant. The precedent of a socialist state sloughing off one political system and taking on pre-existing political, economic, social, and security institutions provided a template for the European Union's rise and eventual enlargement, NATO's renewal of purpose and eventual enlargement (Sarotte 2010), and an international environment defined by the expansion of political and economic liberalism, meaning democratization and free market capitalism (Fukuyama 1989, Huntington 1991, Frieden 2007).

During same time, Russia's own integration efforts with the West failed to succeed (Stent 2014), and, as critically, the chance to achieve historical reconciliation with new regional neighbors also passed (Stan 2009), leaving both Russia and its neighbors as insecure as before, without a collectively bargained security space and with Russia in a temporarily much weakened state (Mankoff 2009). As Marten (2017) notes, Polish efforts to secure the pathway towards NATO membership were endogenous to beliefs that this period of Russian weakness was not destined to last forever; Poland needed to be in NATO ahead of any future Russian resurgence and revanchism.

The attractiveness of the West as an institutional source (Cameron 2007, Börzel and Sedelmeier 2017) and traditional security fears emanating from the East incentivized Central European states to join Western institutions as quickly as possible to protect themselves against a future Russia potentially bent on projecting its power once again. Russia could only complain about its interests not being addressed (Pushkov 1997) while being forced to watch a former rival bloc coming "closer and closer" to its borders and being told that it had nothing to fear (Putin 2007, Lukin 2014). Some Russian voices pushed the country to adopt the posture of a nation-state with limited global aims, most poignantly Andrei Piontkovsky, director of the Moscow-based Center for Strategic Studies, who said that the NATO-Russia May 1997 Founding Act's provision for "respect for sovereignty, independence, and territorial integrity of all states and their inherent right to ensure their own security" and thus the right for states to choose their own alliances permitted "a turning point in Russia's choice between being an imperial power and a nation-state. It marked a strong decision to reject empire" (Van Herpen 2015, 283). Russia simultaneously signed, however, a Union State treaty with Belarus that hedged its imperial bets and eventually permitted a shift in official Russian opinion to reject, implicitly and then explicitly, the ability of "near abroad" neighbors to choose their own alliances (Deyermond 2004). The opposing interests between empire and regional integration created an "integration dilemma" by the West integrating former Warsaw Pact members and increasing the insecurity of those left outside (Charap and Troitsky 2013). When Russia could not join on terms different to other post-communist states—Stent (2015) quotes an unnamed Bill Clinton-era official as calling Russians "lousy joiners" when they had little appetite for entering institutions whose rules and practices they could not determine themselves—it sought to remake an entirely new hierarchical order that ultimately relied upon Ukraine as the key member.

The Rubber Hits the Road in Ukraine

The significance of Ukraine to the ongoing "cold war" is that eastward European expansion and westward Eurasian expansion turned Ukraine into an object of international rivalry: a zero-sum battle to pluck the juiciest fruit left on the vine. The European Union and Russia failed to use Ukraine as a bridge, and they jointly and unwittingly revealed the limits to both European and Eurasian integration and the underlying systemic confrontation that had developed over the previous generation.

Whereas the West transformed the rest of Europe by using its favorable postwar power position to create a durable order that attracted regional states fairly quickly and efficiently (Dinan 1999, Goldgeier 1999), Russia's own attempts at regional integration proceeded alongside its more overt attempts at bilateral cooperation and accommodation with the Euro-Atlantic alliance. The first significant Russian attempt at regional integration during the 1990s was through leadership of the Commonwealth of Independent States, which failed to gain traction as an international institution, with member states ratifying only about 10% of thousands of resolutions that were passed at the interstate level. In a time of staggering internal challenges, Russia failed to solve transnational coordination problems, provide public goods, or increase soft power attraction through pursuing historic reconciliation (Krickovic and Weber 2017).

While accommodation and cooperation failed to provide Russia a greater role in the international order either in the early years of the Boris Yeltsin presidency or immediately after the terrorist attacks of September 11, 2001, when Putin was the first foreign leader to call George W. Bush and offer significant assistance in the fight against Al-Qaida, the run-up to the Iraq War provided an opportunity to attempt another foreign policy approach: balancing. When American leaders pushed to turn the internationally recognized and supported operation against Al-Qaida and the Taliban in Afghanistan into a larger war against Iraq under the same anti-terrorism aegis, a great deal of international opposition formed. While individual states had idiosyncratic reasons for opposing a U.S.-led war against Iraq—be it commercial interests, domestic disapproval, or structural concerns over American overreach—the nearly pan-European aversion to the war permitted Putin an opportunity to put Russia in the political mainstream by joining the balancing coalition that was led by France and Germany. The collective ability of Europe to stymie or slow down the American efforts to invade and reorder Iraq proved insufficient, and the balancing coalition failed. Then-National Security Advisor Condoleezza Rice summarized U.S. reaction to those efforts as "punish France, ignore Germany, forgive Russia" (Judt 2005).

Both attempts at accommodating the United States directly and forming a coalition to balance it failed to achieve for Russian policymakers their main goal of bringing Russia back into the highest levels of international decision-making. Without financial or military hard power capabilities sufficient to alter international politics and with clearly insufficient international status, Russia's leaders returned to regional integration to try to revise the international order (Krickovic 2016). Their second, and more successful, attempt at regional integration took place through more explicitly "Eurasian" structures encompassing political, economic, and security institutions. Instead of trying to recreate proto-Soviet institutions like the Commonwealth of Independent States, Russia deepened bilateral relations with as many countries as possible, sometimes pleasantly (Ivanov 2004) and others times a bit more heavy-handedly (Stulberg 2008). Moreover, Russia pursued smaller multilateral groupings to create a more concentrated Eurasian alliance. The chief structures included the Eurasian Customs Union that eliminated customs and tariffs; the Collective Security Treaty Organization that boasted rapid response functions and prohibited members from alternative security alliance membership; and the Eurasian Economic Union (EEU) to supersede the Customs Union through additional institutional harmonization, a free trade zone, and a crisis fund to serve as an alternative lender of last resort instead of the International Monetary Fund (Blockmans et al., 2012, Tarr 2016).

The significance of why conflict emerged over Ukraine becomes easier to understand in the zero-sum context identified above by Sakwa (ibid. and 2008). The expansion of the Western order directly contested the expansion of the Eurasian order, and Ukraine itself was central to the success of the Eurasian Economic Union. Its industrial base was still heavily integrated into the Russian economy, and it posed heretofore no security threat to Russia. Without Ukraine, Russia's attempt to create a transnational bloc that would be able to compete at the regional level would reach its zenith, unable to go further or higher and destined to plateau at best without any more natural regional partner. This consequence would mean Russia's ability to revise the post-1991 international order as the leader of Eurasia would be effectively curtailed.

Table 4 depicts Russia's reliance on Ukraine. Ukraine's potential addition to the Euro-Atlantic bloc or the Russian-led bloc would provide the same absolute gain because it is the same country, but in relative impact it would add an average of 3% of hard power capability to the U.S.-led bloc and almost 22% to the Russia-led bloc.[6] In the chart below, the column marked "UKR" is Ukraine's worldwide share of hard power capabilities as discussed above, starting with about 2.3% of international hard power capabilities in 1991 when the Soviet military-industrial complex was still very large. By 2012, Ukraine's hard power had declined to 0.82% of global hard power capabilities, a 65% decline that not only demonstrates the collapse and tepid recovery of Ukraine but the disproportionate importance it holds to Russia versus the Western blocs as shown in the other columns. In the third column, the Euro-Atlantic alliance (the United States and its allies) comprised 46.83% of capabilities in 1991 and 40.83% in 2012, a change attributable

---

[6] Careful observation also demonstrates the perhaps caustic insight that the war in Ukraine is one neither Russia, Ukraine, nor the West can "afford to win," as Gaddy and Ickes (2014) put it. Ukraine's material contribution declines in absolute and relative terms as the country both becomes poorer and opposing blocs become stronger and wealthier.

almost entirely to the development of India and especially China. By combining the second and third columns in the fourth column to evaluate the difference Ukraine would make to the Western bloc, the fifth column shows a high of nearly five percent (4.95%) in 1991 declines by more than half to just a little over two percent (2.02%) in 2012, with an average of nearly three percent (2.97%) over the entire period.

The same exercise in the sixth through eighth columns demonstrates the impact Ukraine would make to the Russian-led Eurasian hierarchical order and just how important it is to Russia. In the sixth column, I report the Russian-led bloc's hard power capabilities as Russia's allies add very little statistically to Russia itself, and that number declines from 13.08% in 1991 to 4.92% in 2012, itself a decline of more than 60% from the end of the Soviet period to the beginning of Putin's third term in office. Ukraine's same absolute hard power capabilities as reported in column 2 are added to the Russian bloc's figures in column 7 to produce a numerical reality of just what Ukraine means to Eurasia. Even declining from highs around 25% in the early 2000s — meaning that Ukraine would make the future Eurasian bloc about a quarter more powerful in realist terms — by 2012, Ukraine would still represent an instant enlargement of one-sixth (16.74%) to Eurasian hard power capabilities. This figure also does not directly measure the efficiency gains of maintaining the existing military-industrial complex in a single bloc, something that has produced a number of difficulties since 2014 (Malmlöf 2016) or the value of Ukraine as any sort of "bridge to Europe" for Russia in its diplomatic maneuvers and capabilities.

Table 4. Ukraine as Potential Addition to Western vs. Russian Blocs, 1991–2012 CINC Scores

Year	UKR	US BLOC	WEST+UKR	% DIFF	RUS BLOC	RUS+UKR	% DIFF
1991	0.0232	0.4683	0.4915	0.0495	0.1308	0.1539	0.1771
1992	0.0228	0.4865	0.5093	0.0468	0.0961	0.1188	0.2369
1993	0.0194	0.4942	0.5136	0.0394	0.0848	0.1043	0.2293
1994	0.0164	0.4849	0.5013	0.0338	0.0906	0.1070	0.1812
1995	0.0154	0.4815	0.4969	0.0320	0.0858	0.1012	0.1798
1996	0.0152	0.4784	0.4936	0.0318	0.0702	0.0854	0.2164
1997	0.0148	0.4789	0.4937	0.0308	0.0672	0.0820	0.2197
1998	0.0139	0.4809	0.4948	0.0288	0.0616	0.0755	0.2252
1999	0.0143	0.4871	0.5014	0.0293	0.0608	0.0750	0.2349
2000	0.0149	0.4781	0.4930	0.0311	0.0589	0.0738	0.2523
2001	0.0151	0.4677	0.4828	0.0324	0.0610	0.0762	0.2480
2002	0.0146	0.4864	0.5010	0.0301	0.0570	0.0716	0.2566
2003	0.0146	0.4793	0.4939	0.0305	0.0568	0.0714	0.2568
2004	0.0137	0.4820	0.4957	0.0284	0.0549	0.0686	0.2490
2005	0.0118	0.4687	0.4806	0.0252	0.0474	0.0592	0.2496
2006	0.0114	0.4619	0.4733	0.0248	0.0501	0.0615	0.2286
2007	0.0112	0.4535	0.4647	0.0247	0.0501	0.0613	0.2233
2008	0.0098	0.4467	0.4565	0.0220	0.0505	0.0603	0.1950
2009	0.0089	0.4236	0.4325	0.0209	0.0485	0.0574	0.1829
2010	0.0088	0.4257	0.4346	0.0207	0.0483	0.0571	0.1824
2011	0.0087	0.4166	0.4253	0.0208	0.0492	0.0579	0.1765
2012	0.0082	0.4083	0.4165	0.0202	0.0492	0.0574	0.1674
AVG	0.0140	0.4654	0.4794	2.97%	0.0650	0.0790	21.68%

In figure 4 below, we can see Russian's core complaint depicted graphically: Ukraine means little to the West, but means a great deal for Russian interests. With the bottom line hugging the x-axis, we see Ukraine's modest but non-zero contribution to world affairs. The next line up is the Russian bloc and the third line just above that is "Eurasia." With the top two lines being the U.S.-led bloc and then the West with Ukraine, there may not be a clearer demonstration of why Ukraine is more important to Russia than it is, in general, to the West.

Figure 4. Ukraine as Potential Addition to Competing Western vs. Russian Blocs, 1991–2012

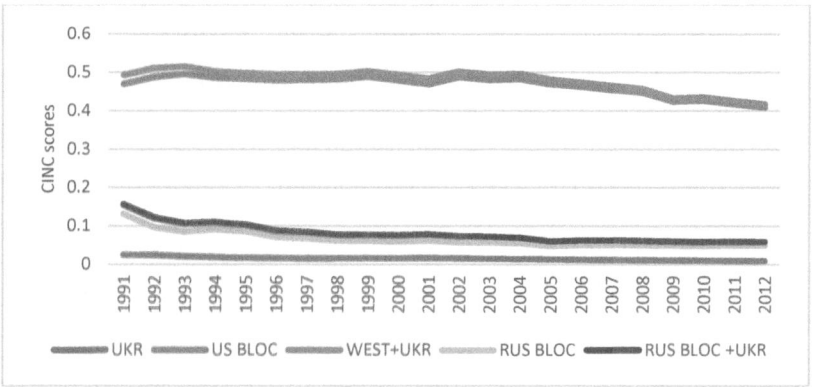

When applied to the European Union, the same analysis demonstrates the value of Ukraine to both blocs, but, again, it is much less important to "Europe" than to "Eurasia."

Table 5. Ukraine as Potential Addition to European vs. Russian Blocs, 1991–2012 CINC Scores

	UKR	EU	EU+UKR	% DIFF	RUS BLOC	RUS+UKR	% DIFF
1991	0.0232	0.1298	0.1530	0.1784	0.1308	0.1539	0.1771
1992	0.0228	0.1319	0.1547	0.1725	0.0961	0.1188	0.2369
1993	0.0194	0.1307	0.1502	0.1488	0.0848	0.1043	0.2293
1994	0.0164	0.1286	0.1450	0.1276	0.0906	0.1070	0.1812
1995	0.0154	0.1378	0.1532	0.1119	0.0858	0.1012	0.1798
1996	0.0152	0.1359	0.1511	0.1118	0.0702	0.0854	0.2164
1997	0.0148	0.1328	0.1476	0.1112	0.0672	0.0820	0.2197
1998	0.0139	0.1351	0.1490	0.1027	0.0616	0.0755	0.2252
1999	0.0143	0.1286	0.1429	0.1110	0.0608	0.0750	0.2349
2000	0.0149	0.1213	0.1362	0.1226	0.0589	0.0738	0.2523
2001	0.0151	0.1193	0.1345	0.1268	0.0610	0.0762	0.2480
2002	0.0146	0.1194	0.1341	0.1225	0.0570	0.0716	0.2566
2003	0.0146	0.1182	0.1328	0.1235	0.0568	0.0714	0.2568
2004	0.0137	0.1311	0.1448	0.1043	0.0549	0.0686	0.2490
2005	0.0118	0.1292	0.1410	0.0915	0.0474	0.0592	0.2496
2006	0.0114	0.1264	0.1379	0.0905	0.0501	0.0615	0.2286
2007	0.0112	0.1285	0.1397	0.0871	0.0501	0.0613	0.2233
2008	0.0098	0.1233	0.1331	0.0798	0.0505	0.0603	0.1950
2009	0.0089	0.1133	0.1222	0.0783	0.0485	0.0574	0.1829
2010	0.0088	0.1096	0.1184	0.0804	0.0483	0.0571	0.1824
2011	0.0087	0.1062	0.1148	0.0818	0.0492	0.0579	0.1765
2012	0.0082	0.1014	0.1096	0.0812	0.0492	0.0574	0.1674
AVG	0.0140	0.1245	0.1384	11.12%	0.0650	0.0790	21.68%

Figure 5. Ukraine as Potential Addition to Competing Blocs, including European, 1991-2012

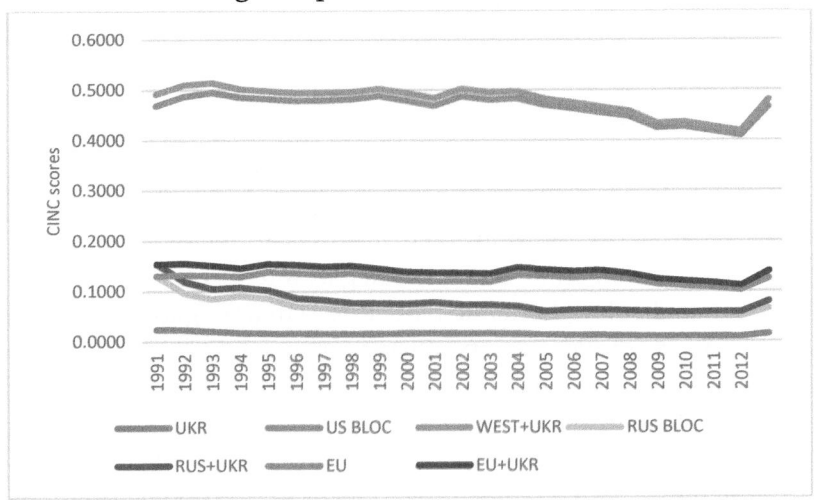

These data demonstrate the centrality of Ukraine to Russia's Eurasian project: with Ukraine in the Russian hierarchical network, Russia can plausibly claim transnational great power status on its own merits. Ukraine in Eurasia instead of Europe would also deny the European Union its last major expansion because Ukraine would not only represent close to a 10% increase to European hard power capabilities, but should Ukraine experience the same economic boom that other post-communist states did, that figure could rise to 15% or more. Without Ukraine, Russia's aspiration to great power status simply dies on the vine because "Eurasia" would be merely modestly larger than Russia itself.

The events of the Euromaidan unveiled those exact fears for Russia. The violence and breakdown of public order forced Viktor Yanukovych's government from power and caused the erstwhile Ukrainian President to flee first Kiev and then Ukraine altogether. For Putin, any subsequent government coming into power on the basis of social revolution would be pro-Western at best and anti-Russian at worst. Whatever the exact outlook or course of events that would then take place, the transition itself meant that Eurasia had reached its zenith and other blocs would increase their relative economic power over Eurasia.

The fall of Yanukovych and the loss of Ukraine as a subordinate ally posed a classic commitment problem: as others would grow more powerful, any promises not to exploit those advantages in the future would not be deemed credible by Putin. This negative shift in future bargaining power provided an incentive for a declining state to fight before it actually became weak (Fearon 1995, Powell 2006). To forestall relative weakening and to maintain the same strategic intent of revising the international political order to place Russia unambiguously into the first rank of world powers, Russia annexed Crimea to secure military assets and maintain power projection capabilities into the Eastern Mediterranean. The country then withstood sanctions, sponsored and increased support to separatists fighting a civil war to destabilize the Ukrainian government and economy, and has now intervened into the Syrian civil conflict.

Sustaining the Challenge

Russia's dissatisfaction with this international order is that, as a great power in many ways but without the status and prestige its leaders believe the country merits, it seeks to conduct an independent foreign policy that includes the ability to set the rules of international political and economic interaction—or to carve out exceptions for itself. Its prestige as a traditional great power and leading nuclear state was not matched by actual abilities to influence international politics for a full generation, and where prestige does not match benefits in international politics, a state can be motivated to revise the international order. The consequences of this dissatisfaction are what we are observing in Ukraine and Syria, where the ability of the Euro-Atlantic alliance to settle conflicts without acceding to Russia's political aims has been noticeably challenged. The cumulative effect is to pit the two systems—the Euro-Atlantic's post-WWII liberal order versus Russia's promotion of regional blocs against one another — raising the threat of a wider war between them.

Russia's active foreign policy, first to admit Ukraine into Eurasia and now its actions to shape Ukrainian politics through war, has secured Russia a seat at the table in European security through the Minsk negotiations it was pursuing for years. Paradoxically, however, the seat at the European table has made it more difficult to get a seat at the global table and reshape its core dissatisfaction with the global order. The commitment problem rears its ugly head once more: if challenging Western interests and the United States through war directly produces results, how could an American president and his or her Western allies trust that any particular agreement with Russia would hold? Why wouldn't Putin, or any other Russian leader (as well as others across the world), not keep challenging the existing order?

The end of the Cold War and the end of the Soviet Union served as two critical junctures from which Western institutional structures spread across Europe without meaningful Russian input. Russian revival and dissatisfaction with the global order led to an assertion of security interests abroad that challenge the Euro-Atlantic alliance and from which a systemic struggle that resembled, in part, the Cold War in miniature could emerge.

Unlike the Cold War of 1947–1989, Russia's current illiberal political model does not inspire mass devotion, even if it appeals to similarly authoritarian and statist leaders in the region (Hale 2013). Russia's economy possesses solid macroeconomic fundamentals following key reforms in the 2000s, but its inability to diversify away from energy exports since the mid-2000s boom has rendered the state even more dependent on that sector to drive growth. In combination, the Russia of today, compared to post-WWII Soviet Union, seeks a global position with a regional economy.

The sustainability of Russia's challenge will depend on adding new subordinate allies, shaping China's foreign policy interests to include Russia in its creation of an alternative to American dominance of the international order, its leaders' abilities to inspire the domestic population to accept lower consumption in return for continuing international relevance, and resolving the Ukrainian crisis on favorable terms. Should any of those fail, the high-risk, high-reward expansionist period seen since Euromaidan might catalyze another devastating retrenchment. Any such retrenchment could then be traced back to the failure of the Eurasian integration strategy to revise the international order stemming from events on the main square of Kyiv. Facing a negative shift in bargaining power, Putin selected the rational strategy—challenge Ukraine before European integration rendered any such challenge non-credible—that will remain in effect for the indefinite future.

References

Anon, 1989. October 25, 1989. 'Sinatra Doctrine' at Work in Warsaw Pact, Soviet Says. Available at: http://articles.latimes.com/1989-10-25/news/mn-745_1_warsaw-pact.

Anon, 1989. BBC ON THIS DAY, December 3, 1989: Malta summit ends Cold War. BBC News. Available at: http://news.bbc.co.uk/onthisday/hi/dates/stories/december/3/newsid_4119000/4119950.stm

Ash, T.G., 1999. *History of the Present: Essays, Sketches, and Dispatches from Europe in the 1990s.* Vintage.

Blainey, G., 1988. *Causes of War.* Simon and Schuster.

Blockmans, S., Kostanyan, H. and Vorobiov, I., 2012. Towards a Eurasian Economic Union: The challenge of integration and unity. CEPS Special Report. Available at: https://www.ceps.eu/publications/towards-eurasian-economic-union-challenge-integration-and-unity

Börzel, T.A. and Sedelmeier, U., 2017. Larger and more law abiding? The impact of enlargement on compliance in the European Union. *Journal of European Public Policy*, 24(2), pp. 197–215.

Braumoeller, B.F., 2013. *The Great Powers and the International System: Systemic Theory in Empirical Perspective.* Cambridge University Press.

Brown, A., 1997. *The Gorbachev Factor.* Oxford University Press.

Cameron, D.R., 2007. Post-communist democracy: The impact of the European Union. *Post-Soviet Affairs*, 23(3), pp. 185–217.

Charap, S. and Troitskiy, M., 2013. Russia, the West and the integration dilemma. *Survival*, 55(6), pp. 49–62.

Corbetta, R., Volgy, T.J., Grant, K.A. and Baird, R.G., 2009. So who gets into the club? The attribution of major power status in international politics. Conference paper, *International Political Science Association Conference*, Santiago, Chile.

Danilovic, V., 2002. *When the stakes are high: Deterrence and conflict among major powers*. University of Michigan Press.

Dinan, D., 1999. *Ever closer union: an introduction to European integration*. Basingstoke, Hampshire: Lynne Rienner.

Deudney, D. and Ikenberry, G.J., 2009. The unravelling of the cold war settlement. *Survival,.* 51(6), pp. 39–62.

Deyermond, R., 2004. The state of the union: military success, economic and political failure in the Russia–Belarus union. *Europe-Asia Studies*, 56(8), pp. 1191–1205.

Fearon, J.D., 1995. Rationalist explanations for war. *International Organization*, 49(3), pp. 379–414.

Frieden, J.A., 2007. *Global capitalism: Its fall and rise in the twentieth century*. WW Norton & Company.

Fukuyama, F., 1989. The end of history? *The National Interest*, (16), pp. 3–18.

Gaddis, J.L., 2005. *Strategies of containment: a critical appraisal of American national security policy during the Cold War*. Oxford University Press.

Gaddy, C.G. and Ickes, B., 2014. Ukraine: A prize neither Russia nor the West can afford to win. Brookings Institution.

Garthoff, R.L., 1994. *The great transition: American-Soviet relations and the end of the Cold War*. Brookings Institution.

Gaidar, Y., 2010. *Collapse of an empire: lessons for modern Russia*. Brookings Institution Press.

Gilpin, R., 1983. *War and change in world politics*. Cambridge University Press.

Goldgeier, J.M., 1999. The US decision to enlarge NATO: How, when, why, and what next?. *The Brookings Review*, 17(3), p. 18.

Goldgeier, J.M. and McFaul, M., 2003. *Power and purpose: US policy toward Russia after the Cold War*. Brookings Institution Press.

Goldgeier, J., 2016. Promises made, promises broken? What Yeltsin was told about NATO in 1993 and why it matters. *War on the Rocks*. Available at: https://warontherocks.com/2016/07/promises-made-promises-broken-what-yeltsin-was-told-about-nato-in-1993-and-why-it-matters/.

Greig, J.M. and Enterline, A.J., 2017. Correlates of War Project: National Material Capabilities Data Documentation, Version 5.0. Available at: http://correlatesofwar.org/data-sets/national-material-capabilities.

Hale, H.E., 2014. *Patronal politics: Eurasian regime dynamics in comparative perspective.* Cambridge University Press.

Hoffman, D., 2009. *The dead hand: The untold story of the cold war arms race and its dangerous legacy.* Anchor.

Huntington, S.P., 1991. Democracy's third wave. *Journal of democracy*, 2(2), pp. 12–34.

Ikenberry, G.J., 2001. *After victory: Institutions, strategic restraint, and the rebuilding of order after major wars.* Princeton University Press.

Ivanov, I.S., 2004. *The new Russian diplomacy.* Brookings Institution Press.

Judt, T., 2005. Europe vs. America. *The New York Review of Books*, 52(2), pp. 1–14.

Korolev, A., 2016. Systemic balancing and regional hedging: China–Russia relations. *The Chinese Journal of International Politics*, 9(4), pp. 375–397.

Korshunov, M., 2014. Mikhail Gorbachev: I am against all walls. *Russia Behind the Headlines.* Available at: https://www.rbth.com/international/2014/10/16/mikhail_gorbachev_i_am_against_all_walls_40673.html.

Kramer, M., 2009. The myth of a no-NATO-enlargement pledge to Russia. *The Washington Quarterly*, 32(2), pp. 39–61.

Krickovic, A., 2016. Catalyzing conflict: The internal dimension of the security dilemma. *Journal Global Security Studies*, 1(2), pp. 111–126.

Krickovic, A. and Weber, Y., 2017. Commitment issues: The Syrian and Ukraine crises as bargaining failures of the post–Cold War international order. *Problems of Post-Communism*, pp. 1–12.

Kydd, A., 2000. Arms races and arms control: Modeling the hawk perspective. *American Journal of Political Science*, pp. 228–244.

Legvold, R., 2016. *Return to cold war.* John Wiley & Sons.

Leitzel, J., 1995. *Russian economic reform.* Psychology Press.

Lukin, A., 2014. What the Kremlin Is Thinking: Putin's Vision for Eurasia. *Foreign Affairs*, 93.

Lynch, A.C., 2002. The evolution of Russian foreign policy in the 1990s. *The Journal of Communist Studies and Transition Politics*, 18(1), pp. 161–182.

Malmlöf, T., 2016. A case study of Russo-Ukrainian defense industrial cooperation: Russian dilemmas. *The Journal of Slavic Military Studies*, 29(1), pp. 1–22.

Mankoff, J., 2009. *Russian foreign policy: the return of great power politics.* Lanham, MD: Rowman & Littlefield.

Marten, K., 2017. Reconsidering NATO expansion: a counterfactual analysis of Russia and the West in the 1990s. *European Journal of International Security*, 3(2), pp. 1–27.

Medvedev, D., 2016. *Munich Security Conference Official Presentation.* Government of Russian Federation. Available at: http://government.ru/en/news/21784/.

North, D.C., 1990. *Institutions, institutional change and economic performance.* Cambridge University Press.

Politkovskaya, A., 2009. *A dirty war: a Russian reporter in Chechnya.* Random House.

Powell, R., 2006. War as a commitment problem. *International organization*, 60(1), pp. 169–203.

Pushkov, A.K., 1997. Don't isolate us: A Russian view of NATO expansion. *The National Interest*, (47), pp. 58–63.

Putin, V., 2007. *Speech and the following discussion at the Munich Conference on Security Policy.* President of Russian Federation. Available at: http://en.kremlin.ru/events/president/transcripts/24034.

Risse-Kappen, T., 1994. Ideas do not float freely: transnational coalitions, domestic structures, and the end of the cold war. *International Organization*, 48(2), pp. 185–214.

Roland, G., 1990. Gorbachev and the common European home: the convergence debate revived?. *Kyklos*, 43(3), pp. 385–409.

Sakwa, R., 2008. 'New Cold War' or twenty years' crisis? Russia and international politics. *International Affairs*, 84(2), pp. 241–267.

Sakwa, R., 2017. Russia's 1989 plea for a new world order was rejected, and so Putinism was born. The Guardian. Available at: https://www.theguardian.com/commentisfree/2017/mar/31/putinism-russia-1989-world-order-rejected.

Sarotte, M.E., 2010. Perpetuating US preeminence: the 1990 deals to "bribe the Soviets out" and move NATO in. *International Security*, 35(1), pp. 110–137.

Sarotte, M.E., 2014. *1989: the struggle to create post-Cold War Europe.* Princeton University Press.

Seabright, P., 2000. *The vanishing rouble: Barter networks and non-monetary transactions in post-Soviet societies.* Cambridge University Press.

Shevel, O., 2011. Russian nation-building from Yel'tsin to Medvedev: ethnic, civic or purposefully ambiguous?. *Europe-Asia Studies*, 63(2), pp. 179–202.

Shifrinson, J.R.I., 2016. Deal or no deal? The end of the cold war and the US offer to limit Nato expansion. *International Security*, 40(4), pp. 7–44.

Singer, J.D., Bremer, S. and Stuckey, J., 1972. Capability distribution, uncertainty, and major power war, 1820–1965. *Peace, war, and numbers*, 19(2), p. 48.

Singer, J.D., 1988. Reconstructing the correlates of war dataset on material capabilities of states, 1816–1985. *International Interactions*, 14(2), pp. 115–132.

SIPRI Yearbook 2016: Armaments, disarmament and international security, 2016. Oxford: Oxford University Press.

Slocum, J.W., 1999. A sovereign state within Russia? The external relations of the Republic of Tatarstan. *Global Society*, 13(1), pp. 49–75.

Stan, L. ed., 2009. *Transitional justice in Eastern Europe and the former Soviet Union: Reckoning with the communist past*. Routledge.

Stent, A.E., 2014. *The limits of partnership: US-Russian relations in the twenty-first century*. Princeton university press.

Stulberg, A.N., 2008. *Well-oiled diplomacy: strategic manipulation and Russia's energy statecraft in Eurasia*. SUNY Press.

Tarr, D.G., 2016. The Eurasian Economic Union of Russia, Belarus, Kazakhstan, Armenia, and the Kyrgyz Republic: Can It Succeed Where Its Predecessor Failed?. *Eastern European Economics*, 54(1), pp. 1–22.

Thompson, N., 2009. *The Hawk and the dove: Paul Nitze, George Kennan, and the history of the Cold War*. Henry Holt and Company.

Tishkov, V.A., 1995. What is Russia? Prospects for Nation-Building. *Security Dialogue*, 26(1), pp. 41–54.

Van Herpen, M.H., 2015. *Putin's wars: The rise of Russia's new imperialism*. Rowman & Littlefield.

Varese, F., 2001. *The Russian Mafia: private protection in a new market economy*. Oxford University Press.

Westad, O.A., 2005. *The global Cold War: third world interventions and the making of our times*. Cambridge University Press.

Woodruff, D., 2000. *Money unmade: Barter and the fate of Russian capitalism*. Cornell University Press.

Tomasz Stępniewski

The Ukraine Crisis, NATO, and Eastern Europe's Grey Zone of Security

This chapter discusses the impact of the Ukraine crisis on NATO's policies towards Eastern Europe. The crisis, a de facto Russo-Ukrainian armed conflict raging since 2014, has resulted in a shift of perception in how Eastern Europe, and Europe more generally, understands security. In addition, the Ukrainian conflict has raised concerns over the end of the post-Cold War international order, which was based on the peaceful coexistence of states, the integrity of borders, and the recognition of international legal regulations. Therefore, the objective of the present chapter is to offer answers to the following research questions: Will Russia's revisionist policy result in NATO's revitalization? Is NATO thinking strategically as far as Eastern Europe is concerned? Does a rationale exist for modifying Eastern Europe's security paradigm (the so-called "grey zone of security")? And finally, will the Russian Federation succeed in revising the US-dominated post-Cold War international order by means of the Ukrainian conflict?

Introduction

Brexit negotiations, initiated in 2017, have resulted in EU decision-makers' attention being drawn primarily to internal affairs (notably, EU and NATO member states' significant overlap). Apart from Brexit, additional crises and problems impacting the condition of the Union have emerged (on crises plaguing the EU, see Łukaszewski 2015; Zielonka 2014). Undeniably, internal affairs are critical from the point of view of the European Union as an organization, its cohesion, and de facto international position. The Ukraine crisis, a de facto Russo-Ukrainian armed conflict raging since 2014, has resulted in a shift of perception in how Eastern Europe, and Europe more generally, understands security. In addition, the Ukrainian conflict has raised concerns over the end of the post-Cold War international order (see, for example, Youngs 2017; Besier & Stokłosa 2017; Onuch & Sasse 2016, 556–587; Bertelsen 2016; Delcour & Wolczuk 2015, 459–478; Haukkala 2015, 25–40; Lannon 2015; Judah 2015; Larrabee, Wilson & Gordon 2015; Sakwa 2015; Polyakova 2014; Menon & Rumer 2015; Shekhovtsov & Umland 2014; Wilson 2014). This international order was based upon the peaceful coexistence of states, the integrity of borders, and the recognition of international legal regulations. The objective of the present paper is to offer answers to the following research questions: Will Russia's revisionist policy result in NATO's revitalization? Is NATO thinking strategically as far as Eastern Europe is concerned? Does a rationale exist for modifying Eastern Europe's security paradigm (the so-called "grey zone of security")? And will the Russian Federation succeed in revising the US-dominated post-Cold War international order by means of the Ukrainian conflict (among others)?

The dissolution of the Warsaw Pact (July 1991) and the fall of the Soviet Union (December 1991) — meaning the structures NATO had perceived as its enemies — resulted in a second post-WWII "geo-military" division of the world. These changes markedly impacted the post-Soviet states. In addition, NATO was forced to redefine its position, utility and role in the new, post-Cold War reality. According to Jerzy Nowak, as a result of the above, NATO "has been constantly evolving its political, military and operational capacity" (2008, 263). Changes in the structure of international relations have forced the organization to adapt to new post-Cold War challenges and problems (e.g., asymmetric threats, the proliferation of weapons of mass destruction, etc.) (Berdal & Ucko 2009, 55–76; Nunn 2010, 13–18). As a consequence, NATO must recognize security threats originating from the region in order to ensure its own security as well as that of the post-Soviet space. Moreover, the situation in the post-Soviet space is complicated by two processes. A deontological imperative, visible especially among the states of the Western world today, constitutes the first of these. This phenomenon revolves around the growing significance of multilateral (and multidimensional) processes and networks, which comes at the expense of states' interests. Decision-makers' return to thinking geopolitically is the second. These two processes have resulted in the emergence of the so-called "new Cold War," i.e., rivalry for influence in areas significant for the interests of key players (Olchowski 2011, 205; Sherr 2008, 141–151; Winrow 2007, 220–222).

As the world moved away from the bipolar divisions of the previous century, the state of its insecurity, ambiguity and unpredictability all deepened. According to Adam Rotfeld, "after the Cold War has ended, internal, ethnic conflicts, religious, and civil wars have been prevalent instead of international ones. Globalization results in these conflicts' negative impact upon international security" (Rotfeld 2014, 31–32). In addition, as a result of the disappearance of this bipolar division, a certain vacuum of security emerged in Eastern Europe. Sławomir Sierakowski labels this vacuum as "the shadow zone" or "the shadow of the Kremlin." According to him, this zone is half-moon-shaped and spans from Helsinki to Tbilisi, and even to Astana. The half-moon encompasses states which, on the one hand, do not desire to remain together — those which failed to develop into a cohesive geopolitical region — and on the other hand, are joined by common interests more than they are divided by differences. This geopolitical shadow zone, located between the West and Moscow, emerged as a result of imperial ambitions resurfacing in the Russian Federation (Sierakowski 2017, 22).

NATO's Interests in Eastern Europe

A modern international system is composed of several regional security complexes (see Buzan & Wæver 2003; Buzan, Wæver & Wilde 1998; Weaver 2011, 1–11; Stępniewski 2011). NATO, as a system of security, collides in Eastern Europe and the Black Sea region with other regional security systems. In particular, three regional security systems crisscross in these areas: the European Regional Security Complex (European RSC), Post-Soviet Regional Security Complex (Post-Soviet RSC), and the Middle Eastern

Regional Security Complex (Middle Eastern RSC). Apart from the above, the Balkan sub-complex and the Caucasus mini-complex are also present (Celikpala 2010, 289).

Dynamic changes occurring in international relations exert an impact upon NATO's structuring of its interests in this area. According to Olchowski (2011, 206), these encompass:

- a shift of European security's center-of-gravity from Central Europe eastwards;
- the presence of several unresolved political, ethnic-based conflicts which have emerged since the fall of the USSR (see also Lynch 2007, 483–496; Flikke 2011, 41–45);
- the post-Soviet space's political, economic and military instability;
- problems in relations with the Russian Federation (see also Antonenko 2009, 259–269; Rumer & Stent 2009, 91–102; Antonenko & Yurgens 2010–2011, 5–11);
- a growing terrorist threat in the Caucasus;
- the geopolitical location of the region at the edges of Europe, Asia, the Near East and the Balkans, which boosts its significance for the transport of energy resources, but also increases its attractiveness as a transfer channel for various criminal groups involved in trafficking drugs, humans, and arms;
- the role and position of Turkey in NATO (this issue has only gained significance after the annexation of Crimea by Russia) (see also Aydın 2009, 271–285; Chappell & Terlikowski 2011, 22–36);
- the (prospective) further enlargement of NATO;[1]
- the geostrategic importance of the post-Soviet space and the Black Sea region—along with the Caspian Sea—not only for NATO, but also for Russia, Turkey, the USA, the EU, Iran, and even China.

---

[1] The eastward enlargement process was halted due to the Russo-Georgian war and Russo-Ukrainian armed conflict.

The fact Russian politicians highlight that under Putin's rule, the Russian Federation has been pursuing a policy of "reclaiming Russian territories," (in other words, a neo-imperial policy), is also noteworthy (see Marciniak 2001; Nowak 2006).

On the other hand, according to John Herbst (2016, 166), the post-Cold War international order in the post-Soviet space is based upon several premises opposed by Putin's Russia:

- states which were subject to Moscow under the Warsaw Pact are now pursuing independent internal and international policies;
- the USSR was dissolved and all its republics became independent states. The fact that the decision was made solely by leaders of Russia, Ukraine, Belarus, and Kazakhstan, is noteworthy. The West did not participate in the decision-making process. In addition, president George H. W. Bush advised against the dissolution of the Soviet Union;
- in order to decrease political tension and promote welfare on the continent, European integration will continue and post-Soviet states will be included in the process;
- Russia and the West became partners. The West, intending to tighten relations with Russia, sponsored Moscow's membership in international organizations, such as the G8 and IMF.

Putin's address during the Munich Security Conference in 2007, and later his comments during the 70th United Nations General Assembly in New York in September 2015, confirmed that the Russian leader believed the present international order requires changes and that Russia will pursue its own objectives. According to Agnieszka Bryc (2015, 95):

> Recapturing the capacity for shaping international order has become an idee fixe of Putin's international activity. It is directly associated with Russia's superpower traditions and imperial nostalgia which has emerged in the aftermath of the fall of the USSR. The Russian Federation's strategy of readiness for political confrontation with the West resulted in the Ukrainian conflict becoming a breakthrough, concluding the post-Cold War period in

international relations which was dominated by a cooperative attitude characterizing Russia's relations with the West.

Twenty five years after the collapse of the USSR, we have witnessed Russia openly questioning the post-Cold War international order in the course of the annexation of Crimea and the war in the Donbas.

The Evolution of NATO's Policy Towards Ukraine and Eastern Europe: From the 1990s to the 2008 NATO Summit in Bucharest

In the early-to-mid 1990s, NATO's policy in the region was focused primarily on improving relations with Russia at the expense of contacts with other post-Soviet states. However, NATO's enlargement in 1999, encompassing Poland, the Czech Republic and Hungary, fundamentally altered the security system in this part of the continent. Furthermore, after the September 11 attacks, the United States and NATO changed their strategy towards the region, with the US increasingly considering the post-communist region to be a "security vacuum" and placing it at the center of its external security policy. As a consequence, specific aid programs for Georgia and Ukraine were developed, and the international visibility of the region increased, which further altered the approach towards security issues (Celikpala 2010, 289; George & Teigen 2008, 339–362). These actions stemmed from NATO's desire to tighten cooperation in the beginning of the 21st century, and to bring countries such as Ukraine and Georgia closer to NATO standards. In addition, the "color revolutions" in Georgia and Ukraine initiated a new debate on the consolidation of democratic transformations in these countries, and actions regarding security in the post-Soviet space in general (Asmus 2008, 95–106). Moreover, the March 2004 enlargement of NATO, which encompassed Bulgaria, Romania, Estonia, Latvia, Lithuania, Slovakia, and Slovenia, resulted in the organization directly encroaching on the post-Soviet space, particularly in the sensitive Black Sea region. By doing so, NATO became responsible for co-shaping (along with Russia) the security situation in the region.

The April 2008 NATO Summit in Bucharest constituted the next milestone in NATO's policy towards Eastern Europe. During the summit, the US sought support among NATO member states to expand the Membership Action Plan (MAP) eastward. It was the US, via NATO, which sought to intensify cooperation with Ukraine and Georgia, the intent being to improve their relations with NATO's member states. Taking into account Russia's efforts directed at destabilizing the post-Soviet states and its declarations regarding what Moscow regarded as its "privileged zone of influence" among the Commonwealth of Independent States (CIS), NATO's pushing MAP for Ukraine was a clear reflection of its interests in Eastern Europe, and more broadly the CIS. However, NATO ultimately decided to not grant MAPs to Ukraine and Georgia. This was motivated by objections on the part of Germany and France, as well as NATO's apprehension concerning a possible deterioration of relations with Russia. Moreover, certain NATO members (again headed by Germany and France) voiced their opposition for any further intensification of cooperation with countries in Eastern Europe and the South Caucasus. They supported their position by claiming that NATO enlargement ought to strengthen the overall alliance rather than weakening it, which is highly probable if Ukraine and Georgia are accepted as members.

Consequently, the Eastern European states may be regarded as existing in a "security vacuum" caused by their being located between the Euro-Atlantic (NATO) and European (EU) security organizations on the one hand, and a neo-imperial Russian Federation on the other. In particular, the geopolitical location of a country such as Ukraine results in it being positioned in two regions: Europe and Eurasia. However, in both cases its location is peripheral. This is especially so as the situation in the post-Soviet space has been very dynamic, especially recently. Russia's war with Georgia in August 2008 (on this, see Zasztowt 2008, 113–120) and its "cold gas war" with Ukraine in January 2009, along with intentionally provocative subsequent actions undertaken by Russia (e.g., its passport policy in Crimea, the Black Sea Fleet being stationed in Sevastopol, and the outbreak of Russo-Ukrainian war, which has been ongoing since 2014) have resulted in Ukraine's internal situation becoming severely complicated. And it has only been further worsened by Russia's hybrid war with Eastern Europe and the West. Additionally, the Donbas conflict will potentially enable Russia to further destabilize the internal political situation in the country by utilizing pro-Moscow separatists from Donetsk and Luhansk.

A Breakthrough? The 2016 NATO Summit in Warsaw

The 2016 Warsaw NATO Summit, and its potential consequences for East-Central Europe, are worth considering in detail. The summit, which took place between July 8–9, 2016, witnessed qualitative international changes, both on NATO's southern and eastern flanks. In addition, 2016 may have been a breakthrough year from the point of view of NATO's policy toward the region. This year saw not only changes in how regional security is perceived, but also a new way of viewing threats by NATO member states. When NATO accepted Poland, the Czech Republic and Hungary into its fold in 1999 and Slovakia in 2004, it overcame long-standing divisions in Europe. As a result, the Warsaw Summit not only reflected the changes occurring in Europe, but also confirmed Poland's significance to NATO and its vision of regional security. Importantly, this meeting was also symbolic, because it was in Warsaw in 1955 that the Warsaw Pact, which divided East-Central Europe into two opposing military camps, was established. As a consequence, a bipolar division of this part of the continent emerged, one which only ceased to exist with the fall of communism in 1989.

When analyzing the message of the Warsaw Summit, the fact that its resolutions are of a military (e.g., the decision to deploy four individual battalion groups in Poland and three Baltic states) and political character (e.g., emphasis on NATO's internal cohesion, increase in defense spending, etc.) needs to be highlighted. NATO also conspicuously reaffirmed its resolve:

> The defense of our territory and societies against an attack, pursuant to article 5 of the Washington Treaty, is of primary importance to NATO. No one ought to doubt NATO's determination in case of security threats to any of its members. NATO will maintain full capacity for deterring and defending against any security threats to our societies, wherever they may emerge (Warsaw Summit Communiqué 2016).

Moreover, while decisions regarding the improvement of NATO's capacity in preventing emerging threats were made during the previous summit in Newport in 2014, this commitment was reiterated in Warsaw with the implementation of the Readiness Action Plan (RAP) and the establishment of the Very High Readiness Joint Task Force (VJTF). There it was concluded that the VJTF (comprised of a force of 5,000 military personnel) would be deployment-ready within a few days' time if need be. Due to these initiatives and improvements in cooperation on land and sea operations (the latter affecting the Baltic, Black, and the Mediterranean Seas), NATO's strategic adaptation to new challenges and threats emerging from both the southern and eastern neighborhoods was confirmed.

However, matters of soft- and cyber-security cannot be disregarded. Russia's hybrid war with Ukraine (de facto a conflict with the West) has compelled NATO member states to face new challenges. It also poses a test of NATO-Russia relations and international security. Importantly, apart from conventional threats, Russia poses a nuclear threat as well. Despite the fact that many analysts claim Russia's attack on any NATO member is highly unlikely, some Russian politicians suggest the country is a nuclear power and may use these weapons against the West. This is a consequence of the fact that since 2014, Russia has considered NATO as the main threat to its interests in the post-Soviet space. Indeed, NATO's announcements regarding the deployment of forces in East-Central Europe are considered by Russia as a means of "enlargement." However, NATO cannot agree with such an interpretation because Poland and the Baltic states are full members of the organization and may independently decide their security policies. Poland and other NATO members may also influence NATO policies, including those regarding the East.

Russia's Military Presence in the "Security Grey Zone" of Eastern Europe

Recent events, occurring both within NATO and the EU as well as internationally, have influenced the policies of these organizations towards their neighbors. In this context, the Eurozone crisis, the prospects of Brexit, continuing fighting in Syria, the overflow of migrants in the Mediterranean region, the issue of the so-called Islamic State (Daesh), and Russia's adoption of a neo-imperial policy (as exemplified by the annexation of Crimea and Moscow's support of the separatists in southern and eastern Ukraine) all ought to be mentioned. These events have resulted in EU member states (and thus effectively NATO) becoming divided geographically along two key dimensions: 1) countries invested in matters of the Mediterranean (meaning the southern European countries and those which are destinations for migrants: Germany, Austria, etc.) and 2) countries focused on the situation in the eastern neighborhood (meaning the Central European states, the Baltics, and Sweden) where Russia and Ukraine pose challenges for their individual security and the security of the whole region. Importantly, Russia's aggression against Ukraine resulted in the reactivation of conversations about the role NATO, as an organization committed to guarding European security, should play in this space.

When viewing a map of Eastern Europe, the fact that Russia's military presence in the region makes it a "security grey zone" ought to be taken into consideration. Frozen conflicts occurring here may indirectly or directly impact the stability and security of Eastern European states and the whole EU as well.

Importantly, as of January 2016, one third of the Donbas region (comprising parts of Luhansk and Donetsk), or close to 3% of Ukrainian territory, is controlled by the combatants (or terrorists) of the so-called "Donetsk People's Republic" and "Luhansk People's Republic," not by Ukraine's government (Shelest & Maksak 2016, 6–7).

When the deployment of Russia's Iskander missile systems in Kaliningrad Oblast is considered, it is evident that they pose a potential threat for northeastern Poland and the Baltic states. Moreover, the Russian multi-level A2/AD system (anti-access/area denial) is worth discussing. This system is capable of detecting and electronically interfering with guidance systems and affecting the spatial orientation and communications of aerial assets, including aircrafts, drones and cruise missiles. In this regard, Kaliningrad constitutes the northernmost threat area for NATO, as Russian anti-aircraft systems based there can reach far into Polish territory and, in case of a crisis, may eliminate NATO relief forces deployed to the Baltics. In addition, after the annexation of Crimea, the Crimean Peninsula constitutes another threat area, with Russia having deployed a powerful A2/AD system there. Consequently, it is capable of controlling virtually the whole Black Sea region (Turkey and its formidable military—the second largest in NATO—constitute a counterbalance). Moreover, Russia has recently built up its A2/AD potential in Syria as well.

Violations of NATO and Scandinavian airspace constitute another problem associated with the conventional security of the region. Analysts observe that "dangerous military-military and military-civilian incidents involving ships or aircrafts of Russia, NATO member states, and third parties continue to pose a serious threat to Euro-Atlantic security" (see Kulesa, Frear & Raynova 2016). The period directly following the annexation of Crimea was a time of particularly intense military activity for Russia, featuring numerous violations of NATO's sea and airspace and a general decline of NATO-Russia relations.

Likewise, the degree to which the Ukrainian army (and other post-Soviet armies) have been infiltrated by Russian forces constitutes yet another field to be discussed in the context of NATO's eastern policy and the potential enlargement of the organization. Such infiltration negatively affects the image of these countries and their potential for NATO membership. The extent of the Ukrainian army's infiltration by Russian forces was confirmed during the annexation of Crimea and its peaceable "handover" by

Ukrainian military. Transcripts (published almost two years after the annexation) of the February 28, 2014 session of the National Security and Defense Council of Ukraine prove that some of the Ukrainian servicemen communicated with the command of the Russian Black Sea Fleet stationed in Crimea. In addition, Ukrainian policemen and military personnel changed sides as well. The transcripts indicate that Ukraine's defense capability in Crimea was minimal, diminished by Russia's consistent and long-term operations in the area.

Conclusions

The objective of the present paper is to present a general overview of the security situation in East-Central Europe, especially as it regards the countries that directly border Russia. On the one hand, many NATO member states have recently decreased their defense budgets (only some, like Poland, have increased defense expenditures). On the other hand, Russia is today rapidly rebuilding and modernizing its military, including its nuclear forces. In addition, it is noteworthy that Russia has been testing new strategies in the course of the Ukrainian conflict. Russia's operations against Ukraine are not only tactical in character, but are determined by Moscow's long-term objectives. NATO is making a mistake when viewing these operations only in light of the Ukrainian conflict (seen as a local, internal problem). NATO members ought to change their approach towards conventional threats in Europe. The situation on NATO's eastern flank is the best evidence of this necessity. As far as conventional threats are concerned, it is Russia and its neo-imperial policy that poses the greatest threat for Europe. Lack of sufficient reflection on the security situation in Eastern Europe may well result in far reaching consequences for NATO as an organization and for its individual member states.

Eastern Europe's security system (broadly, the post-Soviet space and the Black Sea region) is exceedingly complex due to its multi-dimensionality, as it encompasses military, energy, and ethno-political dimensions, among others (on this, see Triantaphyllou 2009, 225–236). And as the result of the growing geostrategic significance of the region, new issues emerge which further complicate matters. NATO's lack of a cohesive strategy towards the post-Soviet space does not contribute to the stabilization of the region and the improvement of its security. Just the opposite is the case. As indicated earlier, NATO's interests in the region revolve around: 1) ensuring geopolitical security (as the destabilization of the region may entail the destabilization of NATO); 2) ensuring the security of natural resources and energy infrastructure; 3) counterbalancing Russia's influence by consolidating the statehood of regional actors and incorporating them into a cooperative security system (Olchowski 2011, 223; Bieleń 2016, 37–50).[2]

It can be said that the recent NATO Summit in Warsaw in July 2016 satisfied the expectations of the East-Central European countries because there was an emphasis placed on ensuring regional security. While Article 5 of the Washington Treaty[3] seems obvious to Western European countries, East-Central European states consider it of critical importance. However, we cannot overlook the fact that many NATO member states have decreased their defense expenditures precisely at a time when Russia is rapidly increasing its military budget. For Poland and other East-Central European states, issues of security and NATO's deterrence policies are of utmost significance. As a consequence, the establishment of the Very High Readiness Task Force (VJTF) in the region constitutes a key element in their national defense policies.

---

2   Due to the Russo-Ukrainian war, this is unlikely to materialize in the near future. Indeed, opinions are being voiced that the involvement of the Eastern European states with NATO has led to the destabilization of the region and contributed to the emergence of tensions between Russia and the West.

3   Article 5 of the Washington Treaty notes that: "Collective defense means that an attack against one Ally is considered as an attack against all Allies."

References

Antonenko, O. & Yurgens, I. (2010–2011). Towards a NATO–Russia Strategic Concept. *Survival*, 52:6, p. 5–11.

Antonenko, O. (2009). Towards a Comprehensive Regional Security Framework in the Black Sea Region after the Russia-Georgia War. *Southeast European and Black Sea Studies*, 9:3, p. 259–269.

Asmus, R.D. (2008). Europe's Eastern Promise. Rethinking NATO and EU Enlargement. *Foreign Affairs*, 87:1, p. 95–106.

Aydın, M. (2009). Geographical Blessing versus Geopolitical Curse: Great Power Security Agendas for the Black Sea Region and a Turkish Alternative. *Southeast European and Black Sea Studies*, 9:3, p. 271–285.

Berdal, M. & Ucko, D. (2009). NATO at 60. *Survival*, 51:2, p. 55–76.

Bertelsen, O. (ed.) (2016). *Revolution and War in Contemporary Ukraine. The Challenge of Change*. Stuttgart: Ibidem-Verlag.

Besier, G., Stokłosa, K. (eds) (2017). *Neighbourhood Perceptions of the Ukraine Crisis. From the Soviet Union into Eurasia?*. Routledge: Oxon and New York.

Bieleń, S. (2016). NATO – czas przewartościowań [NATO – Time for a Revaluation]. *Stosunki Międzynarodowe – International Relations*, no. 1 (v. 52), p. 37–50.

Bryc, A. (2015). Putinizm jako doktryna odbudowy imperium? [Putinism as a Doctrine for the Restoration of the Empire]. In: Bieleń, S. & Skrzypek, A. (eds.), *Rosja. Rozważania imperiologiczne [Russia. Deliberations on Imperialism]*. Warszawa: Aspra-JR, p. 95.

Buzan, B. & Wæver, O. (2003). *Regions and Powers: The Structure of International Security*. Cambridge: University Press.

Buzan, B., Wæver, O. & de Wilde, J. (1998). *Security: A New Framework for Analysis*. London: Lynne Rienner Publishers.

Celikpala, M. (2010). Escalating Rivalries and Diverging Interests: Prospects for Stability and Security in the Black Sea Region. *Southeast European and Black Sea Studies*, 10:3, p. 289.

Chappell, G., Terlikowski, M. (2011). Turcja w Sojuszu Północnoatlantyckim i jej stanowisko wobec polityki bezpieczeństwa i obrony Unii Europejskiej [Turkey in NATO and its Position in the EU's Security and Defense Policy]. *Sprawy Międzynarodowe*, no. 4 (LXIV), p. 22–36.

Delcour, L. & Wolczuk, K., (2015). Spoiler or Facilitator of Democratization? Russia's Role in Georgia and Ukraine. *Democratization*, vol. 22.

Flikke, G. (ed.) (2011). *The Shifting Geopolitics of the Black Sea Region: Actors, Drivers and Challenges*, "NUPI Report", Oslo: Norwegian Institute of International Affairs, p. 41-45.

George, J.A. & Teigen, J.M. (2008). NATO Enlargement and Institution Building: Military Personnel Policy Challenges in the Post-Soviet Context. *European Security*, 17:2-3, p. 339-362.

Herbst, J. (2016). Assessing and Addressing Russian Revanchism. *PRISM*, 6:2, July 18, p. 166, http://cco.ndu.edu.

Judah, T. (2015). *In Wartime: Stories from Ukraine*. London: Penguin.

Kulesa, Ł., Frear, T. & Raynova, D. (2016). *Managing Hazardous Incidents in the Euro-Atlantic Area: A New Plan of Action*, "Policy Brief," November, European Leadership Network, http://www.european leadershipnetwork.org.

Lannon, E. (2015). More for more or less for less: From the rhetoric to the implementation of European Neighbourhood Instrument in the Context of the 2015 ENP review. *IEMed Overview*. Barcelona: European Institute of the Mediterranean.

Larrabee, F. S., Wilson, P. A. & Gordon, IV J. (2015). *The Ukrainian Crisis and European Security: Implications for the United States and U.S. Army*. Santa Monica, CA: RAND Corporation.

Łukaszewski, J. (2015). *Unia i Polska w świecie wstrząsów i przemian [The EU and Poland in the world of commotion and changes]*. Lublin: Instytut Europy Środkowo-Wschodniej.

Lynch, D. (2007). De Facto "States" around the Black Sea: The Importance of Fear. *Southeast European and Black Sea Studies*, 7:3, p. 483-496.

Marciniak, W. (2001). *Rozgrabione imperium. Upadek Związku Sowieckiego i powstanie Federacji Rosyjskiej [Plundered Empire. The Fall of the USSR and Emergence of Russian Federation]*. Kraków: Arcana.

Menon, R. & Rumer, E. B. (2015). *Conflict in Ukraine: The Unwinding of the Post-Cold War Order*. Boston: MA, MIT Press.

Nowak, A. (ed.) (2006). *Rosja i Europa Wschodnia: „imperiologia" stosowana [Russia and Eastern Europe: Applied Imperialism]*. Kraków: Arcana.

Nowak, J.M. (2008). NATO: główne dylematy i pytania o przyszłość NATO [Chief Dilemmas and Concerns for the Future]. In: Rotfeld, A.D. (Ed),

Dokąd zmierza świat? [Where is the World Headed?]. Warszawa: PISM, p. 263.

Nunn, S. (2010). NATO Nuclear Policy and Euro-Atlantic Security. *Survival*, vol. 52, no. 2, s. 13–18.

Olchowski, J. (2011). Interesy Sojuszu Północnoatlantyckiego w regionie czarnomorsko-kaspijskim [NATO's Interests in the Black Sea and the Caspian Sea Region]. In: Bojarczyk, B. & Stępniewski, T. (eds.), *Obszar czarnomorsko-kaspijski w stosunkach międzynarodowych [The Black Sea and the Caspian Sea Region in International Relations]*. Lublin: UMCS Publishing House.

Onuch, O. & Sasse, G. (2016). The Maidan in Movement: Diversity and the Cycles of Protest. *Europe-Asia Studies*, 68:4, p. 556–587.

Polyakova, A. (2014). From the Provinces to the Parliament: How the Ukrainian Radical Right Mobilized in Galicia. *Communist and Post-Communist Studies*, 47:2.

Pugsley, S. & Wesslau, F. (eds.) (2016). *Russia in the Grey Zones*, London: European Council on Foreign Relations, 1.09.2016, www.ecfr.eu.

Rumer, E. & Stent, A. (2009). Russia and the West. *Survival*, 51:2, p. 91–102.

Rotfeld A. D. (2014). Porządek międzynarodowy. Parametry zmiany [International Order. Conditions of Change]. *Sprawy Międzynarodowe*, 4 (LXVII), p. 31–32.

Sakwa, R. (2015). *Frontline Ukraine: Crisis in the Borderland*. London: I.B. Tauris.

Shekhovtsov, A. & Umland, A. (2014). Ukraine's Radical Right. *Journal of Democracy*, 25, 3.

Shelest, H. & Maksak, H. (2016). Ukraine's Security Options: Time for Strategic Choices, Smart Partnerships, and Comprehensive Reforms. Caucasus Institute for Peace, Democracy and Development/CIPDD. Tbilisi, June 2016, http://eap-csf.eu/wp-content/uploads/Annex-7.-Ukraine-security.pdf.

Sherr, J. (2008). Security in the Black Sea Region: Back to Realpolitik?. *Southeast European and Black Sea Studies*, 8:2, p. 141–151.

Sierakowski, S. (2016). Długi cień Kremla [The Long Shadow of the Kremlin]. *Polityka*, no. 30 (3069), 20.07–26.07, p. 22.

Stępniewski, T. (2011). *Geopolityka regionu Morza Czarnego w pozimnowojennym świecie [The Geopolitics of the Black Sea Region in the*

Post-Cold War World]. Lublin–Warszawa: Instytut Europy Środkowo-Wschodniej.

Triantaphyllou, D. (2009). The "Security Paradoxes" of the Black Sea Region. *Southeast European and Black Sea Studies*, 9:3, p. 225–236.

Warsaw Summit Communiqué (2016), NATO, Warsaw, 8–9 July, http://www.nato.int/cps/en/natohq/official_texts_133169.htm.

Weaver, C. (2011). Black Sea Regional Security: Present Multipolarity and Future Possibilities. *European Security*, 20:1, p. 1–11.

Wilson, A. (2014). *Ukraine Crisis: What It Means for the West*. New Haven, CT, Yale University Press.

Winrow, G. (2007). Geopolitics and Energy Security in the Wider Black Sea Region. *Southeast European and Black Sea Studies*, 7:2, p. 220–222.

Youngs, R. (2017). *Europe's Eastern Crisis. The Geopolitics of Asymmetry*. Cambridge: University Press.

Zasztowt, K. (2008). Zmiany w polityce regionalnej Turcji, Armenii i Azerbejdżanu po konflikcie zbrojnym w Gruzji w sierpniu 2008 roku [Changes in Regional Policies of Turkey, Armenia and Azerbaijan in Light of Russo-Georgian War of August 2008]. *Rocznik Instytutu Europy Środkowo-Wschodniej*, no. 6, p. 113–120.

Zielonka, J. (2014). *Is the EU Doomed?*. Cambridge, MA: Polity Press.

Jussi Laine

The Ukraine Crisis and Ontological (In)Security: Implications from a Finnish Perspective

In today's networked world developments in distant areas may rapidly emerge as broader security issues with multiple, and multi-layered, implications. This paper examines the crisis in Ukraine not as a single isolated incident, but rather as a more profound "game-changer" that has had a broad impact on the security environment in Europe and beyond. In its aftermath changes in the broader security environment have often been interpreted as heralding the "return of the Cold War," and there has been a consequent need to consider security threats increasingly in terms of a realist reading of geopolitics and military preparedness. In contrast to such a reading, this paper underlines the need for a more nuanced perspective that takes into account the pronounced complexity and unpredictability of the contemporary security scene. A broader view of security requires us to focus more on changes in the international order at the supranational level as well as on processes that penetrate everyday life at the national and local levels. This paper examines this situation from the perspective of Finland, and shifts the focus from traditional geopolitical concerns to questions related to everyday ontological security and identitary bordering. It argues that borders, both formal and informal, provide a prism through which security challenges at different levels and in different contexts may be understood, analyzed, and interpreted. Borders are crucial to this analysis, for they reflect the complexity of the present security environment and echo some of the greatest challenges that contemporary Europe faces.

Introduction

The conflict in Ukraine and the general change in Russia's foreign and security policy indicate a tipping point in the security debate in Europe. The pan-European security architecture, which was based on the Helsinki Final Act of the Organization for Security and

Co-operation in Europe (OSCE)[1] during the Cold War, yet reconfirmed and expanded on many occasions since—has been severely tested. Russian actions in Ukraine have called into question its main tenets, including refraining from the threat or use of force, respect for the territorial integrity of states, and the inviolability of borders. Instead of security based on cooperation, friendly relations, and openness, as once envisioned in the Helsinki Principles, Russia has turned back to power politics (Stubb 2015), leaving the EU uncertain how to react.

Russia now defines its security in ways that make many of its neighbors feel increasingly insecure, if not threatened outright. Instead of following jointly agreed-upon rules, Russia has set out its own rules which reflect its increasingly assertive geopolitical strategies. On the EU side these actions have led to widespread proclamations of the return of Cold War geopolitics, which for many strongly imply an emphasis on military security and territorial defense. A common Western take on the matter has been to condemn Russia's actions with the accusation that the country has retreated into nineteenth century imperial modes of thinking. This conception has its merits, but it also suggests a desire to seek to explain the current situation based on past experience, which seems both completely outdated and inadequate for a thorough explanation of the current situation. It fails to acknowledge that, particularly in the aftermath of the Ukraine crisis, the security environment has become clearly more volatile and complex. The traditional approach to security, which focused on states' political-military security practices, is increasingly allied with approaches which also take economic and political interdependences, globalized markets, collective security, and multilateral cooperation into account, and the general emergence of increasingly transnational security concerns (e.g., Browning 2014).

The impact of the Ukraine crisis is an illustration of how in today's networked world developments in distant areas may rapidly emerge as broader security issues with multiple, and multi-

---

1 See: http://www.osce.org/helsinki-final-act

layered, implications. Consequently, this chapter examines the crisis in Ukraine not as a single isolated incident, but rather as a more profound "game-changer" that has had a broad impact on the security environment in Europe and beyond. As Hyde-Price (2015, 5) has suggested, the Ukraine crisis has been a catastrophe for the entire European security system in the classical Greek sense of the word (i.e., an "overturning"). The Russian annexation of Crimea and the subsequent, and still ongoing, conflict in eastern Ukraine have overturned the fundamental assumptions on which the post-Cold War European security order was established. They have reversed the earlier expectations that Russia would be a willing partner in a joint and cooperative security system, and challenged the principles of territorial integrity and national sovereignty as the cornerstones of the European political order. In short, the Ukraine crisis marks a new era in the relationship between Russia and the West: an era in which there are no shared rules (Raik 2014).

Examining this situation from a Finnish perspective, this article shifts the focus from traditional geopolitical concerns to questions related to everyday ontological security and identitary bordering. The focus is not on the Ukraine crisis as such, but rather on its wider implications. The common reading of the situation has been that Ukraine's vulnerability to Russian aggression has sent a strong message to other countries bordering Russia, such as Finland (Laine 2017). To avoid the fate of Ukraine and to survive in the absence of shared rules, urgent attention has had to be paid to ensuring domestic stability, the resilience of democracy, the sustainability of the economy, and the credibility of national defense (Raik 2014). Furthermore, now more than ever, unity is required from the EU member states in their stand against Russia, not just to survive but to defend the key values and norms on which the whole of Europe and its security has been built.

In Finland, the crisis has provoked a broad debate on Finland's place in a transforming Europe, but also concerning everyday security at the nexus of external-internal security threats affecting the functioning of basic societal processes and cross-border flows, as well as the social and political stability of Finnish society at large.

The security environment of Finland — which shares a 1340 km land border with Russia — now possesses more risk factors of various kinds, which together form an intertwined border-related security challenge. As is often argued in Finland, the choices made continue to be determined by the border, which makes Finland's position more geopolitically vulnerable than is the case with other Western European states. In addition to the increased Russian military presence along Finland's borders (land as well as maritime), repeated airspace violations, and the utilization of cyber-attacks and other forms of "hybrid" warfare, the presence of Russian intelligence operatives and misrepresentative propaganda have increased in Finland in recent years, returning security to the heart of the debate.

With the collapse of the Soviet Union, the neighbor to which Finns had grown accustomed, for better or worse, suddenly disappeared. The Soviet Union had not been the easiest of neighbors, but at least the risk associated with living next to a sleeping giant could be assessed and managed, and the dangers could be judged (Laine 2017). With its successor, the Russian Federation, the rules of the game changed and the probabilities became harder to estimate. This increased unpredictability, as opposed to a straightforward threat, has arguably reawakened feelings of insecurity, if not in the form of outright fear, then certainly of an existential anxiety. The role of borders has been brought into the discussion, for they reflect the complexity of the present security scene and thus provide a prism through which security challenges at different levels can be analyzed and interpreted.

Changes in the Security Environment

This tenser security situation, brought on by Russia's actions and the conflict between Russia and Ukraine, has had far-reaching impacts on relations between the EU and Russia and on Europe's overall security. It would be no exaggeration to claim that as a result of the crisis in Ukraine relations between Russia and the EU are now worse than at any time since the end of the Cold War. Earlier visions of a common EU-Russia neighborhood now seem far-fetched, but the original premise remains, making cooperation possible to envision even if the pursuit of this end now seems difficult to accomplish.

The EU-Russia relationship was certainly troubled even before the Ukraine crisis. Ambitious, jointly agreed upon plans for closer political, societal, and economic links in the form of Common Spaces and Road Maps, while themselves important achievements, led to almost nothing and were barely implemented. Instead, Russia and the EU drifted into direct geopolitical competition. Despite the EU's strong rhetorical commitment to regional partnership and multilevel cooperation, these goals have clearly become subordinated to the dictates of geopolitical expedience, and the EU has grown increasingly critical of, and frustrated by, Russia's internal developments. Russia, in turn, has expressed its opposition increasingly forcefully, in particular to the EU's Eastern Partnership agenda of forging closer links and a more central geopolitical role with former Soviet countries.

While the EU and Russia have had competing agendas over the shared neighborhood for a decade and a half, it is only recently that Russia has asserted itself as a strong countervailing force against the EU's structural foreign policy (Gowens & Timmins 2009; Sasse 2013) and has sought to gain influence over EU decision-making. As with Georgia in 2008, with Ukraine Russia is responding to what it perceives as Western encroachments into its "near abroad" by demonstrating its hard power, which the EU, being a soft power, can neither afford to provoke nor counterpoise. These insights notwithstanding, much critical discussion of EU geopolitics has been somewhat introspective, interpreted from post-colonial European perspectives or from the perspective of the bordering practices of the EU itself rather than engaging with external perceptions of Europe (Hobson 2007; Scott 2017). Moving beyond a self-centered view in trying to understand the agency of "others" in the formation of the EU's geopolitical identity, Morozov and Rumelili (2012) have depicted Russia as a "Europe-Maker" by challenging the EU's power to define the normative meaning of Europe.

As an EU member, Finland is automatically part of this broader EU-Russia equation. The EU is an important security community for Finland, and the EU's objective of strengthened international influence can also be seen as serving Finnish interests. At the same time, however, Finland has sought to continue to maintain bilateral relations with Russia. Based on a shared past as well as geographic proximity, Finland has traditionally depicted itself as a bridge between the EU and Russia and claimed to understand both. While Finland has stood firmly behind the EU's common positions on Russia's actions and directly condemned them, it has at the same time worked towards improving relations between the EU and Russia, and sought to safeguard the continuation of the long lasting socio-cultural forms of cross-border cooperation and pragmatic relations with Russia.

Finnish foreign and security policy emphasizes the ability to adapt to a changing world situation while at the same time, somewhat paradoxically, relying on traditional, historically conditioned notions of security. As Salonius-Pasternak and Limnéll (2015) explain, Finns tend to view security through a historical lens based on their experience of World War II, when battle lines were relatively clear, the enemy's actions affected the civilian population only sporadically, and acts of war generally consisted of physical acts of violence. However, today's altered security environment means that it is increasingly important also to take into account the various forms of cyber and hybrid warfare (see Limnéll 2015; Lehto & Limnéll 2016) that have become not only increasingly prominent but also intelligent and efficient ways to wage war, because they hold the power to achieve political goals without the extensive use of armed force and violence.

The contemporary security scene is characterized by pronounced unpredictability as well as a complex combination of traditional geopolitical challenges and new security threats that are not necessarily connected to interstate relations. At the same time local interpretations of global security concerns and the general perceptions of security and threat that underpin them are directly connected to social and political stability, economic conditions, and degrees of democratic legitimacy. Accordingly, a broader view of global security requires us to focus more on both the supranational-level changes in the international order and the processes which penetrate everyday life at the national and local levels. It has become clear that the global security environment can no longer be understood and analyzed merely in terms of interstate relations (see, for example, Hough 2014). Accordingly, there is an apparent need to recognize the need for new, multi-layered approaches to security that can capture both global processes which may turn into external security challenges and the new supranational and transnational developments which penetrate everyday life at the national and local levels (Abrahamsen & Williams 2009; Buzan, Wæver & de Vilde 1998).

There is also a need to distance ourselves from conventional political approaches to security which interpret the multi-layered nature of security challenges simply in terms of transferring images of external threats from one level to another. Rather, this chapter pays particular attention to how the threat images are present at each level in their particular ways and how the understanding of security must also take into account subjective perceptions of threat and broader social dynamics of identity formation. The essentialized imaginaries of security threats based on exaggerated representations and imaginaries of foundational differences between people, cultures, and states (Rumelili 2015a) cannot be ignored, because within contexts of socio-economic stress and geopolitical instability the sense of insecurity can dramatically increase, regardless of whether the assessment made is rational or not. Resolving conflicts by convincing people the "Other" is no longer a threat, or not as dangerous as it once was, may actually generate high levels of anxiety (Hansen, 2012; Browning & Joenniemi 2015; 2017). A well-defined and stable threat can be easier to manage and live with than constant unpredictability and instability, which generate uncertainty in the general population and eventually lead to political goals. A stable threat may come with a certain sense of familiarity and be if not psychologically comforting at least identity confirming, that is, as long as uncertainly fuels anxiety and can disrupt the conventional systems of meaning and the sense of self-integrity.

Reframing (In)Security

Security is a multifaceted and context-specific concept, and there has been an ongoing debate about who or what should be protected and the risks that should be prepared for, by whom, and for what purpose (Laine 2015). In the field of international politics security has traditionally meant a state's defense against external threats, i.e., national security (Heiskanen 2013, 201). "Security" as a political value has no independent meaning and is related to individual and societal value systems (Brauch 2007). In common parlance security can mean different things. It is often used to refer to the state of being which is free of various dangers and risks and also from care, anxiety, and doubt—the absence of threats (Wæver 1995, 52).

Throughout history security has been one of the most compelling driving forces in politics (Limnéll 2009, 3), and it continues to play a central role in thinking and theorizing about international relations (Nyman & Burke 2016, 4). The idea of security, Limnéll (2009) posits, is constructed in relation to perceived threats which are, by definition (even if it is claimed that they are real), products of estimates and interpretation, and which cannot be defined in terms of objective reality. Publicly presented threat perceptions are deliberately constructed in specific ways, which means that the content of the threat perception is politically determined. Threat perceptions are also flexible according to current political interests and resources. Security can therefore be produced by constructing threats that are suitable (i.e., manageable). Limnéll explains that we are living in an era in which the concept of security is continuously expanding, which has made threat perceptions increasingly controversial (2009, 44). The ever-expanding concepts of security have become part of everyday politics, yet the tradition of consensus-building remains quite visible in Finland, and the role of Russia in this regard is still crucial. The threat perceptions of domestic security, especially, have made their way into the sphere of security policy, whereas international, and especially Western, security trends have strongly influenced the securitization of non-military threats. Limnéll underlines that there are also pragmatic reasons for the production of new threats and the maintaining of old ones: threat perceptions are useful in maintaining the political status of engaged players, in the allocation of related resources, and in reinforcing certain political issues (2009, 395.)

This article uses the concept of ontological security to better understand how the individual's gaining of security is at risk in the turbulent and unpredictable environment of the contemporary era. The concept of ontological security was already used by Laing (1960) to refer to "a continuous person" who enjoys a stable and whole existence in reality, as opposed to suffering from the anxiety and loss of meaning that can threaten everyday experiences and the self's integrity. This idea was developed further by Giddens (1990; 1991), who pays particular attention to psychological needs, the importance of a continuous narrative, and the maintenance of routine. He underlines the stability of the self's existence, the "sense of self," and the confidence that most human beings have in the continuity of their self-identity and in the constancy of the surrounding social and material environments of action.

At its most fundamental level ontological security concerns the ability of actors to "go on" with their lives without succumbing to paralyzing anxieties and insecurities about the nature of existence (Browning & Joenniemi 2014, 4; Browning 2016). It emphasizes a concern with the continuity of the self and the "security of being, a sense of confidence and trust that the world is what it appears to be" (Kinnvall 2004, 746). Much of this reasoning derives from Giddens, who explains that social actors need basic trust in the continuity of the factors that give them their sense of identity if they are to have agency, set objectives, define interests, and act strategically (1991, 98). Without a belief in the continuity, reliability, and consistence of him or herself, other people, and other factors closely tied to his or her daily life, a person is unable to develop a sense of trust in the nature and stability of the social and structural environments he or she inhabits. In an existential sense an ontologically secure person has a stable and unquestioned sense of self and of his or her place in the world in relation to other people and objects, while an ontologically insecure person does not accept the reality or existence of things (Giddens 1991; Hewitt 2010, 511). An ontologically secure self can feel whole and act within taken-for-granted coordinates of daily life, gaining power, predictability, and creating common sense in the system, as long as these coordinates remain unchallenged (Giddens 1991, 37; Chernobrov 2016, 3).

Scholars of international relations (e.g., Mitzen 2006a, b; Krolikowski 2008; Berenskoetter 2014; Browning & Joenniemi 2014, 2017; Rumelili 2015a, b) have sought to extend the concept to argue that states as well as individuals seek security in ways that ensure a consistency in the narratives, myths, and stories they tell about who they are, what they do, and why in order to create a consistent sense of self that is recognized by others. Mitzen (2006a, 341) explains that in addition to physical security states also seek ontological security. She refers to security "not of the body but of the self, the subjective sense of who one is, which enables and motivates action and choice" (Mitzen 2006a, 344). This entails knowing not only what one is doing, but also why one is doing it (Steele 2005, 526). Stability and continuity of being is crucial here, for ontological security arises from a sense of being safely in control of a cognitive situation (Roe 2008, 783), and entails having a consistent sense of self and having that sense affirmed by others (Zarakol 2010, 6)

A focus on ontological security is of use here, for it allows us to tie the logic of security to the production and reproduction of identities, rather than merely utilizing it in the traditional sense of avoiding or defending against physical threats. As Browning and Joenniemi (2014, 4) explain, a condition of ontological security need not imply that the environment of the ontologically secure actor is one of peace or that it is completely lacking in tension, but what really counts is the stability of expectations surrounding particular relationships. Building on Mitzen (2006a), they assert that while tension and security dilemmas often indicate the existence of a precarious threat environment where war is understood as a persistent possibility, at the ontological level such security dilemmas may actually reinforce the sense of being and identity of the actors involved. In this respect, ontological security arises in a situation when actors, be they individuals or states, can treat their significant Others in predictable ways—whether as friends or enemies.

The fundamental cause of the security dilemma is uncertainty (Mitzen 2006a, 341). Uncertainty makes it difficult to create and sustain the self-conception, leading to the deep, incapacitating state of not knowing which dangers to confront and which to ignore (i.e., ontological insecurity) (Mitzen 2006a, 345). Instead, states-as-actors prefer relationships they have practiced and can recognize, even if attachment to these relationships maintains conflict or reproduces other harmful, but recognizable and certain, situations (Mitzen 2006a; Steele 2008). The familiarity of the threat can thus be both attractive and dangerous: It creates an illusion of predictability, but at the same time prevents seeing other dimensions of the problem and may thus lead to a known and well-rehearsed routine of policy escalation and popular suspicion (Chernobrov 2016, 3). This is to say that states may override rationality in their search for continuity and routine, and "pursue social actions to serve self-identity needs, even when these actions compromise their physical existence" (Steele 2008, 2). A breakdown of such a stable relationship, then, can become a source of existential anxiety and fear (Roe 2008, 782).

Giddens (1991, 44–45) has reasoned that anxiety results when our systems of meaning and sense of self-integrity have been challenged or destabilized. What separates anxiety from fear is that while fear emerges in response to a specific threat and therefore has a definite object that can be prepared for, anxiety lacks such an object of focus since it emerges when one's self of integrity, systems of meaning, or self-esteem are placed in question (Giddens 1991, 43–45). Given the precarious nature of existence and the innumerable threats and risks that constantly face us, anxiety may easily become overwhelming and even paralyzing (Browning 2016). Ontological security is thus grounded in developing mechanisms which protect the subject from otherwise potentially debilitating anxieties, allowing subjects to create a sense of certainly and predictability, and to make order out of chaos (Browning 2016). What is often overlooked is that ontological security is a mere matter of asserting stability and reinforcing a sense of certitude about the existence and the nature of the social world and the self, but it also necessitates adaptability and an ability to cope with change (Craib 1998, 72). A capacity for self-reflexivity is required to enable the subject to respond creatively and innovatively to a changing world (Giddens 1991, 40-1). Stable identities do not exist (Kinnvall 2004, 747-8), nor is the social world what it used to be. It is thus adaptability that allows stability and security to be found in changing circumstances.

While peace may enhance the overall sense of physical security, it may also provide fundamental challenges to the established grounds upon which identities have been constituted (see Rumelili 2015a). This is especially evident in the context of long-established conflicts, where conflicts over material issues have transformed into conflicts over reinforcing mutually opposed identities (Wæver 2008). The current critical literature on security has, however, failed to properly theorize the identity/security nexus, because the differentiation between ontological security (security-as-being) and physical security, defined as the freedom of a pre-constituted Self from harm, threat, or danger (security-as-survival), remains unclear and thus obscures the ways in which identity constructions both enable and limit desecuritization (Rumelili 2015b, 56). After all, the processes of desecuritization are ultimately about "shifting interrelatedness," which, if they are to be possible, "must instantiate the non-threatening identity of the Other" (Hansen 2012, 533).

However, Browning and Joenniemi (2014, 7) assert that the ontology of ontological security also has dimensions that go beyond this. They argue that ontological security is also tied to socially constructed understandings of subjectivity, whereby the nature of any specific Self-Other relationship may itself be a function of perceived threats to these other foundations of ontological security; apparent for example in how the contemporary ideas about nationalism have impacted upon understandings of the requirements and needs of national identity. This applies well in the Finnish context, as contemporary ideas about nationalism can be seen to have had a strong impact on Finnish understandings of the requirements of national identity during the late nineteenth century project of national awakening, which became tied to an understanding that, to be complete, nations needed to possess a distinctive culture, territory, and, ultimately, sovereignty over that territory (Browning & Joenniemi 2014). This is also why the border between Finland and Russia has played such an important role in its various forms since Finnish independence—and continues to amidst the complexity of the present security environment

The Ukraine Crisis as a Watershed

Rather than a single, isolated event, the Ukraine crisis must be assessed as a profound game-changer, "a moment of truth" (Sakwa 2016), that has had a broad impact in Europe, but also more globally. It is true that there had already been continuing tension and political turbulence in the EU's neighborhood during the previous twenty-five years (Biscop 2016), which might lead one to argue, in hindsight, that the crisis was something that both the EU and Russia should have seen coming (Forsberg & Haukkala 2016, 8). Indeed, Russian behavior can actually be seen to have shown a degree of consistency in terms of a rejection of a liberal-values and rules-based international system, and in its pushback against the influence of both the EU and NATO in what Russia regards as its rightful sphere of influence in its "near abroad" (Hyde-Price 2015, 6). Even if the EU had been slow to reappraise its policies in response to significant changes in Russia over the years and failed to understand the exceptional nature and position of Ukraine and the shared neighborhood, the rapid unravelling of events took many by surprise and forced the European states to "sleepwalk" into the current crisis (House of Lords, EU Committee 2015, 6).

The frequent comments about the return of the Cold War seem simplistic, and hide much of the actual contemporary substance of the current crisis and its implications under the cover of the past. Effectively, much of the inner complexity of the crisis is overshadowed by the more comprehensible and familiar routine of Cold War politics, and is thus placed within a rhetoric that seems inadequate and incapable of explaining its actual substance.

Nevertheless, the severity of the situation cannot be understated. While strong, concrete reactions to the invasion of Crimea have been few and far between, and those now in place took remarkably long to materialize, in terms of rhetoric the epochal nature of the conflict has been actively underlined. "The world will never be the same again," said European Council President Herman van Rompuy at the Brussels Forum in April 2014 of the EU's geopolitical awakening to the stark realization that territorial aggression in Europe was not after all obsolete, but that instead of "responsible stakeholders" the leaders of the EU now found themselves dealing with revisionist powers.[2] Strengthened Russian assertiveness and use of power politics have resulted in a fading of the European vision of cooperative security, which has been confronted by the Russian model of an international order based on a balance of power between the leading states consolidating their right to spheres of interest.

In terms of Europe's security environment, the Ukraine crisis has been no passing storm, but rather full-blown climate change (Hyde-Price 2015). In his assessment of the situation NATO Secretary-General Anders Fogh Rasmussen (2014a,b) called the current crisis a "wake-up call" and "the gravest threat to European security since the end of the Cold War," lambasting the Russian

---

2   Statement by the European Council President Herman van Rompuy during the panel "The global consequences of the Ukraine crisis" held at the European Council on Foreign Relations on 10th July 2014. Audio available at: https://www.mixcloud.com/ECFR/europes-unstable-periphery-the-global-consequences-of-the-ukraine-crisis/

annexation of the Crimean Peninsula as illegal and illegitimate. Developments in Ukraine, Mr. Rasmussen stated, "are a stark reminder that security in Europe cannot be taken for granted" and that "tough decisions in view of the long-term strategic impact of Russia's aggression on our own security" needed to be taken. In the same vein the NATO Summit Declaration of September 2014 noted that "Russia's aggressive actions against Ukraine have fundamentally changed our vision of a Europe whole, free, and at peace."[3]

While the general failure to establish a genuinely inclusive and equal European security system after the asymmetrical end of the Cold War created tensions that have ultimately contributed to what is now called the Ukraine crisis (Sakwa 2015), there is also something fundamentally new in the current conflict. In addition to challenging the cornerstones of European political order and the ontological narrative of the multipolar and pluralistic concept of Europe, the conflict in Ukraine can be seen as a clear culmination of longstanding stresses in EU-Russia relations. It has rendered the European "Grand Narrative of EU-Russia relations" void (Haukkala 2015, 12) and shattered the last hopes for an EU-Russian strategic partnership, along with any EU attempts to tie Russia into cooperative structures. In the words of the EU High Representative Catherine Ashton (2014), the illegal Russian annexation of Crimea was "an act of aggression" and a "breach of Russia's international obligations and its commitments" that have forced the EU to ponder both the relative merits of its own policies and the future prospects for meaningful relations with Russia (Ashton 2014). The need to rethink relations has also been voiced by the Russian side, with the Russian Ambassador to the EU, Vladimir Chizhov, remarking that there should be no return to "business as usual" (Chizhov 2015).

---

3   Wales Summit Declaration. Issued by the Heads of State and Government participating in the meeting of the North Atlantic Council in Wales on 5 Sep. 2014. Available at: http://www.nato.int/cps/en/natohq/official_texts_112964.htm?mode=pressrelease

The present situation effectively signals the end of the Kantian order, and can at best be characterized as a "Cold Peace" (Hyde-Price 2015, 6; Sakwa 2016) or a "Cool War" (Larrabee, Wilson & Gordon 2015, 17). It thus seems safe to argue that the Ukraine crisis marks the end of an era of cooperation and suggests a move to a much more contested, even conflictual setting. This entails serious dangers for both the EU and Russia, as well as the countries between them (Haukkala 2015, 37). It is particularly in these latter countries that the questions of ontological security and national identity have come to the fore as Russia's disregard for the established system of norms has markedly increased distrust and unpredictability. The deterioration in political and diplomatic relations has been accompanied by growing Russian military assertiveness and a series of military incidents between Russia and its western neighbors. In addition to increased political confrontation and military tension, the security situation in many of Russia's neighboring countries, such as Finland, has become more vulnerable in terms of an ontological awareness of danger and insecurity.

The official Finnish position regarding Russia remains largely unaffected, yet the tone and wording with which it is communicated has become increasingly direct and critical. As outlined by the Prime Minister's Office (2016, 22), in its relations with Russia Finland promotes cooperation and maintains a dialogue regarding international matters, issues associated with the Baltic Sea region and various other bilateral topics, while the EU's common positions on Russia form the basis for Finland's actions. Although it is acknowledged that improved cooperation between the EU and Russia would strengthen the security and economy of Europe as a whole and that Russia's isolation serves no one's interests, this seems unattainable as Russia is perceived as not complying with the precepts of international law and its other international obligations (Prime Minister's Office 2016).

Finland seeks to maintain stable and well-functioning relations with Russia and support its democratic development and stability, yet as summarized by the Prime Minister's Office (2016, 11):

> During the past decades the foundation of the security system in our neighbourhood has been cooperation that was based on the principles of shared security as well as arms reduction treaties and confidence-building measures. During the past ten years or so Russia, through its actions and interpretations, has challenged the essence of the security regime to an extent, and has destabilised it. The West and Russia have very different opinions on how to restore stability to the security regime.

Finnish Reactions to the Ukraine Crisis

The crisis in Ukraine, or more precisely the actions of Russia, can be seen as a tipping point that not only heralded an unforeseen change in both Finland's official and public rhetoric, but also impelled it to adopt a completely new foreign policy and security position. As the Government Report on Finnish Foreign and Security Policy explains, the security of Europe and the Baltic Sea region has deteriorated largely *because* Russia annexed the Crimean Peninsula and created the crisis in Eastern Ukraine (Prime Minister's Office 2016, 11). According to official assessments, Russian actions in Ukraine have generated a vicious cycle that has led to increased tension and military activity in the Baltic Sea region and along Russia's border with Finland.

Various opinion polls suggest the crisis has caused Finns' perceptions of Russia to become considerably more negative, which is corroborated by the appearance of sharply critical opinion pieces in newspapers and throughout social media. Regarding the latter, the crisis in Ukraine has even caused a new kind of virtual unrest among concerned citizens (Huhtinen 2014). Furthermore, at a more official level there has been a noticeable departure from the previously friendly and diplomatically cautious tone. As the recent *Review on Finland's Security Cooperation,* published by the Ministry for Foreign Affairs of Finland (2015, 20), states:

> Russia, through its actions in Ukraine, has breached international law and the fundamental principles of European security, which include inter alia the right of states to independently take decisions regarding their own

> security policy guidelines. While Russia's precise goals and intentions are unknown, great-power posturing and spheres-of-influence thinking seem to be guiding its action. Relations between the West and Russia have deteriorated and are pervaded by mistrust. Furthermore, military tension has increased. These also impact Finland's immediate security environment. Russia's internal development is worrying.

A more detailed assessment, very similar in tone, was published in the Government Report on Finnish Foreign and Security Policy, published by the Prime Minister's Office a year later (2016, 14–15). The chosen wording is indicative of the increased emphasis of cultural-civilizational and even normative difference in defining non-Europe:

> Russia's leadership aim to strengthen a superpower status for their country. On the whole they perceive international relations a geopolitical zero-sum game. Their view is that the West has largely ignored Russia's considerations and security interests, and that it has opposed Russia by challenging it through many actions. Russia has mostly abandoned the cooperation-based security thinking. Rather, it now challenges the European security system. Russia has publicly promoted its goal of a sphere-of-influence-based security regime and demonstrated the will and capacity to employ military force in prosecuting its objectives. Russia's leadership try [sic] to avert internal disorder, and have [sic] been unable to reform the economy, which, in the short term, will suffer from energy price fluctuations and, in the long term, from different structural problems.

On this basis, it was determined that for the sake of its security Finland must carefully monitor the military capabilities and aspirations of actors that have an impact on its immediate surroundings, where the situation, so far, has remained relatively stable. Another cause for concern has been the realization that Russia uses "a wide range of military and non-military instruments in advancing its interests" and the "use or threat of military force against Finland cannot be excluded" (Prime Minister's Office 2016, 11). Accordingly, the "picture of war" has become more complex, as in addition to the developing military situation, the affairs of other countries can rapidly begin to be influenced, even under normal conditions, by the instigation of pressure, damage, uncertainty, and instability, blurring the line between internal and external security (Prime Minister's Office 2016, 15). This description of the situation derives from the forms of hybrid warfare practiced by Russia in Ukraine and the concern that something similar could happen in Finland. Particularly germane from Finland's perspective was the swift implementation-capacity and decision-making procedure of the Russian state leadership, which escalated the situation rapidly (Salonius-Pasternak & Limnéll 2015; Lehto & Limnéll 2016).

Russia's aggressive behavior in Ukraine was keenly followed, but it was the anxiety over the country's increasing military presence and more aggressive meddling in the Nordic and Baltic region that really hit home for Finns. Although Russia had certainly been a challenge for the previous two decades, Russian policy in Ukraine, the increased activity of the Russian Navy in the Gulf of Finland, and the rapid increase in Russian military flights over the Finnish coast made it appear more of an actual threat, a perception that in Finland carries a strong historical burden from the Soviet era. Russia's increased military operations in the Baltic Sea caused anxiety not only among the general public, but to an extent also within the government. Perhaps most notably, Finland's Minister of Defense Jussi Niinistö (2015) fanned the flames by arguing that Finland should reappraise its defense policy in light of Russian actions, suggesting that Finland's armed forces were already shoring up the defenses of the Åland Islands against "little green men" and making preparations for a possible occupation of the islands by Russia.

One of the key issues of the debate was whether Finland should finally devote serious consideration to joining NATO. While this discussion has been taking place in Finland since the collapse of the Soviet Union, it was reified and intensified by the events in Crimea. Russia is not, therefore, only an unknown, unpredictable factor, but also the reason Finland is now contemplating NATO membership. Given that the Kremlin has made it very clear that Finland can expect serious difficulties from Russia should it join NATO, the implications of membership for its security are debatable. While NATO membership is marketed as insurance against a possible attack from Russia, those opposed to it tend to argue that only NATO membership could cause such an attack. Despite heated debate, a majority of the population is still against NATO membership, and opinion continues to support a defense partnership with Sweden. In April 2015 the five Nordic countries (NATO members Norway, Denmark, and Iceland, and non-NATO members Sweden and Finland) announced a new defense-cooperation agreement aimed explicitly at confronting Russia.

Discussion of the topic grew increasingly tense and heated but lacked consensus, which was a new feature of the Finnish security policy debate, as there had traditionally been a generally accepted and united view of Russia in Finland. Although relations between the two countries had become more "normal" compared with the forced friendship of the Soviet era, during the 1990s and 2000s Finland had actively sought to continue its special relationship and remain among the "good" countries from the Russian perspective. An alternative avenue for the management of relations with Russia was provided with Finland's 1995 accession to the European Union (EU), as a result of which previously bilateral activities abruptly became part of the broader dynamics of international politics and EU-Russia relations, giving Finland increased political and economic leverage. These new and bigger circles brought much needed treatment for the Finnish long-common-border-syndrome in advocating a departure from the geo-deterministic premise that the geography of Finland predetermined its choices concerning its political actions. However, at the same time there was a tacit understanding that well-functioning bilateral relations formed a better basis for pragmatic forms of cooperation and interaction than working through Brussels could.

Although lacking a clear consensus on how to deal with Russia, the Finnish foreign policy elite seemed to reject the manner in which the EU's Russia policy was formulated following the Ukraine crisis. Moreover, a common and quite accurate understanding of the situation was that before the Ukraine crisis had escalated into a major conflict between Russia and the Western powers, it had arisen as a protest against the government's dropping of plans to forge closer trade ties with the EU. This was taken as an indication that in practice Finland, as an EU member country, was now part of the broader conflict because of its membership in the EU—a realization that served to restore the focus on the Finnish parallel bilateral relationship with Russia, in spite of the fact that the management of this more familiar avenue had also suddenly become more complicated. Deviating from the EU approach would have consequences too, but Finland was more likely to suffer than the other EU member states should relations with Russia cool further.

Finland was perceived to have much more at stake than the other EU countries, and this explains much of the somewhat paradoxical actions taken (Laine 2017). The EU's sanctions policy, Finland's Minister of Foreign Affairs Timo Soini (2015) explained, was costly not only for Russia but also for the countries that are subject to its counter-sanctions. For this reason, despite severe concerns regarding the development of Russia's domestic policy, its assertive actions in Ukraine and Finland's commitment to act within the EU sanctions framework, seeking and maintaining dialogue and good bilateral relations with Russia has been considered necessary, particularly at the level of functional politics. The decades-old balancing act was thus taken to a new level, as Finnish politicians actively tried to salvage what they could from the depleted trade with Russia, and the Border Guard sought new measures to speed up border inspections, while at the same time the official government rhetoric grew increasingly critical and public debate hovered somewhere between resentment and fear.

The situation can be seen to underline the continued benefits of eastern trade, which in turn largely explains the Finnish eagerness to keep economic and security interests separate (Raik et al. 2015). While a failed state in Ukraine would be tragic and costly for the whole of Europe, economic collapse and political chaos in Russia, together with the loosening of ties with the West and a readiness to pay a high price to pursue its imperialist ambitions, seem an even more dangerous prospect to many in Finland (Raik 2014). This paradox is evident in regularly published opinion polls such as the one conducted by the Finnish Business and Policy

Forum EVA (2015), which suggested that the number of Finns concerned about Russia had increased from 42% to 75% since the beginning of the Ukraine crisis, the feeling of insecurity had grown, the vast majority of Finns considered Russia unstable and unpredictable, and as much as half the population, the highest figure in years, perceived Russia as a military threat—yet most (87%) continued to see Russia as an important trading partner. Indeed, as Salonius-Pasternak (2015) makes clear, most Finns have no problem in maintaining two seemingly contradictory ideas: considering Russia a neighbor with whom it is worthwhile to trade and strengthen socio-cultural ties, while regarding Russia as the only potential existential threat to Finland and the Finnish people. Given the latter idea, it may be even more difficult to explain to an outsider why many Finns believe that joining NATO would be an unnecessary provocation (Raik et al. 2015, 5).

Security from What or for Whom?

Research in the humanities and social sciences has detected a substantial transformation in both the nature and the concept of borders as a result of globalization and, in particular, the process of European integration. Much of the flows and interactions, whether those of people, ideas, goods, capital, or services, have, in effect, been de-bordered; i.e., the established structures and frames of reference for setting the limits of society have been called into question. Paradoxically, flows and de-bordered spaces have also become the major cause of insecurity and instability. While globalization has fueled the emergence of complementary forms of borders which depart from the norms of territorial linearity, it has not led to a borderless world. In spite of the euphoric dreams of the early post-Cold War era, the contemporary world is involved in an extensive process of securitization and re-bordering. While there have been a number of developments and incidents—from territorial disputes to the surge of refugees and displaced people, from the rise of national populism to protectionist behavior and policies—suggesting that we cannot simply conceptualize space and borders in a postmodern way, the Ukraine crisis has revealed that there has not been a clear-cut shift towards post-national borders, but that state borders prevail, even if in reconfigured form, and continue to matter. The Russian annexation of Crimea and the subsequent conflict in Ukraine has shifted the focus back to the issues of sovereignty and territorial integrity, as well as the EU's failure to defend them and its own credibility in its eastern neighborhood, and to counter Russia's grave violations of international norms.

In Finland the implications of the crisis have been broad, and have led the country to redefine its own place in the wider constellation of regional geopolitics and international order. The debate on the cornerstones of Finnish foreign and security policy and Finland's position and place in the region has been intense. While a significant part of the population endorsed the Finnish government's decision to take the unprecedented step of condemning Russia's actions in Ukraine and actively participate in the EU's anti-Russian economic sanctions, others approached these decisions with great caution, as such a direct and open confrontation with Russia, they argued, was unquestionably a state of affairs that went beyond the Finns' customary comfort zone (Laine 2017). In stark contrast with President Paasikivi's (1946–56) famous formulation of Finnish foreign policy (continued by his successor Kekkonen [1956–82]), which turned its back to the East while bowing to the West and vice versa, President Niinistö (2012–present) has clearly positioned Finland in the West and distanced it from Russia since the Ukraine crisis began. As President Niinistö stated at the opening of parliament on 2 February 2017, while the Finnish foreign policy administered by Paasikivi and Kekkonen had been necessary to secure the existence of Finland alongside the Soviet Union, the world has gradually but fundamentally changed. Good foreign policy, President Niinistö (2017) made clear, has been and is based on the art of the possible:

> Finland is part of the West and is a country of western traditions. Nobody is questioning this. Our existence is based on the values of democracy, human rights and equality. These are also the foundations of our foreign policy. (…)

the EU must speak out on geopolitical matters—it has now become clear that the voice of Europe is also much needed in championing western values. Our security policy can have only one objective—how best to ensure a secure life for Finnish people. Neither Finland nor the Nordic countries in general are a source of danger that any unrest would break out in our own back yard because of us or that would be directed against us in particular. However, we do need to be prepared for problems originating elsewhere. This is where our foreign and security policies converge; we need to build our security in all places and in all ways. We must secure our own continued existence, in case the worst occurs.

While much of the debate continues to reflect various threats to conventional forms of state security, beneath the surface there is a greater concern and anxiety about security, predictability, stability, the self's existence, belonging, and identity. As President Niinistö stated, the main objective of Finnish security policy is to ensure a secure life for Finnish people, which is very different from securing the existence of the Finnish state as the goal was defined during the Cold War. But how exactly to go about securing daily life, then? It seems fair to assume that everyone is keen to find a solution and make arrangements which they believe will enhance their security. The difficulty lies, however, in agreeing upon which arrangements increase security and which ones reduce it, as well as in finding reliable information on the basis of which to make such an assessment.

Security is largely about information, its production, consumption, and interpretation. Information may be false or misleading and it may cause reactions and feelings that seem irrational or unfounded. True or false, information affects how we feel, behave, perceive others, and go about our daily life. Our actions and feelings, especially around (in)security, may indeed be irrational or even imagined, but this does not make them any less real. While the official Finnish position, voiced by President Niinistö on numerous occasions, is that Russia poses no military or other threat to Finland and that there is no need be afraid of Russia, public debate on the topic is undoubtedly more agitated. What this accentuates is that fear and anxiety are psychological, not political, phenomena. However, fear is easily politicized (Rumelili 2015b; Browning & Joenniemi 2017) and thus disconnected from its root causes. The idea that what occurred in Crimea might happen to us may make little political sense, but the mere dismissal of the concern does not make it go away. Fear and anxiety are not relieved by the claim that they are unfounded or irrational. What is needed is assurance that despite unpredictability and instability one's daily life can go on without major interruptions and that uncertainly can be managed.

The events in Ukraine point to a need to strengthen societal preparedness in Finland. This, in turn, calls for a holistic view of societal security, requiring citizens and various societal actors to be prepared to live and continue operating in abnormal conditions for extended periods of time. The feeling of insecurity and unpredictability has become the new normal, on the basis of which preparations for the strengthening of society's overall resilience, both mental and physical, must be made. To prepare for what is unexpected is difficult, but as the world is changing, so too must our approach to it change. In this process a careful balance must be sought, which also takes into consideration more ontological notions of security, because simply securitizing everything may in fact only create a heightened and unwarranted sense of insecurity.

Borders provide an illuminating laboratory for analysis, because they reflect the complexity of the present security environment and echo some of the greatest challenges contemporary Europe faces. The securitization of borders, both physically and administratively, is seldom a functional solution, as it does little to address the actual root cause of the perceived problem at stake, be it irregular migration, smuggling, or the unwanted influences of the outside world. However, at a time of global unrest, economic instability, and rapid social transformation borders have begun to represent an important symbolic element of security, which in itself is important socially and psychologically for the individual. Feelings of personal insecurity are reflected in rhetoric about closing state borders in an attempt to make borders feel ontologically safe. This may have less to do with actual control or protection from a perceived threat from the other side, and more with the psychological comfort borders bring about and the role they play in identity construction.

References

Abrahamsen, R., & Williams, M. C. (2009). Security Beyond the State: Global Security Assemblages in International Politics. *International Political Sociology*, 3(1), 1–17.

Ashton, C. (2014). Remarks by EU High Representative Catherine Ashton following the extraordinary Foreign Affairs Council on Ukraine, Brussels, 3 March 2014, 140303/02. Retrieved from http://eeas.europa.eu/statements/docs/2014/140303_02_ en.pdf

Berenskoetter, F. (2014). Parameters of a National Biography. *European Journal of International Relations*, 20(1), 262–288.

Biscop, S. (2016). Game of Zones: Power Struggles in the EU's Neighbourhood. *Global Affairs*, 2(1), 1–11.

Brauch, H. G. (2007). Security Threats, Challenges, Vulnerability and Risks. *In*: Ú.O. Spring (Ed.), *International Security, Peace, Development and Environment*, Oxford: EOLSS-UNESCO.

Browning, C. S. (2014). The Hidden Opportunities within Finland's Country Brand. *In*: V. Sinkkonen & H. Vogt (Eds.), *Utopia ulkopolitiikassa: sarja visioita Suomen asemasta maailmassa [Foreign Policy Utopias: Visions of Finland's Position in the World]*, pp. 53–63. Jyväskylä: Ministry for Foreign Affairs of Finland.

Browning, C. S. (2016). Ethics and Ontological Security. *In*: J. Nyman & A. Burke (Eds.), *Ethical Security Studies: A New Research Agenda*, pp. 160–73. London and New York: Routledge.

Browning, C. S. & Joenniemi, P. (2014). Karelia as a Finnish-Russian issue: Re-negotiating the Relationship between National Identity, Territory and Sovereignty. *CEURUS EU-Russia Papers*, No. 18.

Browning, C. S. & Joenniemi, P. (2015). The Ontological Significance of Karelia: Finland's Reconciliation with Losing the Promised Land. *In*: B. Rumelili (Ed.), *Conflict Resolution and Ontological Security: Peace Anxieties*, pp. 154–171. New York: Routledge.

Browning, C. S. & Joenniemi, P. (2017). Ontological Security, Self-articulation and the Securitization of Identity. *Cooperation and Conflict*, 52(1), 31–47.

Buzan, B., Wæver, O., & De Wilde, J. (1998). *Security: A New Framework for Analysis*. Boulder: Lynne Rienner Publishers.

Chernobrov, D. (2016). Ontological Security and Public (Mis)Recognition of International Crises: Uncertainty, Political Imagining, and the Self. *Political Psychology*, 37(5), Early View Online version DOI: 10.1111/pops.12334

Chizhov, V. (2015). Address by the Permanent Representative of the Russian Federation to the EU Ambassador Vladimir Chizhov at the Alpbach Forum panel 'The EU and Russia: Rivals, Opponents, Partners?', Alpbach, 31 August 2015. Retrieved from https://www.russianmission.eu/en/ambassador-vladimir-chizhovs-address-alpbachforum-2015

Craib, I. (1998). *Experiencing Identity*. London: Sage.

Finnish Business and Policy Forum EVA (2015). *Ken on maassa jämäkin? EVA:n Arvo- ja asennetutkimus 2015*. EVA Report 1/2015. Helsinki: Taloustieto.

Forsberg, T. & Haukkala, H. (2016). Could It Have Been Different? The Evolution of the EU-Russia Conflict and its Alternatives. LSE IDEAS – Dahrendorf Forum Special Report. March 2016, 8–14.

Giddens, A. (1990). *The Consequences of Modernity*. Cambridge: Polity Press.

Giddens, A. (1991). *Modernity and Self-Identity: Self and Society in the Late Modern Age*. Stanford, CA: Stanford University Press.

Gower, J. & Timmins, G. (2009). Introduction: The European Union, Russia and the Shared Neighbourhood. *Europe-Asia Studies*, 61(10), 1685–7.

Hansen, L. (2012). Reconstructing Desecuritisation: The Normative-political in the Copenhagen School and Directions for How to Apply It. *Review of International Studies*, 38(3), 525–546.

Haukkala, H. (2015). From Cooperative to Contested Europe? The Conflict in Ukraine as a Culmination of a Long-Term Crisis in EU-Russia Relations. *Journal of Contemporary European Studies*, 23(1), 25–40. DOI: 10.1080/14782804.2014.1001822.

Heiskanen, M. (2013). *Rajakeisarin uudet (v)aatteet: Käsiteanalyysi rajaturvallisuudesta [The Border Emperor's New Clothes: Concept Analysis of Border Security]* Doctoral Dissertation. Acta Electronica Universitatis Lapponiensis 124. Rovaniemi: University of Lapland.

Hewitt, B. A. (2010). Ontological Insecurity. *In*: R.L. Jackson & M.A. Hogg (Eds.), *Encyclopedia of identity*, pp. 511–512. London: Sage.

Hobson, J. M. (2007). Is Critical Theory Always for the White West and for Western Imperialism? Beyond Westphalian towards a Post-racist Critical IR. *Review of International Studies*, 33(SI), 91–116.

Hough, P. (2014). *Understanding Global Security*. 3rd Edition. London: Routledge.

House of Lords, EU Committee (2015). *The EU and Russia: before and beyond the crisis in Ukraine. (House of Lords, European Union Committee, 6th Report Session 2014-15, HL Paper 115)*. Technical report. London: The Authority of the House of Lords.

Huhtinen, A-M. (2014). Ukrainan kriisi romahdutti suomalaisten käsitykset Venäjästä [The Ukraine Crisis Crumpled the Finnish Perceptions of Russia]. Retrieved from http://yle.fi/uutiset/3-7521314

Hyde-Price, A. (2015). European Security and the Ukraine Crisis: Between Globalisation and Geopolitics. *Katse* 2/2015, 5-8.

Kinnvall, C. (2004). Globalization and Religious Nationalism: Self, Identity, and the Search for Ontological Security. *Political Psychology*, 25(5), 741-767.

Krolikowski, A. (2008). State Personhood in Ontological Security Theories of International Relations and Chinese Nationalism: A Sceptical View. *The Chinese Journal of International Politics*, 2(1), 109-33.

Laine, J. (2015). Threats, Challenges, and Finnish-Russian Cross-Border Security Cooperation: A Finnish Perspective. *Eurolimes* 20, 125-142.

Laine, J. (2017). Shifting Borders: Unpredictability and Strategic Distrust at the Finnish-Russian Border. *In*: G. Besier & K. Stokłosa (Eds.), *Neighbourhood Perceptions of the Ukraine Crisis: From the Soviet Union into Eurasia*, pp. 90-104. Routledge: London.

Laing, R. D. (1960). *The Divided Self*. London: Penguin.

Larrabee, F. S., Wilson P. A. & Gordon IV J. (2015). *The Ukrainian Crisis and European security: Implications for the United States and U.S. Army*. Santa Monica, CA: RAND Corporation.

Lehto, M. & Limnéll, J. (2016). Cyber Security Capability and the Case of Finland. *In*: Proceedings of the 15th European Conference on Cyber Warfare and Security, ECCWS 2016 (Vol. 2016-January, pp. 182-190). Curran Associates, Inc.

Limnéll, J. (2009). *Suomen uhkakuvapolitiikka 2000-luvun alussa [The Finnish Threat Perception Policy iat the Beginning of the 2000s]* Helsinki: National Defence University.

Limnéll, J. (2015). European Cybersecurity Must Be Strengthened. *European Cybersecurity Journal*, 2(1), 41.

Ministry for Foreign Affairs of Finland (2015). *Review on Finland´s Security Cooperation*, Publications of the Ministry for Foreign Affairs 3.

Mitzen, J. (2006a). Ontological Security in World Politics: State Identity and the Security Dilemma. *European Journal of International Relations*,12(3), 341–70.

Mitzen, J. (2006b). Anchoring Europe's Civilizing Identity: Habits, Capabilities, and Ontological Security. *Journal of European Public Policy*, 13(2), 270–85.

Morozov, V. & Rumelili, B. (2012). The External Constitution of European Identity: Russia and Turkey as Europe-makers. *Cooperation and Conflict*, 47(1), 28–48.

Niinistö, J. (2015). An interview with Lännen Media regional news service. Kaleva 30 July 2015.

Niinistö, S. (2017). Speech by President of the Republic Sauli Niinistö at the opening of Parliament on 2 February 2017. Speeches, 2/2/2017. Office of the President of the Republic of Finland, Helsinki. Retrieved from http://www.presidentti.fi/public/default.aspx?contentid=357586

Nyman, J. & Burke, A. (2016). Introduction: Imagining Ethical Security Studies. *In*: J. Nyman J & A.D: Burke (Ed.), *Ethical Security Studies: A New Research Agenda*, pp. 1–14. London: Routledge.

Prime Minister's Office (2016). Government Report on Finnish Foreign and Security Policy. Prime Minister's Office Publications 9/2016.

Raik, K. (2014). How Should Europe Respond to Russia? The Finnish view. Commentary, European Council on Foreign Relations, 18 November 2014.

Raik, K.; Aaltola, M; Pynnöniemi, K, & Salonius-Pasternak, C. (2015). Pushed Together by External Forces? The Foreign and Security Policies of Estonia and Finland in the Context of the Ukraine Crisis. FIIA Briefing Paper 167.

Rasmussen, A. F. (2014a). Speech at the Brookings Institution, Washington, DC. 19 Mar 2014.

Rasmussen, A. F. (2014b). Joint press point with NATO Secretary General Anders Fogh Rasmussen and the Prime Minister of Ukraine, Arsenii Yatseniuk, 6 Mar 2014. Retrieved from http://www.nato.int/cps/en/natolive/opinions_107842.htm

Roe, P. (2008). The 'Value' of Positive Security. *Review of International Studies*, 34(4), 777–94.

Rumelili, B. (2015b). Identity and Desecuritisation: The Pitfalls of Conflating Ontological and Physical Security. *Journal of International Relations and Development*, 18(1), 52–74.

Rumelili, B. (ed.). (2015a). *Conflict Resolution and Ontological Security: Peace*

Anxieties. London: Routledge.

Sakwa, R. (2015). *Frontline Ukraine: Crisis in the Borderland*. London: I.B. Tauris.

Sakwa, R. (2016). The Ukraine Crisis Has Become More Dangerous Than Just a New Cold War. Russia Direct June 02, 2016. Retrieved from http://www.russia-direct.org/qa/ukraine-crisis-has-become-more-dangerous-just-new-cold-war

Salonius-Pasternak, C. (2015). Finland's Balancing Act. *The Journal of International Security Affairs*, 28.

Salonius-Pasternak, C. & Limnéll, J. (2015). Preparing Finland for Hybrid Warfare: Social Vulnerabilities and the Threat of Military Force. FIIA Comment 6/2015.

Sasse, G. (2013) Linkages and the Promotion of Democracy: the EU's Eastern Neighbourhood. *Democratisation*, 20(4), 553–591.

Scott, J. W. (2017). Constructing European Neighborhood: Critical Perspectives from EU-Ukraine Interaction and Civil Society Actors. *Journal of Borderlands Studies*, 32(1), 23–39.

Soini, T. (2015). Interview with radio programme Yle Ykkösaamu. 18 August 2015.

Steele, B. J. (2005). Ontological Security and the Power of Self-Identity: British Neutrality and the American Civil War. *Review of International Studies*, 31(3), 519–40.

Steele, B. J. (2008). *Ontological Security in International Relations: Self-Identity and the IR State*. New York: Routledge.

Stubb, A. (2015). Prime Minister Alexander Stubb's speech at the seminar "European Security and Conflict in Ukraine" 30 March 2015. Government of Finland Communications Department. Retrieved from http://valtioneuvosto.fi/artikkeli/-/asset_publisher/10616/paaministeri-alexander-stubbin-puheenvuoro-euroopan-turvallisuus-ja-konflikti-ukrainassa-seminaarissa-30-maaliskuuta-2015?_101_INSTANCE_3wyslLo1Z0ni_languageId=en_US

Wæver, O. (1995). Securitization and Desecuritization. *In*: R.D. Lipschutz (Ed.), *On Security*, pp. 46–87. New York: Columbia University Press.

Wæver, O. (2008). Fear and Forgetting: How to Leave Longstanding Conflicts through De-securitization. Paper presented for the first Research Seminar of CAST, Copenhagen University, 29 Oct 2008.

Zarakol, A. (2010). Ontological (In)Security and State Denial of Historical Crimes: Turkey and Japan. *International Relations*, 24(1), 3–23.

George Soroka

Assessing Domestic Security Challenges in Post-Maidan Ukraine: Two Critical Dimensions

A critical aspect of domestic security has to do with whether or not those inhabiting a given state accept the validity of the political arrangements under which they live. In the case of Ukraine, polarized reactions to the Maidan protests, as well as the subsequent annexation of Crimea and the outbreak of fighting in the Donbas, have clearly demonstrated that the societal understanding of what constitutes a legitimate political community is fractured. Consequently, this chapter explores the nature of this fracture from two complementary yet distinct perspectives, focusing on internal security issues related to problems of nation-building and stateness, on one hand, and the degree and quality of Ukraine's governance, on the other. In particular, I argue that while ethno-linguistic cleavages (and the cultural, religious and historical factors associated with them) do represent a challenge for Ukrainian security going forward, the more consequential challenge revolves around Ukrainian leaders' seemingly endemic inability to rule the country in a manner that is transparent, accountable, and fair to all citizens.

It is one thing to appreciate the implications of divisive identity politics in an abstract sense, and quite another to do so on the basis of lived experience. Although I had already been studying the post-communist region for nearly a decade by then, it was only after several months of fieldwork in Kyiv during the height of the Great Recession that I began to truly appreciate how deeply felt—even at times of acute economic crisis—rifts over such matters as language, history and religion were in Ukrainian society, and how much they affected Ukraine's present and future possibilities. Emblematic of this was an exchange I witnessed one blustery February afternoon while waiting for a bus at Kontraktova ploshcha, in the very heart of the city. Two women, both on the downhill side of middle age, suddenly began arguing loudly. I did not hear what initiated their dispute, but the resulting commotion was impossible to ignore. One woman was screaming in Ukrainian, the other in Russian, both of them refusing to make the slightest linguistic concession, even if only to exchange insults in a common tongue (though it was perfectly obvious that they understood each other). What especially stands out in my mind was how the Russian speaker, after hurling a tirade of invective at the Ukrainian speaker, finally enjoined her to "go back west!" Not to be outdone at sending others into rhetorical exile, the latter — animatedly making the sign of the cross over herself the whole time, as if to ward off evil — retorted that it was her adversary who should instead return to Moscow, prompting the indignant Russian speaker to exclaim "I was born HERE!" Thankfully, the altercation soon ended as the bus pulled up and the gathered crowd began jostling aboard, but not before the Russian speaker let her aggrieved interlocutor (and everyone else within earshot) know that Ukraine needed the return of a figure like Stalin, as such nationalist nonsense would then not be tolerated. ("He would've had you shot!" were her actual parting words.)

A dramatic vignette, to be sure, but also one that serves to illustrate the ideational fractures and ethno-cultural divisions that continue to permeate Ukraine, a country where the unreconciled traumas of the past, particularly those of the Soviet era, remain painfully palpable. These lingering ghosts should not surprise us. Wherever one stands on the antiquity of a distinctive Ukrainian *ethnie*, as a polity Ukraine is quite young, never before having enjoyed sovereignty within its post-Soviet borders.[1] Indeed, in many respects the Ukraine that emerged after the Soviet Union's dissolution constituted an improbable state. Not only was this newly independent entity faced with the daunting task of

---

1   Ukraine attained the geopolitical configuration it would have at independence in 1991 only after Soviet authorities transferred the administration of Crimea from the Russian SFSR to the Ukrainian SSR in 1954. Moreover, much of what is today western Ukraine was only incorporated into the Soviet Union as the result of WWII.

implementing sweeping political, economic and social reforms, but it had to concurrently deal with having its legitimacy impugned from two interrelated sides: by those nostalgic for the USSR and unable to accept new realities, and those who refused to recognize Ukrainians as distinct from Russians. Moreover, significant internal fault lines in its political geography, stemming not only from differences in how Ukraine's inhabitants self-identify but also such structural factors as an industrial base that is concentrated in the eastern part of the country and a prominent rural-urban divide, were superimposed over the mnemonic echoes and institutional traces of discordant imperial legacies—among them Russian, Austro-Hungarian, Polish and Ottoman—and the divergent historical experiences, recollections, and expectations arising from these. Exacerbating this cacophony of cleavages, how one interprets the 2013-2014 Maidan protests, along with Russia's annexation of Crimea and the outbreak of fighting in the Donbas, has become an additional source of contention. As a result, since gaining independence Ukraine has been beset by internecine power struggles between factions that do not always recognize the boundaries of the political unit they inhabit as congruent with the mental maps to which they pledge allegiance. And even among those who accept Ukraine's borders as they were fixed in 1991, controversy remains over exactly what sort of entity it should be. Consequently, a fundamental security dilemma facing post-communist Ukraine is how to minimize the centrifugal forces pulling it apart (e.g., the precedence of regional and transnational loyalties, including to a Soviet empire that no longer exists), while maximizing the centripetal forces causing it to cohere.

At the same time, it is important to recognize there simultaneously exists another, more cosmopolitan and pluralistic, Ukraine. Timothy Snyder captures this competing reality when, in reflecting on the Maidan, he writes: "Has it ever before happened that people associated with Ukrainian, Russian, Belarusian, Armenian, Polish and Jewish culture have died in a revolution that was started by a Muslim?" (2014). The latter reference is to Mustafa Nayyem, the Kyiv-based journalist whom Snyder credits with precipitating the protests (which began on November 21, 2013) by posting messages on Twitter and Facebook urging people to gather on the capital's *Maidan Nezalezhnosti* ("Independence Square") to register their displeasure after President Viktor Yanukovich abruptly reneged on concluding an Association Agreement with the EU. Left unremarked is that Nayyem, who was born in Afghanistan, made these social media posts in Russian, not Ukrainian.

Indicative of the existence of this other Ukraine and its parallel priorities, those demonstrating cut across generational, confessional and ethnic boundaries, with the average protestor being an educated, middle-class male in his mid-thirties (Onuch and Sasse 2016; Onuch 2014).[2] Neither language nor ethnicity were significant determinants of participation (Onuch and Hale 2018; Onuch and Sasse 2016), rendering the movement a "decidedly more civic than ethnic" political phenomenon (Onuch 2014, 49). Moreover, while Kyiv represented the epicenter of the protests, anti-government demonstrations occurred throughout the country, including in Crimea.[3] As to what the protestors were demanding, despite the movement often being depicted as championing an unambiguous turn towards Europe and the institutional life of the West, after the first attempt to violently disperse them on November 30, 2013 failed, they were more focused on criticizing the Yanukovych government's performance than advocating a coherent vision for Ukraine's geopolitical future (Onuch and Sasse 2016; Onuch 2014).[4]

---

[2] However, the protest cycle evinced distinct stages, and the composition of the protestors was not fixed.

[3] Though a regional divide was clearly discernible, with secondary protests disproportionately taking place in the western and central provinces of Ukraine and counter-protests concentrated in the south and east. Indeed, Onuch found that most of the Maidan protesters from outside the Kyiv region (42%) hailed from the west or center of the country (2014, 48; see also Reznik 2016).

[4] This mirrors my observation that while the proximate cause of the Maidan protests may have been Yanukovych's *volte face*, the movement was sustained not by a yearning to join the EU for its own sake, but rather contempt for, and exhaustion with, the endemic corruption that has plagued Ukraine's political

In light of all this, it is apparent that the domestic security challenges facing Ukraine are complex and multifaceted. Nevertheless, they may be distinguished based on whether they stem primarily from tensions related to competing ethnic and linguistic identities (which frequently coincide with differences in how Ukrainian history is interpreted), or dissatisfaction with the performance of elected officials and state bureaucrats. Expressed succinctly, the internal security problems Ukraine faces revolve around two main arenas: *nation-building and stateness*, and the *degree and quality of governance*. Admittedly, these are porous and partially overlapping categories. [5] Nonetheless, sub-setting them in this

---

and economic life since independence. Under these circumstances, the signing of the Association Agreement appears to have been perceived by many, first and foremost, as a means through which to alter the course of domestic affairs rather than Ukraine's international allegiances.

5   For example, problems with state capacity (i.e., the ability of the state to project power and enforce its will) may be related to deficits in nation-building and stateness as well as the degree and quality of governance. The peaceable handover of Crimea by Ukrainian troops to Russian forces occurred not only due to the balance of military power between the two sides heavily favoring the latter in any potential confrontation, but also because soldiers under Ukrainian command were not sufficiently invested in maintaining the geographic integrity of Ukraine to make Crimea worth their fighting over. Similarly, while Kyiv did not possess the penetrative reach necessary to retain control of the breakaway regions of Luhansk and Donetsk, this outcome did not merely stem from insufficient material capabilities. While survey evidence (discussed below) suggests separatist sentiments were only held by a minority in these areas, the lack of identification with Ukraine as a polity was still meaningful enough to support (even leaving aside Russia's considerable interference) the outbreak of hostilities. Thus, although the conflict was abetted by the arrival of foreign fighters and paramilitary groups, the initial crisis of state capacity was endogenous. It is also important to recognize that state capacity – both in terms of fostering sufficient allegiance to the state to ensure its mandates *will be carried out*, as well as the state having sufficient resources to assure they *can be carried out* – is not necessarily evenly distributed. Had Russia instead attempted to annex Volyn or Zakarpattia, the results would almost certainly have been different. The point is that good governance may increase state capacity in myriad ways, including by bolstering defensive capabilities (e.g., ensuring military officers are promoted on merit rather than political connections), but by itself this is insufficient; there is also a need to have those tasked with

fashion remains heuristically useful, as it allows for thinking about the appropriate level at which security threats must be analyzed and ultimately addressed.

Developing this typology further, nation-building and stateness are predominantly *mass-level* phenomena; this is because, regardless of whether one believes collective identities need to arise organically or that they may be aided (or even created) by government policies, it is within society at large that the results are expressed. In this instance, therefore, the dependent variable is the relative strength of a common group identity and the parameters of its inclusiveness, meaning not only whether the primary supra-familial loyalty of Ukraine's citizens lies with the political community they formally belong to, but also the extent to which they share an affective sense of "we-feeling" among themselves (Stepan, Linz, and Yadav 2011). In contrast, when considering issues related to the degree and quality of governance, we are principally interested in assessing *elite-level* performance; here, the dependent variable is how well elected officials and bureaucrats live up to what is expected of those occupying such offices. These too are not fully segregated domains, as there exists a measure of permeability between levels.[6] Still, it is analytically useful to disaggregate them in terms of the principal actors affected.

Framed in this manner, I make two hierarchical — in the sense that I believe the latter to be more consequential than the former — arguments pertaining to Ukraine's security, one predominantly socio-cultural (corresponding to nation-building and stateness evinced at the mass level) and the other predominantly institutional

---

    defending the state feel a sense of loyalty to the underlying socio-political unit that it represents.

6   Nor does distinguishing between mass and elite levels on the outcome side presuppose attendant claims regarding causal variables. Thus, while the success or failure of nation-building manifests on the mass level, it may result from the implementation of top-down policies, bottom-up "grass-roots" initiatives, or some combination thereof. Likewise, while governmental performance is adjudicated at the elite level, both top-down initiatives (e.g., anti-corruption campaigns) as well as bottom-up efforts (e.g., ordinary individuals refusing to engage in bribery) can influence it.

(corresponding to the degree and quality of governance evinced at the elite level).[7] An assumption underlying both is that Ukraine will not relinquish its claims to either the separatist-held areas of the Donbas or Crimea (though the latter appears lost to Kyiv for the foreseeable future). First, I contend Ukraine will remain politically fragile unless and until a robust and inclusive Ukrainian identity develops among its citizens. Second, I assert that while Ukraine's pronounced societal divisions do indeed harm its security, they are not nearly as consequential as shortcomings in the way it is governed.

As regards the scope of this inquiry, since the annexation of Crimea and the start of the conflict in the Donbas domestic and international security issues have effectively become two sides of the same coin for Ukraine, with events beyond its borders ineluctably affecting not only objective assessments of security, but also how its attainment is subjectively defined. However, in this chapter I concentrate on internal issues.[8] This focus not only represents a much-needed counterpoint to accounts claiming Ukraine's options are essentially binary and civilizational in nature (i.e., develop a closer partnership with the West or deepen ties to Russia), but likewise highlights that the security situation appears different when viewed from Kharkiv, L'viv or Odessa than it does

---

[7] Here I use the term *institutional* to refer to both the formal and informal "rules of the game," the latter shading into political culture but distinguished from it by a focus on "shared expectations rather than shared values" (Helmke and Levitsky 2004, 728). This is not to suggest that individual agency or culture are epiphenomenal with regard to governance — far from it. Rather, I focus on institutions for reasons of theoretical and empirical tractability: agency is ungeneralizable except in the most basic sense, while political culture is, at least over shorter timespans, largely anterior to institutions, more likely to be *expressed through* them rather than *shaped by* them.

[8] Ukraine's 2015 National Security Strategy specifically mentions the following threats: 1) Russian aggression; 2) ineffective systems of national security and defense; 3) corruption and poor governance; 4) the economic crisis; 5) energy insecurity; 6) information insecurity; 7) cyber-security threats; 8) threats to critical infrastructure; and 9) environmental problems. Many of these fall squarely within the realm of domestic security, and all of them have a bearing on it (Zakonodavstvo Ukraïni 2015).

from Brussels, Washington or Moscow. Concomitantly, it takes into account that the threat Ukraine faces from the Russian side is not fully exogenous given the myriad historical and contemporary entanglements the two countries share and the extensive transboundary networks that exist between them. Finally, emphasizing the internal aspects of the security equation acknowledges the under-theorized intermediary role domestic actors play in advancing or retarding the designs of more powerful states. Undoubtedly, whether or not Ukraine joins the EU and/or NATO will have a substantial impact on its security, as will Russia's response to these contingencies. But as events surrounding the Maidan have shown, while external forces may attempt to incentivize certain outcomes over others, it is vital to consider how "the preferences of rent-seeking domestic elites mitigate the effect of the EU and Russia on domestic change" (Langbein 2016, 20).

Below I proceed by enumerating the internal security issues facing Ukraine and their potential solutions. Considered first are challenges related to nation-building and stateness, and how these may be attenuated by the deepening and strengthening of a Ukrainian identity that cuts across existing socio-political cleavages. The latter half of the analysis, meanwhile, focuses on problems associated with Ukraine's degree and quality of governance, and assesses what may be done to improve how the country is ruled.

Nation-Building and Stateness: Defining and Implementing Concepts

Identifying as a nation "means, above all, that *it is proper* to expect from certain groups a specific sentiment of solidarity in the face of other groups" (Weber 1978, 922).[9] When national belonging is based on shared ethnicity, such solidarity manifests across multiple dimensions, with cultural and linguistic factors being particularly pertinent. Ethnic conceptions of nationhood are also linked to

---

9   Emphasis in original.

consanguineal descent (whether real or imagined), and thus bolster cohesiveness by imbuing the idea of the nation with a primordial gravitas.[10] Contrariwise, nationhood predicated on civic principles only demands the acceptance of a comprehensive system of shared ideological premises to achieve solidarity. Under its terms, allegiances are voluntary, rooted in mutually affirmed ideals and values; defining the nation in this context becomes a collectively constitutive act. In both instances, however, the process of nation-building involves conspicuous othering: for every claim "we are x," there exists a corollary counterclaim about those who are "not x."[11] It likewise encompasses an inherent relationality; individuals must not only view themselves as part of the nation, but they must also, in turn, be recognized by others within that community as rightfully belonging to it (Gellner 1983, 7). As a result, nation-building is successful when the centrality of the national unit (regardless of the terms in which it is conceived) in commanding individuals' aggregate loyalty is no longer disputed, but simply taken for granted.[12]

However, whereas the nation possesses "no autonomy, no agents, no rules, but only the resources derived from the psychological identification of the people who constitute it" (Linz and Stepan 1996, 22), the state is defined precisely by its autonomy, agents and rules. As such, a state provides the space *within which*, as well as the institutional mechanisms *through which*, nations are

---

10 This is precisely the genius of ethno-nationalism: it appears so natural even when it often is not, making it easy to forget, for example, that Germans and Italians did not think of themselves as such until relatively recently. However, once established, civic as well as ethnic nations function in a temporally transcendent fashion, establishing ties with those long dead and those not yet born through historical myth-making and symbolic politics.

11 On the differences between ethnic and civic conceptions of nationhood, see Smith 1986, 134-138. However, these are best understood as ideal types given that, in reality, ethnic and civic elements of nationhood are routinely combined within states (Stepan, Linz and Yadav 2011).

12 As Bloom (1993, 58) observes, this does not mean that other sub-national or supra-national loyalties cease to be meaningful, but they do have to be subsumed to the interests of the nation, in the sense that they can no longer form a competing center of legitimacy.

actualized as political entities.[13] State-building, therefore, involves developing an institutional apparatus of governance that claims exclusive authority over a delimited territory.

But although state-building is not synonymous with nation-building, the two processes exhibit multiple synergies. For instance, ethno-nationalism is based on the expectation that the geographic territory regarded as the group's homeland should be coterminous with its political borders (Gellner 1983, 1). But while this form of nationalism may bolster state-building under certain circumstances, it may thwart it in non-ethnically homogenous contexts, with aggressive nationalizing policies proving especially destabilizing when pursued in states with a sizeable ethnic minority.[14] Conversely, when the reification of the state precedes that of an underlying nation, the former may provide the "container" in which national identity coheres *ex post* (Bloom 1993, 54–59; Dalberg-Acton 1949, 183–194).[15] Problems of nation-building consequently occur when individuals do not identify with one another in either an ethnic or civic sense. In contrast, problems of stateness, which Linz and Stepan define as disputes over territorial boundaries and matters of citizenship (1996, 16), manifest when the

---

13 For the classic definition of the state, conceptualized as "a compulsory association with a territorial basis" that monopolizes the legitimate use of force, see Weber 1964, 156. Note, though, that while more than one ethnic nation may exist within a state (as the imperial model has demonstrated), this is not possible for a full-fledged civic nation.

14 This is of particular concern when the ethnic minority "is, or could be, considered by a neighboring state as an irredenta," as this may "fan extremist nationalism in the neighboring country" and incentivize the pursuit of militant policies aimed at ostensibly protecting co-ethnics residing abroad (Linz & Stepan 1996, 26).

15 This is characteristic of many of the states that resulted from European decolonization efforts in the latter half of the 20th century, and conforms to the distinction Stepan, Linz and Yadav (2011) make between "nation-states" and "state-nations," the latter entities wherein a national identity (to the extent that it exists at all) has emerged after the formation of the state. Many civic nations (e.g., the United States, Canada) were established via this pathway, but it may also serve as the means through which ethnic nations form. Recall the exhortation of the 19th century stateman Massimo d'Azeglio: "We have made Italy, we now have to make Italians."

inhabitants of a state refuse to recognize it as legitimate, or else identify with a national project incongruent with its borders.

Of particular significance to determining the degree of stateness a polity possesses is its ability to act independently. Relative to the international environment, the state needs a high degree of autonomy from outside influences to operate effectively, even realizing that the exercise of sovereignty by weaker states will always *de facto* if not *de jure* be constrained to some extent by more powerful neighbors, and that international treaties and agreements will likewise limit a state's ability to act in an unfettered manner. Domestically, meanwhile, the state's essential duties must remain autonomous from subversive forces that would privilege themselves at the expense of the wider body politic. The state needs to function as a state, in other words, and not the personal piggybank of its putative representatives, business elites, or criminal figures and their syndicates.

Socio-Cultural Identity and Its Determinants

Post-Soviet Ukraine was formally established on civic rather than ethnic principles, with the 1990 Declaration of State Sovereignty explicitly referencing the "people of Ukraine" rather than the "Ukrainian people." And upon achieving independence in 1991 Ukraine adopted liberal citizenship policies, granting full membership in the political community to anyone living within its borders, regardless of ethnicity. These commitments were reiterated in the 1996 Constitution, which described it as a multi-ethnic polity based on shared ideological commitments.[16] Practically, however, Ukraine has since independence experienced continual tension between the inclination to promote preferential recognition of the titular (and numerically superior) ethnic group and its professed dedication to a more inclusive identity.

One way of visualizing how identity variables relate to political performance is via electoral maps, wherein voting patterns correlate prominently to ethno-linguistic cleavages in a country

---

16 See Wolczuk 2001.

whose western region is overwhelmingly Ukrainophone and ethnically Ukrainian, whose center is linguistically and ethnically mixed, and whose eastern and southern regions are largely Russophone and home to a considerable number of ethnic Russians.

The first map is of the 2004 presidential election, in which Viktor Yushchenko beat out Viktor Yanukovych after the fraudulent results of the prior election were nullified.[17]

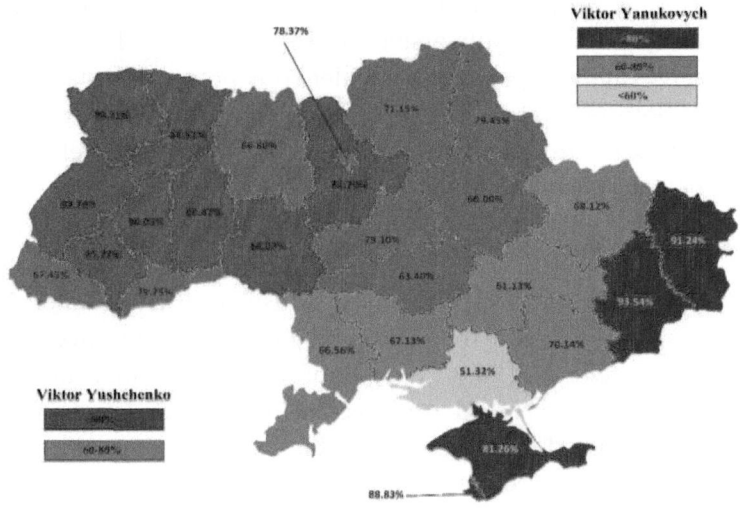

The next map is of the 2010 election, which Yanukovych, whose base of support was located in the Donbas, won in a second-round runoff against Yulia Timoshenko, who identified more with ethnonationalist and pro-European positions.

---

17   I wish to thank Fei Carnes of Harvard University's Center for Geographic Analysis for her assistance in creating these maps. Vote percentages are taken from Ukraine's Central Election Commission (www.cvk.gov.ua).

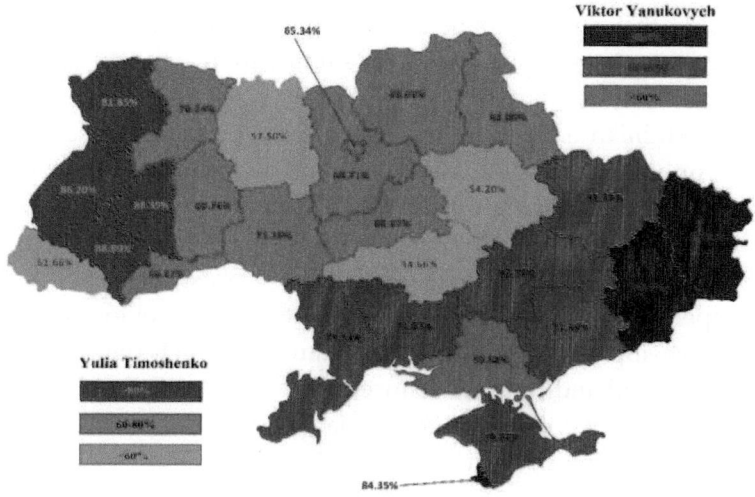

The final map is of the 2014 election, which brought a first-round victory for Petro Poroshenko, an oligarch who hails from Vinnytsia, a city on the banks of the Southern Bug River in west-central Ukraine.

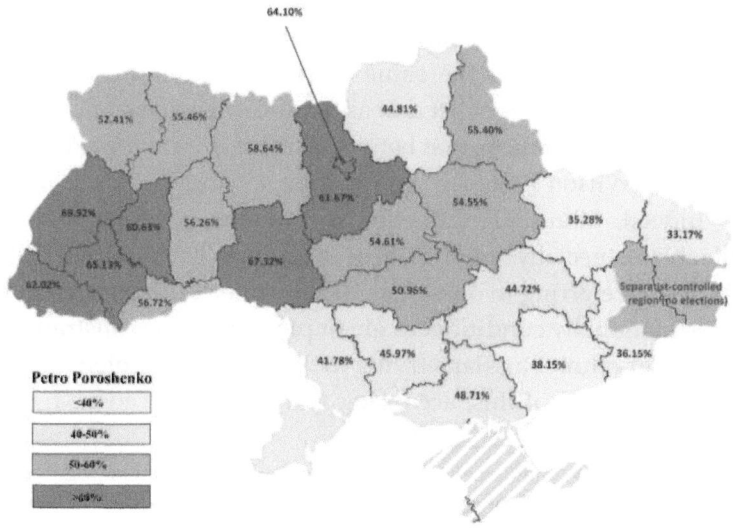

However, while these political divisions are entrenched and durable, they should not be overstated to the point of caricature. In particular, characterizing Ukraine's bifurcation along an east/west axis as solely attributable to pro-Russian sentiments in the former and Ukrainian ethno-nationalism in the latter is overly simplistic. Not only does it elide discussion of considerable *intraregional* variation in political affinities (Osipian and Osipian 2012), but it also overlooks the polarizing role of other factors, which may be concentrated in various geographic constellations or be independent of them altogether (e.g., the existence of localized and industry-specific trade networks, many of which date from the Soviet period and continue to incentivize cooperation with Russia). Moreover, if we accept that Galicia and the Donbas function as antipodes in the Ukrainian cultural imaginary and "exclude such unique and distinctive multiethnic regions as Crimea, Bukovina, and Transcarpathia," it becomes apparent that the "nature, climate, landscape, economy, practices of everyday life, urban and rural architecture, identities, and balance of languages transition smoothly from northwest to southeast within the main body of Ukraine" (Osipian and Osipian 2012, 627). And while staunch ethno-nationalists may hold that "Ukraine and Russia are diametrical opposites and their cultures and histories are essentially antagonistic," many in the country "believe that the two peoples can coexist in the same cultural continuum, creating a division between nationalist and anti-nationalist Ukrainians that is arguably as important as that between ethnic Ukrainians and ethnic Russians" (Wilson 1996, 1).

Indeed, ethnic identification in Ukraine is amorphous and malleable, especially among those of mixed background (Kuzio 1998, 96).[18] Referring to oneself as Ukrainian or Russian is therefore often situationally conditioned, given physiognomic constraints do not hamper ethnic Russians trying to "pass" as Ukrainians (or vice versa). Indicative of this, according to 1989 Soviet census figures,

---

18 A 1997 survey found that, depending on how the question was worded, between 6% and 27% of respondents identified with a composite "Ukrainian-Russian" identity (as cited in Shevel 2002, 394).

alongside 37.42 million ethnic Ukrainians, there were some 11.36 million ethnic Russians living in Ukraine (Brubaker 2011, 1791; Stebelsky 2009, 82). However, between 1989 and the 2001 Ukrainian census, the number of self-identified Russians declined by more than a quarter. Out-migration alone cannot account for this drop, implying many chose to re-identify as Ukrainians during this period (Brubaker 2011, 1793; Stebelsky 2009; Arel 2002, 237–238).[19]

Nonetheless, the boundaries of ethnic identity are not only conditioned on "esthetically conspicuous differences of the physical appearance," but also "perceptible differences in the *conduct of everyday life*" (Weber 1978, 390).[20] Given Ukrainians and Russians exhibit none of the former and relatively few of the latter raises the salience of the cultural differences that do exist, ensuring language, history and religion a prominent—and contentious—place in identity debates. It also makes counter-narratives potentially more threatening, as there exists a greater probability that they will be perceived as legitimate.[21]

Regarding linguistic distinctions, Ukrainian and Russian are not as mutually intelligible as frequently depicted, but many if not most residents of Ukraine are functionally bilingual, with Russian occupying a prominent role in commerce and other spheres. Consequently, it should not be assumed that Russian speakers in Ukraine (a category that includes a large number of ethnic Ukrainians) necessarily want to be part of a "greater Russia," any more than Spanish-speaking Guatemalans necessarily want to be

---

19   Ethnic self-categorization was especially fluid due to the high rates of intermarriage evinced between Ukrainians and Russians (according to the 1989 Soviet census, mixed Ukrainian-Russian families accounted for 22.3% of the total number of families in Ukraine [Stebelsky 2009, 97]), with intermarriage particularly common in the Donbas during the late Soviet period (Pirie 1996, 1086, 1090).
20   Emphasis in original.
21   For example, no serious person would claim that Hungarian is a dialect of Russian, but such claims are routinely encountered regarding Ukrainian due to the more pronounced similarities between them.

part of Mexico. At best, language is a noisy and imperfect proxy for political sentiment; at worst, it is a misleading one.[22]

Additionally, while language usage in Ukraine may appear bimodal due to researchers presenting respondents with the exclusive options of Ukrainian-speaking or Russian-speaking, in reality there exists significant gradation, with individuals frequently utilizing a patois known as *surzhyk* rather than standard Russian or Ukrainian.[23] Nevertheless, the prominence of Ukrainian has increased significantly in public life since independence.[24] Between 1991/92 and 2008/09, for example, the percentage of schools utilizing Ukrainian as the language of instruction went from 45% to 82.7%, while those utilizing Russian fell from 54% to 17.7% (Pogrebinskii et al. 2010).

Relative to historical interpretation, the Soviet legacy has proven an enduring source of societal divisiveness, as a nationwide survey conducted in May 2013 (just six months before the Maidan protests commenced) demonstrates:[25]

---

22 Especially as what individuals report to be their "native" language may not be what they utilize in everyday interactions or speak at home (Kulyk 2013, 282, 286; Brubaker 2011, 1794-1795; Arel 2002).

23 Khmel'ko notes that in 2003 the use of *surzhyk* ranged from 2.5% in western Ukraine to 21.7% in the east-central region (n.d., 13 table 13). More recent sources have estimated it is used on a daily basis by some 16-18% of the population, most frequently in central Ukraine (Olszański 2012, 12-13). However, given that *surzhyk* usage is widely perceived to signify lower educational and economic attainment, under-reporting is likely.

24 As for the use of Ukrainian in private life, the reported gains have been more modest. "Long-term research," Olszański notes, "reveals that the percentage of citizens using only Ukrainian in their family life grew from 37 to 42% between 1992 and 2010, the percentage of those who used only Russian decreased from 39 to 35% and the share of those using both languages declined from 32 to 22%" (2012, 19).

25 Graph and chart based on Fond Demokratichni 2013. Alongside regional differences a generational effect was also observed, with nostalgia for the old system increasing with respondent age (note: some respondents were too young to have been born in the USSR).

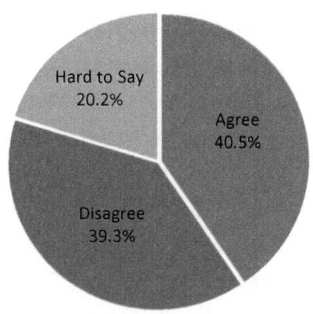

Better if Everything had Remained as It was in the Soviet Union until 1985

Hard to Say 20.2%
Agree 40.5%
Disagree 39.3%

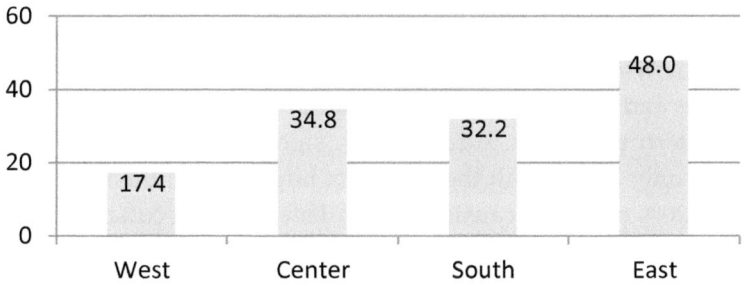

Percentage of Respondents who Feel Greater Affinity for the Soviet Union than Ukraine

Region	%
West	17.4
Center	34.8
South	32.2
East	48.0

However, exhibiting nostalgia for the USSR should not be conflated with supporting irredentism.[26] While secessionist appeals are not new, having played a prominent role in the 1990s and being reinvigorated by the 2004 Orange Revolution,[27] the frequency with which they were heard had actually *decreased* in the years immediately before the Maidan (KIIS 2017, 20–21). Supporting this

---

26 By the summer of 2014, support for Russia's leadership had dropped precipitously even in the south and east, where it fell to 12% from 57% the year before (across Ukraine it fell from 43% to 5%) (Ray and Esipova 2014).

27 It was not only in Crimea and eastern Ukraine that such demands were heard; they also manifest among Rusyns/Ruthenians and Hungarians in Zakarpattia (Giuliano 2018, 171; Szczygło 2010, 9).

contention, at the height of separatist tensions in April 2014, only 15.4% of those polled in the southern and eastern provinces of Dnipropetrovsk, Donetsk, Luhansk, Kharkiv, Kherson, Mykolayiv, Odessa, and Zaporizhia wanted to join Russia, with Donetsk and Luhansk registering the highest levels at 27.5% and 30.3%, respectively (KIIS 2014). Moreover, a December 2014 survey undertaken across these same provinces (with the exception of Donetsk and Luhansk) after the separatist conflict had already commenced found that even among self-identified ethnic Russians, the majority did not favor holding a referendum on whether the Donbas should become part of Russia (Toal 2017, 270–272).[28]

Undeniably, there are individuals throughout Ukraine who identify strongly with Russia in political as well as cultural terms, but for many others what appears to be operative is a longing for an idealized USSR,[29] or else a localized identity counterpoised to Ukrainian ethno-nationalism. As for why Soviet nostalgia is more prevalent in the east, this region was part of the Russian Empire for centuries and came to be incorporated into the USSR far earlier than the western provinces. Additionally, significant settlement in the Donbas only began with the advent of large-scale industrialization in the 20th century, causing it to develop a peculiarly Soviet working-class identity (Wilson 2016, 636).[30] Likewise, massive demographic shifts afflicted the Ukrainian SSR during this time. Not only did the 1932–1933 famine (Holodomor), which claimed several million lives, pave the way for ethnic Russians to re-settle

---

28 Although in Russian-held Crimea over 83% regarded the annexation positively (Toal 2017, 234).

29 An April 2014 survey (Crimea was not sampled) found that while 61% of respondents in the Donbas rued the collapse of the Soviet Union (versus 33% across Ukraine), this position was correlated with age, education level, and income; essentially, the older, less-educated and poorer you were, the more likely that you would view the demise of the USSR in a negative light (Reiting 2014, 2, 6).

30 As a result of its heavy industry and coal mines, it also remained better integrated with the post-Soviet Russian economy than other regions, functioning "almost as a third space between independent Ukraine and Russia" (Toal 2017, 203) and consistently exhibiting more anti-market and anti-Western attitudes than the rest of Ukraine.

the hardest-hit areas in the east, but Stalin's mass deportation of Crimea's indigenous Tatar population in 1944 drastically altered the peninsula's ethnic composition.[31]

Interestingly, what support does exist for separatism in the Donbas appears more closely correlated with economic than ethno-linguistic factors, with micro-regions highly dependent on exports to Russia not only falling under rebel control faster, but also experiencing greater overall levels of fighting (Zhukov 2016).[32] Lending further credence to the idea that the appeal of post-Soviet Russia is to a large degree instrumental, support for unification has varied extensively over time, suggesting that rather than being deeply rooted in ethno-cultural affinities, it reflects responses to more fleeting indicators of economic and political performance.[33]

---

31 It has been estimated that anywhere from 75% to 90% of Crimea's population arrived after WWII, resettled there from other provinces of the USSR (Pleshakov 2017, 90; Kuzio 1998, 87).

32 Giuliano 2018 also notes a significant economic component in support for separatism. Similarly, a 2013 survey conducted in Luhansk oblast—the fieldwork for which ended approximately one month before the Maidan protests began—suggests "geopolitical identities in the Donbas are a matter of social class rather than of national identity," with the less-well-off harboring both anti-Western and anti-liberal sentiments at higher rates than the economically advantaged (Gentile 2015, 212-214).

33 For region-by-region data for the period 1995-2014, see HURI's *MAPA: Digital Atlas of Ukraine*. Of those who voted in Ukraine's December 1, 1991 referendum on independence, 92.3% supported it, including 54.19% in Crimea, 83.90% in Donetsk, and 83.86% in Luhansk (TsDAVO Ukraïni n.d.). However, in the eastern regions this support was not linked to a normative desire for Ukrainian sovereignty, but rather the expected economic benefits that would accompany it (Pirie 1996, 1094-1099), as "the common belief was that the economic strength of Ukraine would bring affluence, deliberately blocked by Moscow, which for decades had exploited Ukrainian industry and agriculture to subsidize the less developed parts of the USSR" (Brudny and Finkel 2011, 825). So, while in western Ukraine the fall in living standards after 1991 was attenuated by the attainment of independence, which played into the nationalizing narrative prominent there, in the Donbas (where Russified Ukrainians make up the majority of the population) and Crimea (where ethnic Russians predominate) the pull of self-determination was not present to anywhere near the same degree. This foregrounded the economic situation, with ensuing problems "blamed largely on either the disintegration of the former USSR or the

So what accounts for the outbreak of secessionist violence in 2014? The answer lies in a combination of agency and apathy. "An active separatist core," notes Kudelia, "coupled with the neutral attitude of the majority created favorable conditions" for separatism to take hold in the Donbas (2016a, 12). In particular, this involved regional business elites and local security organs siding with the rebels, a process facilitated by the patronage networks of the Party of Regions (Kudelia 2016a) and the influence of Russia and "Russian-backed agents" (Giuliano 2018, 163). Wilson (2016) similarly stresses the role elite actors played in precipitating the devolution of long-standing but mostly inert tensions into outright hostilities, noting that far from being a preordained conclusion, the conflict in the Donbas was facilitated by the intervention of the Yanukovych "Family" (especially the ousted president's son Oleksandr) and oligarchs aligned with it, which provided critical funding and organizational support for the separatist movement. Kyiv's response to the separatists' demands, at first hesitant then heavy-handed, likewise lessened its legitimacy in the eyes of those residing in the disputed territories, while fears connected to the perceived rise of radical Ukrainian ethno-nationalism (Guiliano 2018; Kudelia 2016a) added momentum to the downward spiral that ultimately led to a shooting war.

Ukrainian society also diverges on more specific points of historical recall. Ernest Renan famously opined "the essence of a nation is that all individuals have many things in common, and also that all have forgotten many things" (1991, 34), but Ukrainians have not yet agreed on what from their complicated past should be set aside. The two most salient mnemonic divides concern the Holodomor and the respective roles played by the Soviet Red Army and the irregular Ukrainian Insurgent Army (UPA) in WWII.[34] For reasons having to do with divergent colonial experiences, western Ukrainians are more prone to valorize the UPA as a force for

---

breakdown in economic ties with Russia caused by the former 'nationalist' President Kravchuk" (Kuzio 1998, 85).

34 Even whether one refers to WWII as the "Second World War" or the "Great Patriotic War" is highly polarizing.

national liberation and castigate the Red Army for imposing Soviet suzerainty, while eastern Ukrainians are more likely to vilify the UPA as a fascist organization for its alliance with Hitler's Germany and complicity in crimes against Poles and Jews. Similarly, the former are more likely to regard the Holodomor as a Soviet-orchestrated genocide, despite these regions not having been part of the USSR at the time of the famine.

Concerning religion, the main sectarian cleavage in Ukraine is between Orthodox Christians and Greek Catholics. Adherents of Orthodoxy predominate, especially in the eastern and central regions, though they are divided among three competing bodies: the Ukrainian Orthodox Church—Moscow Patriarchate (UOC-MP); the Ukrainian Orthodox Church—Kyiv Patriarchate (UOC-KP), and the much-smaller Ukrainian Autocephalous Orthodox Church (UAOC). The UOC-MP has traditionally had the largest membership, as neither the UOC-KP nor the UAOC are recognized as canonical by the other national Orthodox Churches. Greek Catholics, meanwhile, make up less than 8% of Ukraine's population according to a 2017 survey (as cited in Soroka 2018, 92) but constitute an influential presence, particularly in western Ukraine.

Post-Maidan: Changes in Ukrainian Society

Although a distinctively Ukrainian socio-political consciousness was already incubating well before the 2013–2014 protests, notable shifts occurred in their aftermath. As Kulyk observes (2016, 607):

> For a decade after the Orange Revolution, Ukrainian society was characterised by the uneasy coexistence of two roughly equal territorial 'halves' with their respective divergent identities and policy preferences. Now the bulk of the population seems to agree on the salience of national identity and main elements [sic] of its content, including a pro-Western foreign policy, the nationalist historical narrative and the legitimacy of both languages with the symbolic primacy of Ukrainian. Those who resolutely disagree differ not so much in their striving for a different, Russian-friendly Ukraine as in their wish to distance themselves from Ukraine as such.

Illustrating this, a poll conducted in late 2015 found 68.4% of respondents were proud to be Ukrainian citizens, up from 56.2% in

2005 (even in the non-occupied areas of the Donbas, a plurality of 43.4% reported pride in their citizenship).[35] Additionally, 40.1% identified first and foremost with Ukraine, while 39.6% chose their place of residence, 11.4% their region, and just 0.6% Russia (Razumkov 2016, 22–23).[36] An August 2018 survey likewise revealed 66% of respondents—and majorities in all regions—self-identified as Ukrainian citizens, while 6% chose Soviet as their identity (the same number as European). A downtrend in the number of those classifying themselves in sub-state or ethnic terms since 2010 was also recorded (Reiting 2018b, 13–15).

Regarding societal shifts in geopolitical orientation, a 2017 survey revealed that after the Maidan a plurality would vote for Ukraine to join the EU (49% for, 28% against) and NATO (41% for, 32% against). Contrast these figures to 2005, when 33% supported and 39% opposed joining the EU and 15% supported and 58% opposed joining NATO (KIIS 2017, 25–26). In this same vein, a June 2018 survey found that if Ukraine could only belong to one organization, 52% wanted it to be the EU, as opposed to 15% who chose the Customs Union with Belarus, Russia and Kazakhstan (those favoring the EU ranged from 80% in the west to 26% in the east) (Reiting 2018a, 36–37). Similar findings held for NATO, with 43% claiming they would vote for accession and 33% that they would vote against it, with support ranging from 73% in the west to 18% in the east (Reiting 2018a, 41–42).

Commitments to a civic understanding of nationality have also risen, with 51% of Ukrainians believing it is better to live in a diverse society, as opposed to 35% who prefer a homogenous one (Pew 2017). Likewise, a clear majority (55.7%, as opposed to 43.1% in 2006) views the Ukrainian nation as composed "of all citizens of

---

[35] Unless otherwise specified, surveys conducted after April 2014 do not sample public opinion in Crimea and the separatist-held areas of Donetsk and Luhansk. This, along with the potential bias that may be introduced by polling internally displaced persons (estimated to number more than 1.6 million individuals), must be borne in mind when comparing results of surveys pre- and post-Maidan.

[36] Even in the non-separatist held areas of the Donbas, only 1.1% identified primarily with Russia (and 1.2% with Europe).

Ukraine, regardless of their ethnic background, the language they speak, and the national traditions they adhere to and are raising their children in," with a further 17.0% (as opposed to 15.1% in 2006) agreeing it includes those, irrespective of ethnicity, who speak Ukrainian and uphold and raise their children in accordance with Ukrainian traditions (Razumkov 2016, 39).[37]

Linguistic indicators also testify to post-Maidan changes, with speaking Ukrainian now serving as a "badge of self-identification" among citizens (Vorobiov 2015) and Russian increasingly coming to be decoupled from political and ethnic identities (Kulyk 2018).[38] Moreover, the use of Ukrainian appears to have risen in private as well as public life. According to a recent survey, 44.5% of respondents spoke Ukrainian at home, while 12.6% spoke Russian; a decade prior, the respective figures stood at 39.3% and 28.1% (Razumkov 2016, 33).[39] Meanwhile, 65.1% of respondents reported being fluent in Ukrainian, up from 57.6% in 2006 (Razumkov 2016, 35).[40]

Changes have also taken place in Ukrainians' historical consciousness, with what were previously regarded as western ethno-national interpretations concerning the past gaining traction

---

[37] In contrast, 11.2% (down from 19.8% in 2006) insisted that members of the nation needed to be both citizens of Ukraine and of Ukrainian ethnicity, and 7.7% (down from 14.2% in 2006) claimed that members of the nation were people of Ukrainian ancestry, regardless of their place of residence or country of citizenship.

[38] As a Facebook user from Kyiv memorably posted: "Ukraine is my homeland. Russian is my native language. And I would like to be saved by Pushkin. And delivered from sorrow and unrest, also by Pushkin. Pushkin, not Putin" (as cited in Plokhy 2015, 351).

[39] In addition, 5.3% reported speaking mainly but not exclusively Ukrainian (6.7% in 2006), 24.7% alternated between Russian and Ukrainian (14.7% in 2006), and 11.1% spoke mainly but not exclusively Russian (9.5% in 2006). Though see Pop-Eleches and Robertson (2018), who suggest on the basis of panel survey data that while civic identification with Ukraine has increased between 2012 and 2015, ethno-linguistic divides remain salient.

[40] The regional breakdown was as follows: 94.1% in the west, 71.5% in the center, 48.9% in the south, 52.3% in the east, and 39.1% in the non-separatist-held Donbas.

in other regions.[41] This is partly attributable to the most dissonant elements having been removed from societal discourse by the annexation of Crimea and establishment of separatist strongholds in Donetsk and Luhansk, and partly to the rally-round-the-flag effect the conflict in the east has produced, making centrists and the previously apolitical more receptive to the symbols, heroes and historical narratives of the ethno-nationalists.[42]

Attesting to this, positive views of Stepan Bandera rose from 22% to 35% between June 2012 and October 2016, while positive views of Ivan Mazepa grew from 44% to 52% (Reiting 2016, 28, 30).[43] Favorable assessments of the UPA have also increased throughout Ukraine since 2013, with the greatest relative gains in those regions traditionally most resistant to such interpretations.[44] Likewise, the number of Ukrainians who believe the Holodomor constituted genocide has risen rapidly in the wake of the Maidan,

---

41   A vivid example being the *Leninopad*, or mass toppling of hundreds of Lenin statues between 2013-2014, which took place predominantly in central and eastern Ukraine (in the west most had been removed before the Maidan). On the broader issue of Ukraine's evolving memory politics, see Shevel 2016.

42   It is said that warfare gives birth to nations, with "the myths and symbols of heroes, battles and their sacred sites" becoming "an essential part of the ethnic fabric" (Smith 1993, 53). Tilly has likewise contended that wars make states (1985). Both processes, however, are undoubtedly aided by losing your most restive populations. Comparing vote totals in the 2010 presidential election relative to the 36 electoral districts that did not take part in the 2014 election due to being under separatist control indicates that the most dependably pro-Russian voters have been removed from participation in Ukrainian elections (D'Anieri 2017). This has led some to argue the Ukrainian state would be better off if it did not pursue the reintegration of separatist-held areas (e.g., Motyl 2017).

43   Bandera headed an eponymous faction of the Organization of Ukrainian Nationalists (OUN), of which the UPA was the military arm. Mazepa, the Hetman of Zaporizhian Host, fought on the side of Sweden against Russia during the 1709 Battle of Poltava. However, regional variation in how these two figures are regarded remains pronounced, with positive assessments of Bandera ranging from 71% in the west to 13% in the east, and of Mazepa from 67% in the west to 33% in the east (Reiting 2016, 31).

44   Sympathetic appraisals of the UPA have grown especially in those territories directly proximate to the separatist conflict, rising from 7% to 35% in Luhansk and 13% to 44% in Kherson between 2013 and 2015 (Plokhii n.d.).

resulting in overwhelming majorities in the west and center of the country recognizing it as such by 2015. And even though many in the south and east continue to contest this characterization, far fewer do so than previously (Plokhii n.d., map 4).

Shifts have likewise occurred in religious affiliation. Although the UOC-MP still possesses the largest number of parishes and monasteries according to official statistics (as cited in Soroka 2018, 92), it no longer boasts the greatest number of adherents.[45] This is no small matter in a country where some seven out of ten people consider themselves to be Orthodox and the Church consistently ranks among the most trusted institutions (Reiting 2018a, 29; Zlenko 2017). The reason for this shift is that the UOC-MP, even though it is formally self-governing, has increasingly come to be seen as a foreign entity due to its ecclesial connection to the Russian Orthodox Church.[46] Archbishop Evstratiy Zorya of the UOC-KP sums up the position of a growing number of Ukrainians when he declares "having a church that is dependent on Russia is. . . a threat to our national security and a threat to our existence as Ukrainians" (as cited in Kinstler 2014).

State and National Identity: Moving Forward

Ukraine's domestic security is inseparable from its nation-building and stateness, but how to facilitate the former and strengthen the latter? Two pathways are available: repress pluralism and accentuate ethno-nationalism or accommodate pluralism through emphasizing a civic concept of socio-political belonging. The preliminary evidence post-Maidan is intriguing in this regard, as it suggests Ukraine's linguistic, mnemonic and religious allegiances have shifted toward what were previously regarded as moderately

---

[45] A March 2017 survey found that among self-identified Orthodox reporting an affiliation, 38.8% belonged to the UOC-KP (22.1% in 2010), 17.4% belonged to the UOC-MP (34.5% in 2010) and 1.5% belonged to the UAOC (essentially unchanged from 2010) (as cited in Soroka 2018, 92).

[46] Though the Russian Orthodox Church (headed by the Patriarch of Moscow) is not a department of the Russian state, but a formally independent body with its own preferences, internal tensions, and rivalries (Soroka 2016).

ethno-nationalist positions. Simultaneously, Ukraine's citizens appear to have become more accepting of a civic conception of nationhood. In effect, the former has served to establish more resilient outward-facing borders, while the latter has diversified the inward-looking sense of what it means to be Ukrainian. This is a highly positive development if it proves sustainable, as Ukraine's deep and complicated historical ties to Russia and sizable ethnic Russian population, along with the long (and lightly fortified) border it shares with its larger neighbor, argue for an ethno-nationally based state being sub-optimal for security. Note, though, that cultivating a Ukrainian state predicated on civic principles does not necessitate reconciling the differences that exist between the various groups that reside on its territory; what it *does* demand is avoiding the political activation of these differences as a source of inter-group competition. It is not the presence of diversity, but rather the degree to which it is tolerated, that matters. Likewise, embracing a primarily civic conception of nationhood does not preclude acknowledging the Ukrainian language and culture as *primus inter pares*.[47] The latter is even desirable from the perspective of reinforcing symbolic boundaries between Ukraine and Russia.

Degree and Quality of Governance: Evaluating the Data

A half-century ago, Samuel Huntington proposed that how well a country is governed is more consequential than its form of government (1968, 1). Proceeding from this, I contend good governmental performance, which presumes a high level of fidelity between codified institutions and observed political outcomes, matters more for Ukraine's internal security than does its geopolitical orientation or even its regime type. This is because a stable state whose governance claims are accepted as valid is critical not only for reinforcing titular ethnics' identification with the

---

47   This corresponds to what Kymlicka terms "liberal culturalism" (2001, 39-48) and Stepan, Linz, and Yadav refer to as "soft" ethno-national policies (2011, 173-200).

political community, but also for ensuring that minorities feel invested in (and thus loyal to) it as well. Good governance is also essential if Kyiv is to tackle the massive obstacles it will face if the separatist-held areas of the Donbas or Crimea ever return to its control, both in terms of convincing the residents of these regions that their future lies with Ukraine and in repairing the former's war-torn infrastructure.

Consequently, how to improve the condition of Ukraine's democracy is not the focus here. While there exist compelling reasons for believing this regime type is advantageous when it comes to mitigating security issues, among them the accountability, responsiveness and societal engagement that a well-functioning democracy fosters, democracies may also introduce their own security challenges, as when competing group identities — which are more readily suppressed in authoritarian systems — become a prominent feature of electoral politics.[48] However, while it is useful to disaggregate the *degree and quality of governance* from specific *forms of governance*, Ukraine's constitutional arrangements render it a liberal democracy, allowing us to legitimately evaluate the former in terms of how well the state performs in providing "democratic goods." As such, the five criteria for assessing democratic consolidation (civil society, political society, the rule of law, the state apparatus and economic society) specified by Linz and Stepan (1996, 3–15) provide a suitable metric.

Currently, Ukraine falls short in all these categories. Civil society, for instance, remains weak despite the societal mobilization evinced around the Maidan, with a recent poll finding that 85.3% of Ukrainians do not belong to any civic groups or political parties and 87.4% have not engaged in volunteer activities in the past year

---

48 Although as D'Anieri (2007) points out, the presence of large, geographically concentrated minorities — provided they perceive themselves as having a voice within the system — may actually prove more of an asset than a liability if the goal is to sustain a liberal polity where a loyal veto player can counter the strength of ethno-national appeals.

(Fond Demokratichni 2018, 5–6), rates far below the EU average.[49] And while more people report trusting non-governmental organizations than not, the figure is still low at 37% (Zlenko 2017).[50]

Nor does the picture improve if we broaden the definition of civil society to include the media. According to Reporters sans frontières' 2017 World Press Freedom Index, Ukraine ranks 102 out of 180 countries. Meanwhile, the percentage of individuals who report trusting Ukraine's domestic mass media varies from a high of 39.3% in the west to a low of 10% in the east (while the commensurate percentage for the Russian mass media ranges from 0.8% in the west to 4.6% in the south) (Zlenko 2017). Similarly, 24% believe Ukrainian television broadcasters "almost always" distort information and 38% that they do so "occasionally" (the respective numbers for Russian broadcasters are 33% and 14%) (Reiting 2018a, 68).[51] Doubts about the veracity of news reporting also arise from the concentrated and politicized nature of media ownership.[52]

With respect to its political society, Ukraine's problems center about representatives that lack the incentive to govern transparently and equitably. Yanukovych's ouster did not bring an end to this; what changed instead was the balance of regional

---

[49] Round 3 (2006/2007) of the European Social Survey found 36.1% of Europeans had volunteered at least once during the prior year (European Commission Directorate General for Education and Culture 2010, 57).

[50] Note, though, that another survey employing slightly different wording found that at the end of 2017, 62% trusted volunteer organizations and 54% trusted civic organizations (Razumkov 2018, 87).

[51] Since 2017, Kyiv has banned many Russian-based media outlets and websites from Ukraine. Additionally, a new media law adopted that year stipulates, among other things, that at least 75% of national- and regional-level television broadcasts must be in the Ukrainian language (60% at the local level).

[52] Ukraine's top five television stations are controlled by three oligarchs (Viktor Pinchuk—ICTV, Novyi Kanal and STB; Rinat Akhmetov—Ukraïna; and Ihor Kolomoyskyi—1+1). In addition, newer outlets like Espreso.tv and NewsOne have been linked to political figures (former Prime Minister Yatseniuk and Interior Minister Arsen Avakov in the first case and *Rada* deputies Vadym Rabinovych and Yevhen Murayev in the second). President Poroshenko himself owns a television station, Channel 5 (Rybak 2018).

power. [53] Consequently, disillusionment did not take long to emerge, with a 2015 poll finding Poroshenko's approval rating was lower than Yanukovych's prior to the Maidan, having dropped from 47% in May 2014 to 17% the following year (Ray 2015). Nor has this trend reversed; in June 2018 only 14% approved of his performance (Reiting 2018a, 19).

"The old Ukrainian politico-economic class, with President Poroshenko himself at the helm," writes Andreas Umland, "is still defending the kleptocratic system of patronage politics, rent-seeking, central control, and informal exchanges that emerged after the collapse of the USSR in 1991" (2017, 261). But while a recent poll found 5.3% of Ukrainians reported trusting parliament and 13.7% the President, trust in the opposition, at 13%, was equally abysmal (Zlenko 2017). This implies the problem is systemic, as illustrated by Ukraine's political parties commonly functioning more like electoral vehicles designed to vault specific individuals into office than stable organizations advocating consistent policy positions.

Some progress, however, has been made, with Ukrainian legislators having overhauled the judicial, educational, healthcare, and pension systems over the course of the last few years. (Nonetheless, the effectiveness of these initiatives remains to be seen, and much-anticipated reforms of the electoral system and agricultural land policy remain in limbo.) Another positive from the perspective of domestic security is that Ukrainian ultra-nationalists have not managed to parlay the highly visible role they played on the Maidan into electoral success. The leaders of Svoboda (Oleh Tyahnybok) and Pravy Sektor (Dmytro Yarosh) received less than 2% of the votes in the 2014 presidential election, and neither party managed to clear the 5% party-list threshold in the

---

53 Immediately after the Maidan, Prime Minister Yatsenyuk's new government was dominated by political elites from western Ukraine, with some 60% of top officials hailing from oblasts formerly under Hapsburg control, where only about 12% of Ukraine's overall population resides. In contrast, while Yanukovych was president and Mykola Azarov prime minister, 75% of politicians at the ministerial level were from southern and eastern Ukraine, and 42% were from Donetsk oblast, Yanukovych's home territory (Darden 2014).

parliamentary elections that same year, the former only winning six single-member-district seats.[54] Meanwhile, Poroshenko (himself born in Odessa, a predominantly Russian-speaking region) has positioned himself as a relative moderate.[55]

The rule of law is also problematic in Ukraine.[56] According to the World Justice Project's 2017–2018 Rule of Law Index, Ukraine ranks 77/113, while Transparency International's 2016 Corruption Perception Index places Ukraine at 131/176. Reflecting the endemic nature of this issue, a 2015 survey found 70.7% of those polled had been extorted, bribed someone, or used personal ties to benefit themselves in the previous year, with 94.4% perceiving corruption (and 93.8% specifically "corruption in government") to be a serious problem (KIIS 2015, 3–7, 18).[57] Complicating matters further, the courts and procuracy remain among the least-trusted institutions in Ukraine (Reiting 2018a, 29).

The state apparatus, for its part, has been unable to adequately address Ukraine's glaring economic, social and environmental problems. Exemplifying this, only 16% of respondents approve of how the National Anti-Corruption Bureau, which began functioning in 2015, is performing (Reiting 2018a, 29). Consider as well that in 2015 male life expectancy at birth in Ukraine was 66

---

[54] Ukraine's unicameral 450-seat legislature, or Rada, is elected through a mixed-member system, with 50% of deputies chosen via a proportional representation system with closed party lists, and the other 50% on the basis of first-past-the-post voting in single-member districts (as a result of vacancies created by the Donbas conflict and the annexation of Crimea, the Rada currently consists of 423 members).

[55] During his June 7, 2014 inauguration speech, Poroshenko switched from Ukrainian to Russian partway through to appeal to the residents of the separatist regions, promising to respect the "right of local communities to their own nuances regarding questions of historical memory, their pantheon of heroes, and religious traditions" (TCH 2014).

[56] A quixotic example: while he was Governor of Dnipropetrovsk Oblast, Ihor Kolomoyskyi admitted in a televised newscast to holding Ukrainian as well as Cypriot and Israeli citizenship. He justified this on the grounds that while Ukraine's constitution prohibits dual citizenship, it says nothing about triple citizenship (Coalson 2015).

[57] These figures were only exceeded by the high cost of living (94.9%) and the military campaign in Donetsk and Luhansk (97.4%).

years for males and 76 years for females versus 79 years and 85 years, respectively, in the Eurozone. Healthcare expenditures, meanwhile, totaled just $203 per capita in 2014, as compared to $893 in Russia (World Bank 2018). And Ukraine places 84th in the world (below Algeria, above Jordan, and tied with Armenia) on the latest UN Human Development Index, indicating broad deficits in social provisioning.

Criticism has also attached to the state for how it has handled what was until February 2018 euphemistically termed the Anti-Terrorist Operation (ATO) in the Donbas, with 51% of those surveyed perceiving the conflict to be the greatest threat to themselves and the future of their children (Reiting 2018a, 33). The unofficial blockades of Crimean cargo traffic and coal shipments from the Donbas by Ukrainian activists and the participation of various paramilitary units in key stages of the fighting also underscore the problems with Ukraine's state capacity.

Concerning the economy, nearly three decades after the collapse of the USSR, "only Ukraine of the fifteen former Soviet republics" has still "not recovered to the level of its Soviet era GDP" (Kuzio 2016, 184), with corruption and predatory rent-seeking having stalled both economic and political reforms. Attesting to this, Ukraine performed far worse (76/190) than Russia (35/190) in the World Bank's 2017 Ease of Doing Business ranking. Indeed, it is estimated that in 2016 nearly 46% of Ukraine's economic activity took place off-the-books, untaxed and effectively unregulated (ACCA 2017, 13).

Meanwhile, Ukraine's average wage is the lowest in Europe, with real-wage growth of -20.2% in 2015 (ILO 2016, 106). Its per capita GNI of $7,361 is also much lower than that of neighboring Poland ($24,117) and Russia ($23,286) (United Nations 2018). As a result, economic out-migration has become a major concern, with the number of Ukrainian workers in Poland alone increasing more than six-fold since 2013 (Razumkov 2018, 110).

Finally, despite attempts to diversify, Russia remains Ukraine's largest single-country trading partner, accounting for €6,203 million in imports and €3,440 million in exports in 2017

(European Commission Directorate General for Trade 2018). And while Ukraine has managed to wean itself off of Russian natural gas, imports of diesel and LPG from Russia have actually risen in recent years (Konończuk 2017).

Post-Maidan Governance: What is to be Done?

A notable challenge facing Ukraine's leaders is how to remedy the above-noted problems without driving wedges between various societal elements.[58] While the mnemonic landscape has changed markedly post-Maidan, polarizing initiatives like the April 2015 ratification of four "de-communization laws" are more likely to exacerbate still-significant societal and regional tensions than further unity.[59] Illustrating this, although now mandated by law, 57% of Ukrainians oppose renaming cities, towns and streets that bear Soviet appellations, with opposition ranging from 33% in the west to 73% in the south (Reiting 2016, 20). Similarly, article 7 of the new education law adopted in September 2017 stipulates Ukrainian as the mandatory language of instruction (with limited exceptions) in secondary schools beginning in 2020. This has provoked a strong reaction from minorities in Ukraine, as well as Russian, Romanian and Hungarian leaders who protested on behalf of their co-ethnics (Stormont 2017).

---

58 Identity politics, whether over history or ethno-cultural markers like language or religion, are tempting for politicians to engage in; not only do they represent a convenient shorthand for mobilizing frequently bundled grievances, but they are also useful as a "politics of distraction," capitalizing on divides that are readily activated due to the emotional energy they are imbued with. Such political prestidigitation ("Don't look here! Look there instead!") is easier to engage in rather than the hard, and typically slow, work of battling endemic corruption or reforming key economic sectors. But activating such divides risks the reification of conflict-prone means of relating to dissenting societal voices (and neighboring states).

59 Two are particularly controversial. One extols the role of irregular groups such as the UPA in the struggle for national liberation and prohibits the public denigration of their members, while the other bans the denial of the crimes of the Soviet and Nazi regimes (tacitly conflating them), prohibits the display of their symbols, and requires that Soviet-themed monuments be removed and place names be changed (see Koposov 2017, 194–204).

Concomitantly, and even more critically, Ukraine's political culture needs to change if its internal security is to be fortified. That the state is not as well-governed as it could be does not represent an indictment of its formal institutions so much as a reflection of the socially deleterious norms and mores under which Ukraine's political and economic elites have grown accustomed to operating. Nonetheless, as research suggests formal institutions have the ability to shape both legal and illegal incentive structures and, therefore, to alter behavior (Hale 2016; 2011; Kudelia 2016b), certain institutional modifications may prove beneficial.

In divided societies where the elite networks competing for political power are regionally based and closely tied to economic interests, winner-take-all presidential systems are maladaptive. However, when informal norms tolerate such behaviors as rent-seeking and clientelism, similar concerns may also apply to prime ministers in parliamentary systems (Hale 2016, 128). Under these conditions, semi-presidentialism, and specifically a *premier-presidential* model, is the least objectionable option.[60] This is because, for all that such a system may generate political infighting and gridlock, in a context where "big businessmen have captured the state" (Åslund 2015, 29), having power reside co-equally in a dual executive maximizes the potential for rival factions to gain representation while minimizing the chances they will seek to enact change extrajudicially (Hale 2016). But while this is technically the system Ukraine already possesses, more can be done to delineate and clarify specific areas of responsibility.[61]

While a full consideration of potential reforms is beyond the scope of this work, Ukraine would benefit from the imposition of further checks on presidential power, which remains outsized in

---

60 The difference between this sub-type and a *president-parliamentary* system concerns the relative distribution of power between executives, and specifically the president's ability to remove the prime minister from office.
61 Ukraine functioned as a president-parliamentary system until 2006 (when reforms adopted in 2004 went into effect), then as a premier-presidential system until late 2010, when it reverted to the former. After Yanukovych was toppled, it once again become a premier-presidential system.

comparison to that of the prime minister.[62] This could, for example, involve allowing the legislature to nominate as well as appoint the prime minister.[63] Likewise, holding parliament responsible for the investiture of the full cabinet, rather than reserving the right to appoint the Ministers of Defense and Foreign Affairs for the president, would help re-center the balance of power.[64] A similar argument could be made for revisiting the presidential prerogative to appoint or dismiss the prosecutor general (which does require legislative consent) and holders of key bureaucratic offices.[65] And given there exists a "lack of consensus among political elites over the role of the president in the political system" (Choudhry, Sedelius and Kyrychenko 2018, 18), it would also be advisable to better define the role of the presidential administration, as well as to revisit the president's wide-ranging ability to issue decrees, veto legislation, propose constitutional amendments, and call referenda.

A related matter is the need to better institutionalize Ukraine's political parties and improve oversight of campaign financing. Specifically, the adoption of a mixed-member modality in 2012 for parliamentary elections has resulted in a greater number of parties vying for seats in single-member districts than on the party lists. It has also permitted unaffiliated candidates to run in the former, both factors that have increased legislative instability (Choudhry, Sedelius and Kyrychenko 2018, 25). Consequently, returning to an exclusively proportional representation system seems sensible,

---

62 This discussion draws heavily on Choudhry, Sedelius and Kyrychenko (2018).
63 Currently, the prime minister is nominated by the president and appointed by a simple majority vote in the legislature, leaving the impression that the prime minister occupies a subordinate position.
64 This is particularly relevant in times of crisis.
65 In May 2016, Poroshenko caused a scandal by appointing Yuriy Lutsenko to the position of prosecutor general, despite Lutsenko having no legal experience or training. Showcasing the wide scope of this mandate, Ukraine's president also (this is only a partial list) appoints half of the members of the Council of the National Bank and State Committee for Television and Radio-Broadcasting, one-third of Constitutional Court judges, and the heads of diplomatic missions and local state administrations.

along with adopting open party-list voting in order to raise the accountability of individual politicians.

The other critical issue concerns the fate of Ukraine's disputed territories. Inevitably, if Crimea and/or the separatist-held areas of Donetsk and Luhansk are to ever be reincorporated into Ukraine, some devolution of power from the center will need to take place. From an institutional perspective this would be a positive development (regardless of whether or not the term federalism were employed), as increasing the political independence of regional actors would have the benefit of making it more difficult to centralize power around any single office or figure (Hale 2016, 139).

Concluding Remarks

The domestic security issues facing Ukraine today are manifold, but there are reasons for cautious optimism. Socio-culturally, Ukraine's best hope for ensuring domestic tranquility lies in pursuing a civic conception of nationhood and ensuring that the state is committed to safeguarding the rights of minorities. This is the only realistic option going forward if the borders of Ukraine are not to shrink further. An explicitly ethno-national state is simply not a feasible prospect politically as things stand right now, and many Ukrainians would not support this vision even if it were. Institutionally, meanwhile, it lies in promoting a more decentralized authority and carefully balancing responsibilities between the president and prime minister. This will help incentivize elite actors to compete within the electoral system rather than seeking to overthrow or circumvent it, while concurrently reinforcing barriers designed to prevent the lopsided seizure and exercise of power. Essentially, the prescription is to "fake it till you make it" with respect to better governance, stabilizing Ukraine through institutional safeguards in the hope that this will eventually augur a meaningful change in its underlying political culture.

However, it is imperative to remember that while regional variation across Ukraine has attenuated since the Maidan, it has not disappeared. Consequently, much will depend on whether (and how) the conflict in the Donbas is resolved. Finally, while the focus of this chapter has been on Ukraine's internal security, it must be reiterated that this does not exist in isolation from the international environment, and both affect one another in profound ways.

References

ACCA. 2017. "Emerging from the Shadows: The Shadow Economy to 2025." June. http://www.accaglobal.com/content/dam/ACCA_Global/Technical/Future/pi-shadow-economy-report.pdf.

Arel, Dominique. 2002. "Interpreting 'Nationality' and 'Language' in the 2001 Ukrainian Census." *Post-Soviet Affairs* 18(3): 213–249.

Åslund, Anders. 2015. *Ukraine: What Went Wrong and How to Fix It.* Washington, DC: PIIE.

Bloom, William. 1993. *Personal Identity, National Identity and International Relations.* New York: Cambridge UP.

Brubaker, Rogers. 2011. "Nationalizing States Revisited: Projects and Processes of Nationalization in Post-Soviet States." *Ethnic and Racial Studies* 34(November): 1785–1814.

Brudny, Yitzhak M., and Evgeny Finkel. 2011. "Why Ukraine is Not Russia: Hegemonic National Identity and Democracy in Russia and Ukraine." *East European Politics and Societies* 25(November): 813–833.

Choudry, Sujit, Thomas Sedelius, and Julia Kyrychenko. 2018. "Semi-presidentialism and Inclusive Governance in Ukraine: Reflections for Constitutional Reform." *IDEA*, April 13. https://www.idea.int/publications/catalogue/semi-presidentialism-and-inclusive-governance-ukraine.

Coalson, Robert. 2015. "Ukrainian Oligarch Tears Into RFE/RL Journalist." *RFE/RL*, March 20. http:www.rferl.org/a/ukraine-kolomoysky-rfe-journalist/26912164.html

Dalberg-Acton, John. 1949. *Essays on Freedom and Power.* Boston: Beacon.

D'Anieri, Paul. 2007. "Ethnic Tensions and State Strategies: Understanding the Survival of the Ukrainian State." *Journal of Communist Studies and Transition Politics* 23(March): 4–29.

---. 2017. "Ukraine's Changed Electorate: Estimates and Implications." Post-Communist Politics and Economics Workshop, Harvard University (November 3).

Darden, Keith. 2014. "How to Save Ukraine: Why Russia is Not the Real Problem," *Foreign Affairs,* April 14. https://www.foreignaffairs.com/articles/russian-federation/2014-04-14/how-save-ukraine.

European Commission Directorate General for Education and Culture. 2010. "Volunteering in the European Union." February 17. http://ec.europa.eu/citizenship/pdf/doc1018_en.pdf.

European Commission Directorate General for Trade. 2018. "European Union, Trade in Goods with Ukraine." April 16. http://trade.ec.europa.eu/doclib/docs/2006/september/tradoc_ 113459.pdf.

Fond Demokratichni initsiativi imeni Il′ka Kucheriva. 2013. "Ukraїni— 22: dumka gromadian: Stavlennia gromadian do Radians′kogo Soiuza." August 21. https://dif.org.ua/article/ukraini-22-dumka-gromadyan.

---. 2018. "Gromadians′ke suspil′stvo v 2018-mu: novi vikliki, novi zavdannia." March 6. https://dif.org.ua/uploads/pdf/1396339816 5a9eef1b022177.77359526.pdf.

Gellner, Ernest. 1983. *Nations and Nationalism*. Ithaca, NY: Cornell UP.

Gentile, Michael. 2015. "West Oriented in the East-Oriented Donbas: A Political Stratigraphy of Geopolitical Identity in Luhansk, Ukraine." *Post-Soviet Affairs* 31(3): 201-223.

Giuliano, Elise. 2018. "Who Supported Separatism in Donbas? Ethnicity and Popular Opinion at the Start of the Ukraine Crisis." *Post-Soviet Affairs* 34(2-3): 158-178.

Hale, Henry E. 2011. "Formal Constitutions in Informal Politics: Institutions and Democratization in Eurasia." *World Politics* 63(4): 581-617.

---. 2016. "Constitutional Performance after Communism: Implications for Ukraine." In *Beyond the Euromaidan*, ed. Hale and Robert W. Orttung. Stanford: Stanford UP.

Helmke, Gretchen, and Steven Levitsky. 2004. "Informal Institutions and Comparative Politics: A Research Agenda." *Perspectives on Politics* 2(December): 725-740.

Huntington, Samuel P. 1968. *Political Order in Changing Societies*. New Haven: Yale UP.

HURI. Nd. *MAPA: Digital Atlas of Ukraine*. http://gis.huri.harvard.edu/contemporary-atlas/ukraine-and-russia-together-or-apart/independentukraine-project.html.

ILO. 2016. "Global Wage Report 2016/17: Wage Inequality in the Workplace." December 15. https://www.ilo.org/global/research/global-reports/global-wage-report/2016/WCMS_537846/lang—en/index.htm.

Khmel′ko, V.E. Nd. "Lingvo-etnichna struktura Ukraїni: regional′ni osoblivosti ta tendentsiї zmin za roki nezalezhnosti." http://kiis.com.ua/materials/articles_HVE/16linguaethnical.pdf.

KIIS. 2014. "Dumki ta pogliadi zhiteliv Pivdenno-Skhidnikh oblastei Ukraïni: Kviten' 2014."http://www.kiis.com.ua/?lang=ukr&cat=reports&id=302&page=1.

---. 2015. "Corruption in Ukraine: Comparative Analysis of National Surveys: 2007, 2009, 22011, and 2015." https://kiis.com.ua/materials/pr/2016 1602_corruption/Corruption%20in%20Ukraine%202015%20ENG.pdf.

---. 2017. "Ukraïns'ke suspil'stvo za 25 rokiv: dinamika deiakikh sotsial'nikh pokaznikiv." December. http://www.kiis.com.ua/?lang=ukr&cat=reports&id=732&page=1.

Kinstler, Linda. 2014. "Russia's Meddling Might Backfire With an Empowered, Unified Ukrainian Church." *New Republic*, July 16.

Konończuk, Wojciech. 2017. "A Dangerous Energy Policy: Ukraine, Despite War, is Making Itself Dependent on Russian Oil." September 8. http://energypost.eu/15647-2/.

Koposov, Nikolay. 2017. *Memory Laws, Memory Wars: The Politics of the Past in Europe and Russia*. New York: Cambridge UP.

Kudelia, Serhiy. 2016a. "The Donbas Rift." *Russian Politics and Law* 54(1): 5-27.

---. 2016b. "Corruption in Ukraine: Perpetuum Mobile or the Endplay of Post-Soviet Elites?" In *Beyond the Euromaidan*, ed. Henry Hale and Robert Orttung. Stanford: Stanford UP.

Kulyk, Volodymyr. 2013. "Language Policy in Ukraine: What People Want the State to Do," *East European Politics and Societies* 27(May): 280–307.

---. 2016. "National Identity in Ukraine: Impact of Euromaidan and the War," *Europe-Asia Studies* 68(June): 588–608.

---. 2018. "Shedding Russianness, Recasting Ukrainianness: the Post-Euromaidan Dynamics of Ethnonational Identifications in Ukraine." *Post-Soviet Affairs* 34(2-3): 119–138.

Kuzio, Taras. 1998. *Ukraine: State and Nation Building*. New York: Routledge.

---. 2016. "Oligarchs, the Partial Reform Equilibrium, and the Euromaidan Revolution." In *Beyond the Euromaidan*, ed. Henry Hale and Robert Orttung. Stanford: Stanford UP.

Kymlicka, Will. 2001. *Politics in the Vernacular: Nationalism, Multiculturalism and Citizenship*. New York: Oxford UP.

Langbein, Julia. 2016. "(Dis-)integrating Ukraine? Domestic Oligarchs, Russia, the EU, and the Politics of Economic Integration." *Eurasian Geography and Economics* 57(1): 19–42.

Linz, Juan J., and Alfred Stepan. 1996. *Problems of Democratic Transition and Consolidation: Southern Europe, South America, and Post-Communist Europe*. Baltimore: Johns Hopkins UP.

Motyl, Alexander J. 2017. "Kyiv Should Give Up on the Donbas." *Foreign Policy*, February 2. https://foreignpolicy.com/2017/02/02/ukraine-will-lose-its-war-by-winning-it/.

Olszański, Tadeusz A. 2012. "The Language Issue in Ukraine: An Attempt at a New Perspective." *OSW Studies* 40(May).

Onuch, Olga. 2014. "Who Were the Protesters?" *Journal of Democracy* 25(July): 44–51.

Onuch, Olga, and Gwendolyn Sasse. 2016. "The Maidan in Movement: Diversity and the Cycles of Protest." *Europe-Asia Studies* 68(4): 556–587.

Onuch, Olga, and Henry E. Hale. 2018. "Capturing Ethnicity: The Case of Ukraine." *Post-Soviet Affairs* 34(2–3): 84–106.

Osipian, Ararat L., and Alexander L. Osipian. 2012. "Regional Diversity and Divided Memories in Ukraine: Contested Past as Electoral Resource, 2004-2010." *East European Politics and Societies* 26(3): 616–642.

Pew. 2017. "Religious Belief and National Belonging in Central and Eastern Europe." May 10. http://www.pewforum.org/2017/05/10/religious-belief-and-national-belonging-in-central-and-eastern-europe/

Pirie, Paul S. 1996. "National Identity and Politics in Southern and Eastern Ukraine." *Europe-Asia Studies* 48 (November): 1079–1104.

Pleshakov, Konstantin. 2017. *The Crimean Nexus: Putin's War and the Clash of Civilizations*. New Haven: Yale UP.

Plokhii, Serhii. Nd. "Goodbye Lenin: A Memory Shift in Revolutionary Ukraine." http://gis.huri.harvard.edu/images/leninfall/Leninfall Paper.pdf.

Plokhy, Serhii. 2015. *The Gates of Europe: A History of Ukraine*. New York: Basic.

Pogrebinskii, Mikhail et al. 2010. "Russkii iazyk v Ukraine--bez emotsii." *ZN.UA*, September 17. https://zn.ua/EDUCATION/russkiy_yazyk_v_ukraine__bez_emotsiy.html.

Pop-Eleches, Grigore, and Graeme B. Robertson. 2018. "Identity and Political Preferences in Ukraine–Before and After the Euromaidan." *Post-Soviet Affairs* 34(2–3): 107–118.

Ray, Julie. 2015. "Ukrainians Disillusioned with Leadership." *Gallup.com*, December 23. https://news.gallup.com/oll/187931/ukrainians-disillusioned-leadership.aspx.

Ray, Julie, and Neli Esipova. 2014. "Ukrainian Approval of Russia's Leadership Dives Almost 90%." *Gallup.com*, December 15. https://news.gallup.com/poll/180110/ukrainian-approval-russia-leadership-dives-almost.aspx.

Razumkov Tsentr. 2016. "Identichnist' gromadian Ukraïni v novikh umovakh: stan, tendentsiï, regional'ni osoblivosti." June 7. http://dontsov-nic.com.ua/wp-content/uploads/2016/07/Identi-2016.pdf.
---. 2018. "Ukraine 2017–2018: New Realities, Old Problems." http://razumkov.org.ua/uploads/article/2018_Pidsumky_ukr_eng.pdf.
Reiting. 2014. "Nostal'giia za SRSR ta stavlennia do okremikh postatei." May 5. http://ratinggroup.ua/files/ratinggroup/reg_files/rg_historical_ua_052014.pdf.
---. 2016. "Stavlennia do okremikh istorichnikh postatei ta protsesu dekomunizatsiï v Ukraïni." November 17. http://ratinggroup.ua/research/ukraine/otnoshenie_k_otdelnym_istoricheskim_lichnostyam_i_processu_dekommunizacii_v_ukraine.html.
---. 2018a. "Dinamika suspil'no-politichnikh pogliadiv v Ukraïni: 26 travnia-10 chervnia 2018." http://ratinggroup.ua/files/ratinggroup/reg_files/2018_june_survey_of_residents_of_ukraine_press.pdf.
---. 2018b. "Dinamika patriotichnikh nastroïv ukraïntsiv: serpen' 2018." http://ratinggroup.ua/files/ratinggroup/reg_files/rg_patriotyzm_082018.pdf.
Renan, Ernest. 1991. *Qu'est-ce qu'une Nation? Texte integral de E. Renan; Littérature et identité nationale de 1871 à 1915*, ed. Philippe Forest. Paris: Pierre Bordas et fils.
Reporters sans frontières. 2017. "World Press Freedom Index." https://rsf.org/en/ranking/2017.
Reznik, Oleksandr. 2016. "From the Orange Revolution to the Revolution of Dignity: Dynamics of the Protest Actions in Ukraine." *East European Politics and Societies* 30(4): 750–765.
Rybak, Vitalii. 2018. "Yes, Ukraine's Oligarchs Own the Airwaves, but Their Days Are Numbered." *Atlantic Council*, January 29. http://www.atlanticcouncil.org/blogs/ukrainealert/yes-ukraine-s-oligarchs-own-the-airwaves-but-here-s-why-their-days-are-numbered.
Shevel, Oxana. 2002. "Nationality in Ukraine: Some Rules of Engagement." *East European Politics and Societies* 16(2): 386–413.
---. 2016. "No Way Out? Post-Soviet Ukraine's Memory Wars in Comparative Perspective." In *Beyond the Euromaidan*, ed. Henry Hale and Robert Orttung. Stanford: Stanford UP.
Smith, Anthony D. 1993. "The Ethnic Sources of Nationalism." *Survival* 35(Spring): 48–62.
---. 1986. *The Ethnic Origins of Nations*. Oxford: Basil Blackwell.
Snyder, Timothy. 2014. "Ukraine: The Haze of Propaganda," *The New York Review of Books*, March 1.

Soroka, George. 2016. "Putin's Patriarch: Does the Kremlin Control the Church?" *Foreign Affairs*, February 11. https://www.foreignaffairs.com/articles/russian-federation/2016-02-11/putins-patriarch.

---. 2018. "A House Divided. Orthodoxy in Post-Maidan Ukraine," *New Eastern Europe* 3-4 (May-August): 90-97.

Stebelsky, Ihor. 2009. "Ethnic Self-Identification in Ukraine, 1989–2001: Why More Ukrainians and Fewer Russians?" *Canadian Slavonic Papers* 51(1): 77–100.

Stepan, Alfred, Juan José Linz, and Yogendra Yadav. 2011. *Crafting State-Nations: India and Other Multinational Democracies*. Baltimore, MD: Johns Hopkins UP.

Stormont, Nathan. 2017. "Ukraine's Education Law May Needlessly Harm European Aspirations." *Freedom House*, October 2. https://freedomhouse.org/blog/ukraine-s-education-law-may-needlessly-harm-european-aspirations.

Szczygło, Aleksander. 2010. *Kwestia jedności Ukrainy w kontekście bezpieczeństwa wewnętrznego i międzynarodowego*. February. Warsaw: Biuro Bezpieczeństwa Narodowego.

TCH. 2014. "Promova prezidenta Ukraini Petra Poroshenka na inavguratsii." June 7. https://tsn.ua/politika/promova-prezidenta-ukrayini-petra-poroshenka-na-inavnuraciyi-povniy-tekst-353552.html.

Tilly, Charles. 1985. "War Making and State Making as Organized Crime." In *Bringing the State Back In*, ed. Peter Evans, Dietrich Rueschemeyer and Theda Skocpol. New York: Cambridge UP.

Toal, Gerard. 2017. *Near Abroad: Putin, the West and the Contest Over Ukraine and the Caucasus*. New York: Oxford UP.

Transparency International. 2016. "Corruption Perception Index." https://www.transparency.org/news/feature/corruption_perceptions_index_2016

TsDAVO Ukraïni. Nd. "Do 15-ï richnitsi Vseukraïns'kogo referendumu: Dokumenti z fondiv TsDAVO Ukraïni." http://www.archives.gov.ua/Sections/15r-V_Ref/index.php?11.

Umland, Andreas. 2017. "The Six Futures of Ukraine: Competing Scenarios for a European Pivot State," *The Brown Journal of World Affairs* XXIV (Fall/Winter): 261–278.

United Nations. 2018. "Human Development Index." http://hdr.undp.org/en/composite/HDI.

Vorobiov, Ievgen. 2015. "Why Ukrainians Are Speaking More Ukrainian," *Foreign Policy*, June 26. https://foreignpolicy.com/2015/06/26/why-ukrainians-are-speaking-more-ukrainian/.

Weber, Max. 1978. *Economy and Society: An Outline of Interpretive Sociology*, ed. Guenther Roth and Claus Wittich. Berkeley: U. of CA Press.

---. 1964. "The Fundamental Concepts of Sociology." In *The Theory of Social and Economic Organization*, ed. Talcott Parsons. New York: Free Press.
Wilson, Andrew. 1996. *Ukrainian Nationalism in the 1990s: A Minority Faith.* New York: Cambridge UP.
---. 2016. "The Donbas in 2014: Explaining Civil Conflict Perhaps, But Not Civil War." *Europe-Asia Studies* 68(June): 631–652.
Wolczuk, Kataryna. 2001. *The Moulding of Ukraine: The Constitutional Politics of State Formation.* Budapest: CEU Press.
World Bank. 2018. *HealthStats.* http://datatopics.worldbank.org/health/.
World Justice Project. 2018. "Rule of Law Index 2017–2018." https://world justiceproject.org/our-work/publications/rule-law-index-reports/wjp-rule-law-index-2017-2018-report.
Zakonodavstvo Ukraïni. 2015. "Strategiia natsional'noi bezpeki Ukraïni." May 26. http://zakon5.rada.gov.ua/laws/show/287/2015/para N14#N4
Zhukov, Yuri M. 2016. "Trading Hard Hats for Combat Helmets: The Economics of Rebellion in Eastern Ukraine." *Journal of Comparative Economics* 44(February): 1–15.
Zlenko, Stanlislav. 2017. "Dovira sotsial'nim institutsiiam." *KIIS*, February 1. http://www.kiis.com.ua/?lang=ukr&cat=reports&id=678.

Yuriy Matsiyevsky

Western Leverage, Russia's Resistance and the Breakdown of the Yanukovych Regime

My contribution seeks to assess Western and Russian influence on the collapse of Viktor Yanukovych's regime. Drawing on the works of Levitsky and Way and Tolstrup, the chapter explains why during the 2014 crisis Yanukovych was able to withstand Western and domestic pressure much longer than Leonid Kuchma did in 2004, and why he was eventually toppled. I argue that Yanukovych's ability to prolong his stay in power was circumscribed by three specific factors: his concentration of power, Russian backing and miscalculated Western threats to impose sanctions. His downfall, however, was ultimately determined from within the state. This chapter contributes to the theory of hybrid regimes by extending the concept of linkage and leverage to non-democracies; it also offers an empirical measure of Russian anti-democratic influence on Ukraine.

Introduction

Ukraine's 2013/2014 crisis is dissimilar to any other crisis in post-independence Ukrainian history. Unlike in 2004, the 2014 crisis was not resolved through compromise and has grown into a revolution. Being under Western, Russian and domestic pressure, Ukraine's former president Victor Yanukovych had long struggled to keep power, but finally lost it. But why was Yanukovych in 2014 able to withstand these pressures for the first three months of the crisis, unlike Leonid Kuchma in 2004, and why did he finally fall? What was his personal role, and what role did external actors play in this process? In other words, how did the interplay of structural and agency-based factors contribute to the regime's prolonged survival and eventual downfall?

While much has been written about the international confrontation over Ukraine both before and after the 2014 revolution (e.g., Wilson 2014; Menon & Rumer 2015; Charap &

Colton 2017; Götz 2018), much less attention has been paid to the actual amount of leverage the West and Russia possessed in relation to Yanukovych's Ukraine. Both the regime's capacity to withstand this pressure for 90 days of crisis (from 22 November 2013 to 22 February 2014) and its sudden collapse need to be properly accounted for.

This chapter draws on the theory of hybrid regime dynamics developed by Steven Levitsky and Lucan Way (2010). Levitsky and Way advanced an overly structuralist argument in explaining why some regimes democratized while others did not. Way, for instance, has been criticized (Bunce & Wolchic 2009) for neglecting the role of agency in explaining regime outcomes. Another caveat is the role of so-called "black knights" — states capable of thwarting democratizing efforts. The authors only mention this, but they do not discuss it. An interesting attempt to further develop the theory is Jakob Tolstrup's concept of "negative external actor" (2009). Although Tostrup applies this concept to compare Western and Russian influence on Ukraine (2014), he does not seek to measure it.

Consequently, this chapter aims to contribute to these discussions in three ways. First, by focusing on domestic and international actors, it provides a context for the central theme of this volume — Ukraine's security. Inter alia, it shows how a failure of all involved to resolve the internal crisis peacefully brought about the largest international crisis since the collapse of Yugoslavia. Second, it tests Levitsky and Way's theory of linkage and leverage by applying it to the case of Yanukovych's Ukraine. Specifically, it extends the integral part of the theory — the concepts of linkage and leverage — to non-democracies to compare Ukraine's ties both to the West and Russia. And third, it offers a single measure for the above-mentioned concepts. (Although this is a very approximate measure, a basis is provided for developing it in a more nuanced way.)

The chapter is divided into three sections. The first section presents Levitsky and Way's concepts of linkage, leverage and organizational power and Tolstrup's concept of "negative external actor." The second section applies them to assess both Western and Russian influence on Yanukovych's government in the period from 2010 to 2013. The third section summarizes these findings and demonstrates why the theory was not able to predict the outcome. Instead, it introduces agency—based factors (Yanukovych's strategic mistakes made under pressure from Russia) to explain why he finally lost power.

Western versus Russian Leverage

Until now the discussion about the reasons for the breakdown and survival of hybrid regimes has not provided definitive answers (Geddes 1999; Gandhi & Przeworski 2007). While agency—centered theories offer insights into past events (Bunce & Wolchik 2011), structural theories seek to predict them. One such account was offered by Levitsky and Way (2010), who built a theory of hybrid regime dynamics by focusing on three variables: the density of ties to the West (linkage), the scope and cohesion of the state and governing party structures (organizational power), and the state's vulnerability to Western democratizing pressure (leverage). Analyzing these factors across 35 states between 1990-2008, they found that democratization was more likely where linkage to the West was extensive, as in Eastern Europe or the Americas during the post-Cold War period. High linkage pushed autocrats to abandon power instead of keeping it by any means. In contrast, where linkage was low, as in the post-Soviet states, Western democratizing pressure was weaker. In these countries regime outcomes were primarily driven by the organizational power of incumbents. Where the state and governing party were well organized, incumbents were able to overcome opposition and retain power. Meanwhile, where the state and governing party were weak, the survival of the regime was threatened. When the organizational power of a regime was insufficient to prevent elite defection or crack down on protest, it was vulnerable to even weak opposition challenges. In such countries the third factor, incumbents' vulnerability to Western leverage, was often decisive.

This, however, can be constrained by "black knights" — counter-hegemonic powers whose political and economic potential help to blunt democratizing pressure. Where considerable antidemocratic leverage took place (as in the case of Russian influence upon Belarus), even weak regimes survived. Conversely, where Western leverage was high, such regimes were more likely to fall. The same has happened in Ukraine and Georgia, where "defective democracies" emerged in the wake of the Rose and the Orange revolutions. However, due to the lack of strong connections to the West, new leaders usually resorted to old practices and with the West acting inconsistently, nascent democracies were not able to consolidate. The matrix in table 1 presents regime outcomes resulting from the interaction of Western leverage and organizational power.

Table 1. Explaining regime outcomes

	High leverage	Low leverage
Strong power	Unstable authoritarianism	Stable authoritarianism
Weak power	Regime change (not always democratization)	Regime survives

Adapted from Levitsky & Way (2010)

These three factors are important, but whether or not hybrid regimes survive is influenced by economic, historical and institutional factors as well. That is why some regime outcomes differed from those predicted by the theory, as was the case with "post-orange" Ukraine (Levitsky & Way 2010, 214, 234). Although in 2005–2010 Ukraine was rated a "free" country by Freedom House, democracy was not consolidated under Victor Yushchenko, Ukraine's democratization being superficial and subject to internal conflicts, such as those between Yushchenko and Yulia Tymoshenko (Harasymiw 2007). Moreover, rent-seeking behavior among Ukrainian elites (Puglisi 2003) prevented them from institutionalizing the rules of the democratic game. This allowed Yushchenko's successor to quickly expand his authority and establish control over the legislature and judiciary. Indicative of this, just a year after Yanukovych gained power Freedom House expressed concern over the curtailing of democracy in Ukraine (2011). This trend only accelerated in the coming years, which were marked by such landmark events as the politically motivated trial and imprisonment of Yulia Tymoshenko (from August 5, 2011 to February 22, 2014), the passage of a package of anti-protest laws (in January 2014), and the killing of more than one hundred protesters in Kyiv in February 2014. Why did the democratically elected president of Ukraine allow this to happen? While many of his decisions require criminal investigation, the role of the "black knight"—meaning Russia—in precipitating these crises deserves closer scrutiny. One such attempt was Jakob Tolstrup's introduction of the concept of a "negative external actor" (2009; 2014). Tolstrup (2009) advanced a list of 18 indicators to assess the impact of a "negative external actor" on a targeted state, but he did not measure it. However, by quantifying Ukraine's linkage to the West and to Russia as of 2013, as well as Western versus Russian leverage on Ukraine and Ukraine's organizational power, we can empirically test Levitsky and Way's theory and construct a single measure for the above-mentioned concepts. This has the potential to provide much broader insights into the interplay of the external and internal factors that led to the collapse of Yanukovych's regime.

Measuring Linkage

In Levitsly and Way's theory linkage refers to the density of the economic, social and communication ties of the country in question to the West (meaning the EU and US). Intergovernmental ties are also subsumed under this rubric. High linkage would point to better chances for democratization. In order to test this theory (i.e., to explain Yanukovych's prolonged survival and rapid downfall), I apply the same methodology that Levitsky and Way (2010, 374-375) utilized. Specifically, I measure each dimension on a scale from 1 to 5 (1 being the lowest score and 5 being the highest) based on Ukraine's ranking relative to all non-Western countries in the world. These scores will then be summed into a composite score and the result recalibrated on a scale from 0 to 1. Points will be given according to the place occupied in the ranking. From 1 to 15 — 5 points, from 16 to 31 — 4 points, from 32 to 47 — 4 points, from 48 to 63 — 3 points, from 64 to 79 — 2 points, and 80 and above — 1 point.

After estimating the linkage score for Ukraine as of 2013 (the last year for which data are available), I compare it with the score obtained by Levitsky and Way for the period 1990 to 2008. The change in these scores should reveal predictable changes in the dependent variable, namely whether the regime survives or is replaced. Given the actual result, namely the ouster of Yanukovych from power, we can see whether their theory is able to predict this outcome.

Economic ties are measured by the extent of Ukraine's trade with the EU countries (European Commission 2013). Communication ties are measured by the share of the Ukrainian population that uses the Internet and by international voice traffic (commensurate domestic traffic was not taken into consideration as there has been a steady reduction in the number of landline users over the course of the last decade, which has paralleled the expansion of alternative channels of communication [UBR 2012]). As of 2012 Ukraine ranked 68th in the world by Internet users (International Telecommunication Union 2013), and as of 2003 it ranked 36th in international voice traffic (Nation Master 2005). Social ties, meanwhile, are measured by looking at the number of Ukrainians living or working in the West (estimated at between 3 — 3.5 million, or 7 — 7.2% of the population) (International Organization for Migration 2011). Trade ties are assessed at 4 points, communication ties at 3 points and social ties at 2 points.

Intergovernmental ties (measured by the potential for membership in the EU) are assessed at 2 points (on a scale from 1 to 5, where 1 means the country has little prospect of joining, while 5 means the country is a candidate state). Ukraine is still not on the list of "potential EU members," as Yanukovych did not sign the EU-Ukraine Association Agreement (AA) and Ukraine does not yet fit the political and economic criteria required to join the EU.

However, on this measure it scores 2 points, as Ukraine shares a border with four EU countries and is covered under the European Neighborhood Policy. These are the "pros" that most of the post-Soviet, as well as some Balkan and most non-European countries, do not possess. After recalibrating the composite score to a scale from 0 to 1, Ukraine's final score was 0.55, which corresponds to a medium level of linkage as defined by Levitsky and Way. The scores are summarized in table 2.

Table 2. Dynamics of linkage*

Linkage (density of ties)	1990/2008	2012/2013
Economic ties	–	4 points
Communication ties	–	3 points
Social ties	–	2 points
Intergovernmental ties	–	2 points
Recalibrated score (0–1)	0.31 (Low)	0.55 (Medium)

* Linkage scores for 1990–2008 were calculated by Levitsky and Way (2010); scores for 2012–2013 were calculated by the author.

Although the value of the linkage score increased in 2013, Ukraine did not cross the threshold of high linkage states (0.69 – 0.97). This might happen, however, once Ukraine succeeds in terminating the war in the Donbas, demonstrates progress with reforms, and utilizes in full the AA, ratified by the EU in July 2017. Higher linkage, according to the theory, suggests that Ukraine has a chance to get back on the democratization track.

Measuring Organizational Power

Organizational power refers to the state's coercive capacity and the strength of the ruling party. Both dimensions are measured by the scope and cohesion of the state and the party. According to Levitsky and Way, "scope refers to the effective reach of the state's coercive apparatus" (2010, 58) or what other authors call its "infrastructural power" (Slayter & Fenner 2011). This is the extent and the quality of the "internal security sector" that includes the army, police, presidential guards, the security service and their special units, and other coercive agencies (e.g., the financial police or tax inspectorate).

Meanwhile, "cohesion refers to the level of compliance within the state apparatus" (Levitsky & Way 2010, 58). For compliance to be effective subordinates must follow their superiors' commands. Similarly, the scope of the party "refers to the size of the party infrastructure, or the degree to which it penetrates the national territory and society" (Levitsky & Way 2010, 64). Cohesion demonstrates the incumbent's ability to secure the cooperation of partisan allies within the government, the legislature and at the local and/or regional levels. Cohesion is greater when it is rooted in "nonmaterial ties" such as a common ethnic origin, belonging to a common social group or a history of shared struggle. Scores for party scope and cohesion and state scope and cohesion (low = 0; medium = 1; high = 2) are summed by the authors into a single composite score (0−8). Scores between 6 and 8 represent high organizational power, 5−medium high, 4−medium, 3− medium low, and between 0 and 2−low. The scores for organizational power are presented in table 3.

Table 3. Dynamics of organizational power*

Organizational Power	1990/2008	2012/2013
State Scope	High (2 points)	High (2 points)
State Cohesion	Low (0 point)	Medium (1 point)
Party scope	Low(0 points)	High (2 points)
Party cohesion	Low (0 points)	Medium (1 points)
State discretionary control over economy	None	None
Total	Low (2 points)	High (6 points)

*Organizational power scores for 1990-2008 were calculated by Levitsky & Way (2010); scores for 2012-2013 were calculated by the author.

The organizational power of Ukraine's regime has grown from low in the 1990s and 2000s to high in 2012/2013. This is a result of the concentration of power and the growth of the *party of power*. After Yanukovych was elected president, he managed to change the constitution so that he had the same power as Leonid Kuchma had before the "Orange Revolution," and then he subsequently expanded it even further. The Index of Presidential Authority, which was developed by Johannsen and Nørgaard (2003) and is measured on a scale from 0-100%, registered presidential authority in Ukraine at 46.9% during the period 2005-2010, rising to 52.7% during the period 2010-2014. This growth signifies a shift from "divided presidentialism" to "executive presidentialism."[1] Such a "blitzkrieg" in the concentration of presidential power was possible due to the devolution of constitutionalism in Ukraine. During the three years of Yanukovych's rule, Ukraine went from a semi-presidential system to super-presidential system of government (Matsiyevsky 2016, 74-75).

The size of Ukraine's coercive agencies (its Security Service numbered 33.500 officers, the Ministry of Internal Affairs 357,000 employees [and its 13 special subunits 12-13,000], and the tax inspectorate 55,000 employees) strongly indicates that the state's coercive power remained high in the period 2010-2013. Moreover, expenditures to maintain this apparatus were growing steadily; for example, beginning in 2010 the Ministry of Internal Affairs received approximately 1 billion additional hryvnias in funding per year, with funding increasing from 13.1 billion in 2010 to 16 billion hryvnias in 2013 (Burlakova 2013). The interference of these coercive agencies in public affairs has been emphasized by Freedom House (2012). However, despite the large size of Ukraine's coercive apparatus and its Soviet style of management, a lack of incentivization and rampant corruption rendered these agencies unable to coerce effectively. Moreover, frequent changes in their leadership suggest that the President was unsure about the loyalty of his subordinates. Nonetheless, these agencies were used to intimidate opposition leaders, as well as to harass small- to medium-sized businesses, public figures and the media and, eventually, to confront the Euromaidan protesters in Kyiv and other cities (Gazeta UA 2013; Den' 2013).

---

1   If the index falls in the range between 60 and 100%, it indicates the maximum concentration of presidential authority (see Matsiyevsky 2016, 67-75).

Although it was extensive in scope, there is little evidence that the state apparatus enjoyed high cohesion. There was no shared ideology or other non-material ties of unity present. Nor was a common ethnic origin or being from the Donbas region (the Russian-speaking portion of Ukraine where Yanukovych's power base was located) a defining factor, as neither ethnicity nor being a Russian speaker constituted the dominant cleavage in the country (*Economist* 2013). The sole element of unity was the fear of being excluded from the extensive network of patronage.

On the other hand, there was no evidence of disobedience among the personnel of the state apparatus. Specifically, there was no wage debt that would point at the low cohesion within the state apparatus. Instead, the number of personnel employed by the state's coercive agencies was growing, as were their wages (TVI 2013). Thus, I estimate the cohesion of the state to be at a "medium" level.

Meanwhile, the scope of Yanukovych's party of power, the Party of Regions (PoR), can be considered high. The governing party was the largest party in Ukraine, with its official membership exceeding 1.4 million (Didushok 2011). During the 2012 parliamentary elections the PoR won more than 50% of electoral districts (115 out of 225), which was an indication of its vast mobilizational capacity. The extensive use of "administrative resources" by the party (local administrations were frequently headed by the leaders of PoR's regional branches, allowing state budgetary funds to be distributed to political clients) (Gazeta.ua 2012) revealed the extent to which it had effectively penetrated society. However, the PoR did not enjoy nonmaterial ties of unity (such as a shared ideology, a shared ethnicity or a history of shared struggle). Some sort of regional loyalty can only be attributed to the "old party bosses" — people like Nikolai Azarov, Volodymyr Rybak or Aleksandr Efremov. Of the nine "Family"[2] representatives who penetrated the political council (*politsovet*) of the PoR in September 2013, only five were from the Donetsk region (*Zerkalo Nedeli* 2013b).

---

2   The "Family" consisted of Victor Yanulovych's closest allies, and was headed by his elder son Oleksandr.

This is a sign that regional loyalty was subverted by patronage and rent-seeking interests. On the other hand, PoR, like most of the Ukrainian parties, was a typical clientelistic party that attracted rent-seekers of all sorts. Having a large number of members in all regions of the state, the party could not maintain the unity of its cadres. As jailed PoR member Ihor Markov has publicly confessed, "the whole faction of the Party of Regions in parliament is controlled exclusively by fear. Someone is threatened of being deprived of his mandate, someone is threatened—by being deprived of business, to others—some other instruments of pressure are applied" (*Zerkalo Nedeli*, 2013a).

The most important indicator of cohesion within a party is whether it is in power or not. Until its sudden collapse in the end of February 2014, PoR controlled all the executive hierarchy. Although the representatives of the "Family" were not the members of the ruling party, they had the greatest influence in the Cabinet of Ministers (*Podrobnosti* 2012). Even before the split of the faction, PoR did not have a clear majority (it had 208 seats out of the 226 needed to form a majority), and even with the help of the Communists, it could not utilize its coalition status to make decisions effectively. There were several individual defections, precipitated by the first violence against the protesters (on November 30, 2013), but the massive "exodus" took place only after the last attempt to disperse the Maidan failed. In just three days (between February 19-21) the PoR legislative faction lost 78 members, dropping from 208 to 127 (Matsiyevsky 2016, 442-443). Considering all of the above, I classify the cohesion of Yanukovych's party of power as "medium." However, due to the concentration of power in the hands of the incumbent, the growth of the security apparatus and the effective penetration of the governing party into society, I consider the regime's organizational power to be "high" (in keeping with Levitsky and Way's terminology).

Measuring Leverage

According to Levitsky and Way, Western leverage is measurable through "governments' vulnerability to external democratizing pressure" (2010, 40–41). The extent to which such leverage is exerted is rooted in the strength of the country's economy and the presence of counter-powers, whose support may function to blunt democratizing pressure.

Leverage is measured along three dimensions: the size of the economy, oil production and possession, and the capacity to use nuclear weapons. Leverage is considered to be low when the country's total GDP exceeds $100 billion USD (1995 figures). Ukraine is neither a major nor a secondary oil producer. Likewise, it does not have nuclear weapons, and until the beginning of the 2013 crisis it was not a direct beneficiary of "black knight" assistance. Thus the only relevant dimension in the case of Ukraine is the size of its economy.

Ukraine's GDP in 2012 was $180 billion USD ($120 billion USD according to the 1995 exchange rate) (IMF, World Economic and Financial Surveys 2012), which exceeds the limit of $100 billion USD. This makes Ukraine a large economy. However, Ukraine's economy to a great extent depends on global commodity prices, particularly for steel and chemicals. These two sectors generate about 30% of its GDP and provide for almost 40% of all monetary income to the country (Gerasymowa 2011). The real growth of GDP in 2013 was 0%, which signaled the country was on the verge of a new recession. Furthermore, by the end of 2013 Ukraine's external debt amounted to 78.8% of its GDP (Macro Economy Meter 2013), while exchange reserves decreased to $20 billion USD (Trading Economics, Ukraine Foreign Exchange Reserves 2003–2017).

In addition, the imposition of personal sanctions on Ukraine's elite became a possibility once protests began in late November 2013, making the threat of their imposition a tool of conditional pressure on the country's ruling group. This tool, however, was not used as it might have been. Personalized sanctions, for instance, might have tipped the balance in favor of the West and precipitated

Yanukovych's downfall. For this lever to be effective—to make Yanukovych abstain from violence and potentially abdicate—at least three conditions would have been necessary. First, personalized sanctions would have had to have been applied when the regime was at its most vulnerable (*timing*). Second, these sanctions would have had to have been extensive, targeting not only the president but also the ruling "Family." The threat of extending the West's "black list" to include Ukrainian oligarchs might also have pushed them to defect to the opposition, which, in turn, could have undermined the unity of the regime (*scope*). Three, any imposed sanctions would have had to have been coherent, reflecting a unified position on the part of the United States and EU (*cohesion*).

The first country to introduce personal sanctions was Canada, which did so on January 28, 2014 (Government of Canada 2014). The EU announced personalized sanctions only on February 20, 2014, and they only came into force on March 6, 2014, more than two weeks after the massive bloodshed in Kyiv. Meanwhile, the US announced sanctions against Yanukovych, Viktor Medvedchuk (a Ukrainian politician and oligarch) and eight Russian officials only on March 17, 2014 (Weigel 2014). These late sanctions hardly affected Yanukovych, as he had already fled to Moscow.

The scope of the sanctions was also limited. The Initial EU list targeted 18 individuals of Yanukovych's inner circle (Council Decision 2014/119/CFSP). Coherence was also undermined as strategic calculations entered the game, affecting not only unified coordination between the US and EU, but also within the EU itself. The Baltic states, Poland and some new EU members were concerned about the geopolitical implications of Ukraine slipping into Russia's orbit, while "old" EU members, at least publicly, were more concerned with values. This is what Levitsky and Way have called "competing foreign policy objectives" (2010, 41).

But why have both the United States and the EU abstained for so long from sanctioning corrupt Ukrainian officials? Apparently, Brussels and Washington had their reasons. While in the EU the "positive incentive" and conditionality were a dominant line of thinking, for the Obama administration Ukraine barely registered on the radar. Both, however, sought to resolve the crisis through compromise, as they had done in 2004.

In the US there were two views regarding sanctions—policy experts and leaders of international organizations such as David Kramer (president of Freedom House) and Steven Pifer (who served as the US ambassador to Ukraine between 1997 and 2000) championed sanctions (UNIAN 2012). In contrast, government officials instead promoted "engagement," seeing it as preferable to isolating Ukraine, the idea being that maintaining dialogue could prevent Ukraine from slipping into authoritarianism and, subsequently into Russia's orbit.

Both the US and the EU understood that even targeted sanctions were a risky bet, and that they could have easily brought about the opposite effect of what was desired. Furthermore, the EU's decision to impose sanctions was not so much complicated by procedural difficulties as by political calculations. The EU's "Open Door" policy towards Ukraine relied on using positive incentives rather than exerting overt pressure. The reactions of the US and EU to the Ukrainian crisis suggest that it was not the sanctions themselves, but rather the threat of imposing them, that was viewed as the West's means of applying "soft pressure" on Ukrainian authorities (Matsiyevsky 2013, 155–56). However, a late and inconsistent response by the West rendered this tool ineffective.

If personalized sanctions (such as a ban on entering the US and the EU, the freezing of bank accounts and launching of financial investigations) had been applied right after the first acts of violence occurred on the Maidan (November 30, 2013), or at least after the Ukrainian parliament passed a package of "dictatorship laws,"[3] they might have encouraged elite defections, preventing the escalation of violence and, potentially, Putin's aggression against Ukraine. In short, if sanctions had been timely, coherent and extensive, they could have prevented the biggest international

---

3   A package of ten anti-protest laws, pushed through the parliament by the PoR on January 16, 2014.

crisis in Europe since the breakup of Yugoslavia. As Michael McFaul asserts, a credible threat of applying sanctions against Kuchma in 2004 prevented him from using violence against protesters and opened the road to the peaceful transfer of power (2007, 71–72). If the policy of engagement reasonably prevailed until the failed Vilnius summit, why did the West retain it for almost 90 days during the crisis? There are at least three factors that can shed some light on this issue.

First, as the crisis deteriorated, the West exhibited no consistent policy towards either Ukraine or Russia. In the EU the dominant belief was that the AA would be signed, as EU officials saw the fate of AA as primarily if not solely dependent on their own will. This overconfidence was reflected in not having a "plan B" regarding the AA. Second, the competing foreign policy objectives of the EU and the US made it difficult to arrive at reasonable strategies to confront Putin. Sanctioning Yanukovych after the failed Vilnius summit would not provide the means to deter Putin in Ukraine. Meanwhile, the West preferred to react as if Yanukovych was a sovereign player. An inability (or unwillingness) to envision Putin's aggressive intentions resulted in Russia's annexation of Crimea. Third, as the EU and US both had "strategic" concerns that sanctions could provoke a spiral of internal violence, they became preoccupied with decreasing Ukraine's "systemic vulnerability" (Doner, Ritchie & Slater 2005). Sanctions could have potentially weakened the organizational power of the regime, but could also have increased anti-governmental protest, leading to internal conflict and the breakup of the state. As sanctions imposed on undemocratic leaders have rarely had a curative effect (Escribà-Folch 2012), the West preferred an evolutionary scenario to a chaotic and unpredictable "people's revolution."

Likewise, the reaction of the former Ukrainian president proved that the threat of imposing sanctions was not credible. The West expected Yanukovych to act rationally, that is, to abandon power after holding of early elections (the central issue of the compromise reached on February 21, 2014) and thereby secure his physical and political survival until then. The President, however, relying on a different logic, made several grave mistakes and finally lost power. The West likewise made at least three strategic mistakes: hesitating to sanction Yanukovych and his close allies; not deterring Putin from interfering in Ukraine; and intervening too late in the crisis. The EU's diplomatic mission to "channel" the crisis through compromise was also futile for several reasons. First, EU officials missed the moment when the crisis turned into a revolution,[4] as they were still trying to negotiate a deal. Revolution, however, could hardly be tempered by compromise. Second, the EU miscalculated the players. While EU diplomats routinely sought to bring "the ruling elite" and "the opposition" to the table, the real player was not the opposition, but the people protesting in Kyiv and throughout Ukraine. This explains the third mistake — the EU's unacceptable offer[5]. For protesters, agreeing to such a compromise was unacceptable, as it would mean they would have to forgive Yanukovych for more than one hundred deaths and tolerate him as a president for another year.

To sum up, two observations may be made. First, poor economic performance and the capacity to apply sanctions increased Ukraine's vulnerability to the Western pressure. Though the nominal leverage was low, the above factors suggest that potential leverage was at a "medium" level.

Second, though potential Western leverage was actually greater than might have been expected, it was not applied in a timely, extensive and coherent manner. The late and inconsistent response to Ukraine's crisis made sanctions an uncredible threat.

Table 4 summarizes the values of linkage, leverage and organizational power prior to the 2013 crisis in comparison to 1990-2008 (as measured by Levitsky & Way).

---

4 Unlike in 2004, in 2014 the author detected 7 out of 11 analytically defined attributes of a revolution, allowing the latter to be defined as a political, but not a social, revolution (Matsiyevsky 2016. 444-449).

5 An agreement on February 21, 2014, facilitated by the EU representatives — Frank-Walter Steinmeier, Radoslaw Sikorski and Eric Fournier — assumed that Yanukovych would stay in power until at least the end of 2014 in exchange for limiting his prerogatives by restoring the constitution of 2004.

Table 4. The dynamics of linkage, leverage and organizational power scores

Dimension	1990-2008	2012-2013
Linkage	0.31 (Low)	0.55 (Medium)
Economic ties	-	4
Social ties	-	2
Communication ties	-	3
Governmental ties	-	2
Leverage	High	Low/Medium
GDP (in billion USD).	137	180
Organizational Power	2 (Low)	6 (High)
State scope	2	2
State cohesion	0	1
Party scope	0	2
Party cohesion	0	1

How do these empirical findings relate to the theory? The theory predicts that under conditions of low/medium linkage and leverage but high organizational power, the regime will be unstable, but will survive. In 2014 as in 2004 the actual outcome — regime change — differed from the predicted outcome. Why is this? With regard to 2004, Levitsky and Way admit that this outcome was rooted more in domestic processes — limited organizational power, elite defection and a strong opposition — rather than external pressure (2010, 213-214, 219). In contrast to Leonid Kuchma, however, Victor Yanukovych managed to stay in power for the first three months of the crisis before finally fleeing to Russia (Wilson 2014, chap. 4; Aslund 2015, 101-109; Dragneva & Wolczuk 2015, 83-99). I argue that Yanukovych's prolonged survival can be explained by three factors: the growth of Ukraine's organizational power, the West's miscalculated approach to sanctions, and Russia's "black knight" support. Two of these three factors have been discussed above. Now I turn to the role of Russia to describe how Putin's policy towards Yanukovych prolonged his stay in power, but ultimately brought about massive anti-regime mobilization, resulting in his eventual toppling.

Turning to the Other Side: Russia's Influence on Ukraine

Clearly, Russia has interests in Ukraine. But how did these interests translate into an ability to influence Ukraine's political process? In terms of Levitsky and Way, what was the role of the "black knight" in affecting the fate of Yanukovych's regime? More precisely, what was the extent of Ukraine's linkage to Russia and what leverage did Russia exercise over Ukraine under Yanukovych? Considering Yanukovych's impulsive decision to not sign the AA in Vilnius (Wood, Pomeranz, Wayne Merry & Trudolyubov 2015, 6–63), the presence of Russian "consultants" (including Putin's aide Vladislav Surkov) in Ukraine for the entirety of the crisis (Wilson 2014, 108–110), the alleged involvement of Russian snipers in the Maidan shootings (Wilson 2014, 89), and Yanukovych's appeal to Putin to send troops to Crimea (Lederer & Spielmann 2014) after he had fled to Russia all indicate that Putin was able to capitalize on Ukraine's linkage to Russia and turn it into leverage (Hughes & Sasse 2016). On the other hand, this leverage was only capable of influencing Ukraine's corrupt elites and part of the population in Crimea and the Donbas; it proved largely ineffective in spreading the "Russian spring" further across Ukraine.

Levitsky and Way acknowledge the role of "black knights" in supporting authoritarian leaders, but they do not develop it theoretically. By extending the concept of linkage and leverage to encompass non-democracies, we may gain valuable insights not only into Yanukovych's extended struggle for power (and his downfall), but also the broader dynamics of post-Soviet hybrid regimes and what may be termed "autocracy promotion."

Let us take a cursory glance at Ukraine's linkage to Russia. Like the linkage to the West, it may be measured along four dimensions: economic ties, social ties, intergovernmental ties, and communication ties. As previously, each dimension below is assessed on a scale from 1 to 5, with the resulting scores summed and recalibrated into a range from 0 to 1. However, while Levitsky and Way ascribe points based on a country's position relative to all non-Western countries in the world, I ascribe points based on Ukraine's ranking relative to the Commonwealth of Independent States (CIS).

As of 2013, Ukraine's economic ties to Russia were greater than just one component (trade) would reflect. Prior to independence, Ukraine was an integral part of the Soviet military-industrial complex. And while Ukraine's share of trade with Russia declined gradually after independence, in 2013 Russia was still its largest trade partner (trade with Russia that year amounted to 38.2 billion USD), while Ukraine was the fourth largest trading partner of Russia (for which trade with Ukraine accounted for 35.5 billion USD). Moreover, Ukraine's negative balance-in-trade with Russia in 2013 was 1.9 billion USD, which made Ukraine's economy highly dependent on the Russian market (Embassy of Ukraine in Russian Federation, n.d.).

As with economic ties, social ties to Russia are greater than just the number of Ukrainians living or working in Russia. However, just along this dimension, Ukrainians in Russia make up the largest single diaspora group. The official Russian census in 2010 reported that 1.9 million ethnic Ukrainians were living in Russia, representing over 1.4% of the total population and making Ukrainians the third most numerous ethnic group in the country after ethnic Russians and Tatars (2010 National Census in Russia). Similarly, until the annexation of Crimea, Russians comprised the largest ethnic minority in Ukraine at 8.3 million individuals, or 17.3% of the overall population of Ukraine (Russians in Ukraine, n.d.). And while the Russian ethnic minority is decreasing in Ukraine, Russia remains the largest external job market for Ukrainians (Malinovska 2014).

With regard to intergovernmental ties, Ukraine was neither a full member of the CIS nor a member of any other economic, political or security organization together with Russia. Russia's effort to make Ukraine a member of the Customs Union (CU), along with Belarus and Kazakhstan, failed largely due to the Euromaidan protest and Yanukovych's escape to Russia.

Finally, communication ties between Ukraine and Russia are not less extensive than economic or social ties, although this dimension is significantly harder to measure. As of 2009 Ukraine had the largest share (32%) of the voice traffic going out of Russia. (Zolotova 2010). Consequently, economic, social and communication ties are assessed at 5 points, and governmental ties at 2 points. After recalibrating their sum to fit a range from 0 to 1, the obtained linkage score was 0.85. Although this is a very approximate measure, Ukraine's linkage to Russia under Yanukovych appeared to be higher than its linkage to the West (0.53).

Strong linkage to Russia explains not just Ukraine's impasse with reforms and democratization; it also explains why for the greater number of elites and many ordinary Ukrainians Russia remained a model state. Little wonder then that even after three years of warfare in the Donbas, some 40% of Ukrainians retain a positive image of Russia (UNIAN 2017). This extensive spider-web of ties to Russia, which extend beyond linguistic, religious and cultural affinities, allowed Putin to turn linkage into strong leverage. But how comparable was Russia's leverage to the West's leverage when it came to Yanukovych's Ukraine? To apply Levitsky and Way's concept of leverage to Russia is problematic, as it was designed to measure Western democratizing pressure. However, one potential way to measure undemocratic leverage is to apply Tolstrup's concept of "negative external actor." In his work, Tolstrup sought to develop an analytical framework to explain Russia's policies of "managed stability" and "managed instability" on neighboring states. By summarizing previous works he selected 18 levers and combined them into three groupings: military, political and economic.[6] Tosltrup, however, does not offer

---

6 The 18 levers are: military interventions; military threats; military bases abroad; military support to secessionist republics; peacekeeping forces; military alliances dominated by Russia; support for anti-Western groups; opposition to pro-Western groups; multilateral organizations dominated by Russia; support for secessionist republics; control of the CIS Election Monitoring Organization; Russian state TV; the Russian diaspora; trade embargos; subsidies; Russia's energy monopoly; credits; and debt payments (Tolstrup 2009, 929).

any quantitative measure for assessing these levers, which makes it difficult to apply them in a comparative case study. As the first step in developing a quantitative measure for the concept of "negative external actor," I ascribe 1 point to each lever that is present/active at the time of Yanukovych's presidency. The resultant scores will be summed into a composite score (range: 0–18). Scores from 1 to 6 would represent low leverage, while 7 to 13 would represent medium leverage, and 14 to 18 would represent high leverage. Acknowledging that not all 18 levers are of the same weight (and that there exist some other potential levers, such as informal ties, bribes and various forms of blackmail), let me call the former "nominal" leverage. This would allow for making a comparison (albeit very rough) between Russian and Western leverage in the case of Yanukovych's Ukraine.

Of the six military levers (military interventions, military threats, military bases abroad, military support to secessionist republics, peacekeeping forces, and military alliances dominated by Russia) only "military bases abroad" was empirically relevant.[7] Of seven political levers, meanwhile, five were visibly present: support for anti-Western groups; multilateral organizations dominated by Russia; control of the CIS Election Monitoring Organization; Russian state TV; and the Russian diaspora. Of the five economic levers, all five were relevant: energy monopoly; trade embargoes; subsidies; credits; and debt payments. For the purpose of this study, let us assume that all levers have an equal weight. Having noted the presence of 11 out of a total of 18 possible levers, we can see that Russian leverage falls in the category of "medium" leverage (range: 7 to 13), suggesting that the West's leverage (medium) was roughly matched by that of Russia.

As mentioned above, this measure reflects what may be termed "potential" or "nominal leverage." As in the case of the West, Russian leverage was actually higher than represented by the calculated score, as the latter does not include vast informal levers,

---

7   Though "military threat" (to annex Crimea) was mentioned in some media outlets, until we have documented proof it was used by Russian authorities to pressure Yanukovych, we cannot include it as a relevant lever.

such as corruption and political or military blackmail. Tolstrup's list also does not include cultural levers (e.g., religion, language) and the identity politics that Russia has actively pursued in Ukraine.

Three conclusions ensue. First, even given the limited number of quantitatively observable levers, we can see why Russia was able to prevent Yanukovych from signing the AA, to annex Crimea and to launch a hybrid war in Ukraine. What Russia could not affect, however, was the reaction of ordinary Ukrainians. Initially mobilized to protest the government's decision to put the signing of the AA on hold, the protesters became radicalized, and the protests assumed a life of their own after the government decided to violently suppress the Maidan. Second, as Russia's leverage over Yanukovych was matched by that of the West, Russia's policy of "managed stability" (i.e., support for Yanukovych) prolonged his stay in power, but could not secure his political survival. After the collapse of Yanukovych's government, Putin swiftly changed his role in Ukraine from one of stabilizing to destabilizing the new government. Third, the answer to the original question (why Yanukovych managed to survive three months of political crisis) can be attributed in part to the Russia's "black knight" role. As this study shows, if the linkage of the country in question [Ukraine] is higher to the "black knight" state [Russia] than to the West— democratization is not likely to occur. And, if Russia's leverage on the country in question [Ukraine] is equal to/or higher than that of the West, Russia's policies of managed stability and instability can be more effective than Western democratizing efforts. By extending the theory to non-democracies and by offering a single measure for Western versus Russian leverage on Ukraine, this study invites the development of more sophisticated techniques for measuring "black knight" leverage vis-à-vis the West. Finally, Levitsky and Way's theory underestimates the role of agency, namely the role leaders, elites and the masses play in explaining regime dynamics. The futility of focusing only on one set of variables is another reason why the theory was unable to predict the outcome of the Ukrainian case. This suggests that it would be worthwhile to develop more integrative accounts of the dynamics of hybrid regimes in post-communist Eurasia (and beyond).

Agency-Based Factors Affecting the Fall of Yanukovych

The factors discussed above help explain why Yanukovych appeared to be immune to both Western pressure and "people power" for almost three months of the crisis. Until the third violent attempt to disperse the Maidan failed (it occurred between February 18–21, 2014) he managed to prevent any significant defections from the three key pillars of his regime: the Party of Regions' parliamentary faction, the "oligarchs," and the security sector. With the West imposing no sanctions and Putin at his side, Yanukovych virtually neutralized structural democratizing pressure. This indicates that Yanukovych could have likely survived until the next presidential elections, whenever they were to be held.

The fall of Yanukovych was triggered by several agency-based factors, most importantly by his personal strategic blunders, which were apparently made under pressure from Moscow.[8] On the one hand Russia provided political support (by publicly denouncing the protests), economic assistance (by providing 3 billion USD out of a promised 15 billion USD bailout and a 30% discount on natural gas), and security (by sending Putin's aide Vladislav Surkov and a group of Russian agents to Kyiv) to support Yanukovych. On the other hand, the growing pressure from Moscow ultimately turned out to be counterproductive. The Kremlin expected state-led violence would disperse the Maidan. The effect, however, was just the opposite: each attempt to crack down on the protesters increased their organizational capacity, numbers, and persistence.

---

8   The decision to use force against the protesters has been attributed to pressure from the Russian government and its political consultants in Ukraine (chief among them Vladislav Surkov). The latter were allegedly composed of two groups of Russian special agents charged with coordinating the "antiterrorist operation" in Kyiv (Wilson 2014, 89).

State-led violence also provoked the radicalization of the protesters. As the Kyiv International Institute of Sociology (KIIS) reported, 69.9 % of the total number of protesters came onto the Maidan in direct reaction to the violence exhibited against the peaceful protest movement on November 30, 2013 (KIIS 2013). A failure to predict the outcome of these harsh decisions, apparently forced on him by the Kremlin, was Yanukovych's greatest strategic mistake. It precipitated the collapse of his regime in five ways.

First, after several failed attempts to violently disperse the Maidan, the regime lost its monopoly on the legitimate use of force. Despite reshuffling the command of the armed forces, there was a constant danger that the officers would not obey orders. After one unsuccessful attempt to mobilize the armed forces against protesters, the military stayed out of the conflict.[9] Second, after the Ukrainian parliament adopted a package of anti-protest laws ("dictatorship laws") on January 16, 2014, 10 western and central regions effectively slipped out of the government's control (as evinced by the occupation of regional administrative buildings). The ensuing "multiple sovereignty," severe political crisis, massive mobilization, and the subsequent split of elites ensured that the crisis would turn into a political revolution.

Third, the power vertical collapsed after the third failed attempt to violently disperse the Maidan. In the wake of massive bloodshed in Kyiv, the Party of Regions faction in parliament crumbled in just three days. However, the first signs of a coming crisis had already appeared two months earlier, when after the first instance of violence in Kyiv two prominent party figures—Inna Bohoslovska and Davyd Zhvania—publicly quit the party. Then on February 19, 2014 seven MPs defected, and later that same day another eleven followed. And on February 20, 2014 the newly appointed head of the Kyiv City State Administration, Viktor Makeyenko, expressed his support for the residents of Kyiv and

---

9   On February 19, 2014 the acting Minister of Defense, Pavel Lebedev, acknowledged sending airborne troops from Dnipropetrovsk to Kyiv. However, due to an accident en route the convoy of 25 trucks did not reach its destination, instead returning to the base (Miakshykov 2014).

quit the PoR. Shortly afterwards more than twenty deputies of the PoR simply left the country. As a result, the Party of Regions faction in parliament virtually ceased to exist. In just three days it had shrunk by almost 40%, going from 205 to 127 deputies (Verhovna rada of Ukraine, n.d.).

Fourth, the collapse of the regime was also precipitated by its defeat in the "information war." Live broadcasting from Kyiv's central square (the Maidan) became a focal point for sustaining mass mobilization. For the entire period of crisis, there were at least three national TV stations (Channel 5, News 24, and Espresso TV) and three online TV channels (Hromads'ke [Public TV], U-stream, and Spil'no TV), in addition to dozens of online streamers, who were permanently broadcasting from the Maidan. Even though they were occasionally disrupted, mobile and internet connections allowed protestors to maintain communication, both between themselves and the outside world.

Finally, although European mediators reached a deal with Yanukovych and the opposition on February 21, 2014, the people on the Maidan refused to accept it after witnessing massive bloodshed. It was the inability of all the parties involved to take sufficient account of the dynamics on the ground that turned this crisis into a political revolution.

Conclusions

This study focused on international competition over Ukraine prior to the 2014 revolution. It combined structural- and agency-based variables to explain why Victor Yanukovych was able to withstand both Western pressure and "people power" for some three months prior to finally abandoning his post and fleeing Ukraine. In particular, it set out to re-conceptualize Levitsky and Way's concepts of linkage and leverage by extending them to Russia, while testing the theory by applying it to the specific case of Ukraine.

The empirical findings yield four conclusions. First, while structural factors (like the growth of the regime's organizational power, Russian leverage over Ukraine and the West's inconsistent approach to sanctions) extended Yanukovych's stay in power, it was agency-based factors (first and foremost his flawed decision to crack down on protesters) that most contributed to his downfall. The latter are not taken into account by Levitsky and Way's theory, which explains why the actual outcome (regime change) differs from the predicted outcome (regime survival).

Second, this study argues that the capacity to apply sanctions on Yanukovych's regime could have made Western leverage more effective. Despite Yanukovych's concentration of presidential power and Russia's support for him, the West could have facilitated the regime transition and prevented the outbreak of political violence if sanctions had been applied not after, but before, Yanukovych actually lost power. Late and inconsistent sanctions affirmed that the West expected Yanukovych to stay in power until the next elections. This expectation proved a mistake, as it sought to repeat the 2004 compromise solution to the crisis. But unlike in 2004, the 2014 crisis spiraled out of control and grew into a political revolution, which led Russia to launch a counter-revolution. The latter now poses not only an existential threat to Ukraine, but also represents a danger to the entire postwar international order.

Third, nominal Russian leverage over Ukraine appeared to be greater than that of the West. This explains why Putin was able to disrupt the signing of Ukraine's Association Agreement with the EU in Vilnius. While the EU attempted to resolve the crisis through compromise, Russia sought to keep Ukraine in its orbit by pushing Yanukovych toward a violent, confrontational scenario. As soon as this plan failed, Putin changed his policy of "managed stability" to "managed instability" in Ukraine.

Finally, although Western and Russian leverage both weakened Yanukovych's regime, its downfall was brought about from within the state. External pressure, especially from the Russian side, had considerable impact on elites, but it hardly affected the majority of Ukrainians. "People power" was stronger than either the West's inconsistent support or Russia's efforts at counter-balancing it. The issue was that the unwanted Ukrainian revolution caught the West by surprise. Having no consistent policy either towards Ukraine or Russia, the West could not prevent Putin from annexing Crimea and igniting a hybrid war in the east of Ukraine. An inability to learn hard lessons from the Ukrainian crisis (and take a unified position to prevent further aggressive steps by Russia) could ultimately become very costly for the West.

References

Aslund, A. (2015). *Ukraine: What Went Wrong and How to Fix It.* Washington, D. C.: Peterson Institute for International Economics.

Bunce, V., & Wolchik, S. (2011). *Defeating Authoritarian Leaders in Post-Communist Countries.* Cambridge: Cambridge University Press.

Bunce V., & Wolchik, S. (2009). Debating the Color Revolutions: Getting Real About "Real Causes." *Journal of Democracy,* 20 (1), 69–73.

Burlakova, V. (2013). Товаріщі поліцейські. Обіцяна реформа МВС не змінить суті української міліції (Policemen fellows. The promised police reform will not change the nature of Ukraine's police), *Tyzhden,* 284 (16), 16–19.

Charap, S., & Colton, T. J. (2017). *Everyone Loses: The Ukraine Crisis and the Ruinous Contest for Post-Soviet Eurasia.* Milton Park, Abingdon, Oxon: Routledge.

Council decision 2014/119/CFSP. (2014, March 6) *Official Journal of the European Union).* Retrieved from http://eur-lex.europa.eu/legal-content/EN/TXT/PDF/?uri=CELEX:32014D0119&rid=1

Den'. (2013, March 18). Міліція розігнала акцію під Генпрокуратурою (Police dispersed the protest action at the General Procurator's Office). Retrieved from http://www.day.kiev.ua/uk/news/180313-miliciya-rozignala-akciyu-pid-genprokuraturoyu

Didushok, I. (2011, October 27). Методом батога і ПР-яника (The method of stick and carrots). *Ukraina Moloda.* Retrieved from http://www.umoloda.kiev.ua/number/1969/180/70086/

Doner, R. F., Ritchie, B. K., & Slater, D. (2005). Systemic Vulnerability and the Origins of Developmental States: Northeast and Southeast Asia in Comparative Perspective. *International Organization,* 59 (2), 327–361.

Dragneva-Lewers, R., & Wolczuk, K. (2015). *Ukraine between the EU and Russia: The integration challenge.* Palgrave Macmillan UK.

Embassy of Ukraine in Russian Federation. (n.d.). Торговельно-економічне співробітництво між Україною та Росією. (Trade and economic cooperation between Ukraine and Russia). Retrieved June 10, 2016 from http://russia.mfa.gov.ua/ua/ukraine-ru/trade

Escribà-Folch, A. (2012). Authoritarian Responses to Foreign Pressure Spending, Repression, and Sanctions. *Comparative Political Studies*, 45 (6), 683–713.

European Commission. (2013). *Client and Supplier Countries of the EU28 in Merchandise Trade (value %)*. Retrieved from http://trade.ec.europa.eu/doclib/docs/2006/september/tradoc122530.pdf

Freedom House. (2011, April). *Sounding the Alarm. Protecting Democracy in Ukraine. A Report on the State of Democracy and Human Rights in Ukraine.* Retrieved from https://freedomhouse.org/sites/default/files/inline_images/98.pdf

Freedom House. (2012, July). *Sounding the Alarm Round 2: Protecting Democracy in Ukraine. A Follow-up Freedom House Report.* Retrieved from https://freedomhouse.org/sites/default/files/Ukraine%202012%20English% 20 FINAL.pdf

Gandhi, J., Przeworski, A. (2007). Authoritarian Institutions and the Survival of Autocrats, *Comparative Political Studies*, 40 (11), 1279–1301.

Gazata.ua. (2012, August 13). Бютівець про тиск адмінресурсом: "Такого не було навіть при Кучмі (The member of BYuT about the "administrative resource" pressure: "This is never happened even during the presidency of Kuchma). Retrieved from https://gazeta.ua/articles/politics/_byutivec-pro-tisk-adminresursom-takogo-ne-bulo-navit-pri-kuchmi/450406

Gazeta UA. (2013, January 15). За графіті з Януковичем активісти отримали по кілька років в'язниці (For the graffiti with Yaukovych activists were sentenced to a several years in prison). Retrieved from http://gazeta.ua/articles/life/_za-grafiti-z-yanukovichem-aktivisti-otrimali-po-kilka-rokiv-v-yaznici/477028

Geddes, B. (1999). What do we Know about Democratization After 20 years?, *Annual Review of Political Science*, 2, 115–144.

Gerasymova, O., (2011, September 6) Спад в металургії обвалить економіку? (Will the decline in metallurgy crumble the economy?), *Ekonomichna Pravda*. Retrieved from http://www.epravda.com.ua/publications/2011/09/6/297213/

Götz, E., (2018) (Ed.). *Russia, the West, and the Ukraine Crisis*. Milton Park, Abingdon, Oxon: Routledge.

Government of Canada. (2014, February 20). *Ukraine: economic sanctions and expanded travel ban*. Retrieved from www.pm.gc.ca/eng/news/ 2014/02/20/ukraine-economic-sanctions-and-expanded-travel-ban #sthash.inA3L3zI.dpuf

Harasymiw, B. (2007). *Ukraine's "Orange Revolution" and Why It Fizzled*. Paper prepared for presentation to the annual meeting of the Canadian Political Science Association, at the 76th Congress of the Humanities and Social Sciences, University of Saskatchewan, Saskatoon. Retrieved from https://www.cpsa-acsp.ca/papers-2007 /Harasymiw.pdf

Hughes, J., & Sasse, G. (2016). Power ideas and conflict: ideology, linkage and leverage in Crimea and Chechnya. *East European Politics*, 32 (3), 314–334.

International Monetary Fund. (October 2012) *World Economic and Financial Surveys. World Economic Outlook Database*. Retrieved from http://www.imf.org/external/pubs/ft/weo/2012/02/weodata/in dex.aspx

International Organization for Migration. (September 2011). *Migration in Ukraine. Facts and Figures*. Retrieved from http://iom.org.ua/ en/pdf /Facts&Figures_b5_en_f.pdf

International Telecommunication Union. (2013). *Measuring Information Society 2013*. Retrieved from http://www.itu.int/en/ITUD/Statis tics/Documents/publications/mis2013/MIS2013_without_Annex_ 4.pdf

Johannsen, L., & Nørgaard, O. (2003). IPA: The Index of Presidential Authority. Explorations into the measurement of impact of a political institution. Aarhus: Department of Political Science, University of Aarhus.

Kyiv International Institute of Sociology. (2013, December 10). *KIIS press releases and reports. Maidan 2013*. Retrieved from http://www.kiis. com.ua/?lang=eng&cat=reports&id=216&page=26

Lederer, E. M., & Spielmann, P. J. (2014, March 4). Ukraine crisis: Fugitive President Viktor Yanukovych 'asked for Russian troops deployment' in Crimea. *Independent*. Retrieved from http://www.independent.co. uk/news/world/europe/ukraine-crisis-fugitive-president-viktor-y anukovych-asked-for-russian-troops-deployment-in-crimea-916743 0.html

Levitsky, S., & Way, L. (2010). *Competitive Authoritarianism: Hybrid Regimes After the Cold War*. Cambridge: Cambridge University Press.

Macro Economy Meter. (2013). *External debt (Percentage of GDP, Ukraine, 2013)*. Retrieved from http://mecometer.com/whats/ukraine/external-debt-percentage-of-gdp

Malinovska, O. (2014, March 13). Скільки українських мігрантів працює в Росії (How many Ukrainian migrants work in Russia) *Forbs Ukraina*. Retrieved from http://forbes.net.ua/ua/opinions/1367144-skilki-ukrayinskih-migrantiv-pracyue-v-rosiyi

Matsiyevsky, Y. (2013). *Западное давление или внутренние ресурсы: санкции и сценарии выживания политического режима в Украине*. (Western pressure vs. domestic resources: sanctions and the scenarios of Ukraine's regime survival). In A. Gil & T. Stempnevsky (eds.) *Перед выбором. Будущее Украины в условиях системной дестабилизации* (Confronting the Choice. Ukraine's future under systemic destabilization) (pp. 123–164). Instytut Europy Środkowo-Wschodniej: Lublin-Lwów-Kijów.

Matsiyevsky, Y. (2016). *У пастці гібридності: зигзаги трансформацій політичного режиму в Україні (1991–2014)*. Trapped in Hybridity: Zigzags of Ukraine's Regime Transformation (1991-2014). Chernivtsi: Books XXI.

McFaul, M. (2007). Ukraine Imports Democracy: External influences on the Orange Revolution. *International Security*, 32 (2), 45–83.

Menon, R., &. Rumer, E. B. (2015). *Conflict in Ukraine: The Unwinding of the Post–Cold War Order*. Boston: MIT Press.

Miakshykov, M. (2014, February 21). Three paratroopers die in car crash near Dnipropetrovsk. *Ukrinform*. Retrieved from http://photo.ukrinform.ua/eng/current/photo.php?id=599901

Nation Master. (2005). *Media.International voice traffic. Out and in Minutes: Countries Compared*. Retrieved from http://www.nationmaster.com country-info/stats/Media/International-voice-traffic/Out-and-in/Minutes

Podrobnosti. (2012, December 24). Формирование Кабмина встревожило украинскую общественность. (The formation of the Cabinet of Ministers worried the Ukrainian public). Retrieved from http://podrobnosti.ua/878546-formirovanie-kabmina-vstrevozhilo-ukrainskuju-obschestvennost.html

Puglisi, R. (2003). The rise of the Ukrainian oligarchs. *Democratization*, 10 (3), 99–123.

Russians in Ukraine. (n.d.) Retrieved June 12, 2016 from Wikipedia, http://en.wikipedia.org/wiki/RussiansinUkraine#cite_note-census-1

Slayter, D., & Fenner, S. (2011). State Power or Staying Power: Infrastructural Mechanisms and Authoritarian Durability. *Journal of International Affairs,* 65 (1), 15–29.

The Economist. (2013, April 6). Linguistically challenged. How Ukraine falls between political, economic and linguistic camps. Retrieved from https://www.economist.com/news/europe/21575786-how-ukraine-falls-between-political-economic-and-linguistic-camps-linguistically-challenged

Tolstrup, J. (2009). Studying a negative external actor: Russia's management of stability and instability in the 'Near Abroad'. *Democratization,* 16 (5), 922–944.

Tolstrup, J. (2014). *Russia vs. the EU: The Competition for Influence in Post-Soviet States.* Boulder, CO: Lynne Rienner.

Trading Economics. (n.d.). *Ukraine Foreign Exchange Reserves. 2003–2017.* Retrieved from https://tradingeconomics.com/ukraine/foreign-exchange-reserves

UBR. (2012, November 2). Украинцы отказываются от домашних телефонов. (Ukrainians abandon land line telephones). Retrieved from http://ubr.ua/ukraine-and-world/society/ukraincy-otkazyvautsia-ot-domasnih-telefonov-175633

UNIAN News agency (2012, November 14). Stephen Pifer: "USA does not perceive Ukraine as democratic state". Retrieved from http://www.unian.ua/news/535602-eks-posol-payfer-u-ssha-bilshe-ne-spriymayut-ukrajinu-yak-demokratichnu-derjavu.html

UNIAN. (2017, July 10). Ставлення українців до Росії залишається кращим, ніж росіян до України - опитування (Ukrainians' attitude towards Russia still better than Russians' attitude towards Ukraine – polls). Retrieved from https://www.unian.ua/society/2021084-stavlennya-ukrajintsiv-do-rosiji-zalishaetsya-kraschim-nij-rosiyan-do-ukrajini-opituvannya.html

Verhovna Rada of Ukraine. (n.d.). *Фракція партії регіонів у Верховній Раді України сьомого скликання - VII скликання (2012–2014).* (The faction of the party of Regions in Verchovna Rada of 7th convention 2012–2014). Retrieved from http://w1.c1.rada.gov.ua/pls/site2/p_fraction_dep_changes?pidid=2355

Weigel, D., Obama Sanctions Ousted Ukrainian President, 10 Others, *Slate* (2014, March 17). Retrieved from http://www.slate.com/blogs/weigel/2014/03/17/obama_sanctions_ousted_ukrainian_president_10_others.html

Wilson, A. (2014). *Ukraine Crisis: What it Means for the West*. New Haven and London: Yale University Press.

Wood, E. A., Pomeranz, W. E., Wayne Merry, E., & Trudolyubov, M. (2015). *Roots of Russia's War in Ukraine*. Washington, D.C.: Woodrow Wilson Center Press with Columbia University Press.

Zerkalo Nedeli, (2013a, October 27). Лишенный депутатского мандата Марков рассказал, как вся фракция Партии регионов держится на страхе. (Deprived of mandate Markov has told how the whole faction of Party of Regions in parliament is kept on fear). Retrieved from http://zn.ua/POLITICS/lishennyy-deputatskogo-mandata-markov-rasskazal-kak-vsya-frakciya-partii-regionov-derzhitsya-na-strahe-129057_.html

Zerkalo Nedeli. (2013b, September 18). В политсовет Партии регионов вошли представители "Семьи" (The "family" representatives entered the political council of the Party of Regions). Retrieved from https://zn.ua/POLITICS/politsovet-partii-regionov-popolnilsya-predstavitelyami-semi-129413_.html

Zolotova, T. (2010, March 29). Молдаване больше, чем армяне. (Moldavians more than Armenians). *Comnews*. Retrieved from http://*www*.comnews.ru/node/20919

2010 National Census in Russia. (n.d.) Всероссийская перепись населения 2010 года. Retrieved June 11, 2016 from http://www.gks.ru/free_doc/new_site/perepis2010/croc/Documents/Vol4/pub-04-01.pdf

2014 Euromaidan regional state administration occupations, *Wikipedia*. Retrieved October 30, 2017 from https://en.wikipedia.org/wiki/2014_Euromaidan_regional_state_administration_occupations#cite_note-globe20140127-3

Joanna Fomina

On Ukraine's Geopolitical Identity: Public Opinion Dynamics on NATO Accession in the Aftermath of the War with Russia

This chapter examines Ukrainians' preferences regarding security and civilizational choices in the context of the annexation of Crimea by Russia and the ongoing military conflict. Specifically, it analyses the dynamics of public perceptions regarding Ukraine's possible membership in the EU and NATO (the latter a traditionally much more controversial alliance) and demonstrates how Ukrainians' geopolitical orientation has become more consolidated in the aftermath of the Maidan protests. Considered as well is the evolving interplay between linguistic and regional identities and questions of wider geopolitics. Finally, the chapter also reverses analytical perspective and discusses public attitudes within select NATO and EU member states towards Ukraine.

Situated between Russia and the EU and having long had economic, cultural and societal ties with both East and West, Ukraine for many years pursued a foreign policy that relied on juggling two vectors of integration that are, arguably, mutually exclusive. That straddled position was well-reflected in public opinion surveys; nearly two decades ago, 56% of Ukrainians wanted to see Ukraine as a member of the EU, but 52% preferred their country to be in a union with Russia and Belarus. One in three Ukrainians did not see any contradiction with Ukraine belonging to both unions simultaneously. NATO was an entirely different matter, predominately perceived as an aggressive military bloc and as a threat by the majority of society (Konieczna, 2001). However, after former President Viktor Yanukovych's U-turn on Ukraine's EU policy instigated the Euromaidan and the Revolution of Dignity, and after Russia's annexation of Crimea occurred and the outbreak of a fratricidal war in the Donbas began, one could expect that major shifts took place not only in Ukraine's foreign policy but also in Ukrainian public opinion.

This chapter looks at how these events affected Ukrainians' preferences regarding both security and civilizational choices, including membership in international alliances and what can be termed as national and "geopolitical" identities. It focuses on the dynamics of public opinion support for NATO membership as a traditionally much more controversial alliance. The argument is two-fold. Ukrainians' geopolitical orientation has become much more consolidated and their position on NATO membership, as a civilizational choice and as a security guarantor, has changed diametrically in the conflict's aftermath. The population in traditionally more pro-Russian regions, the East and South, has become increasingly supportive of NATO membership and very skeptical about any alliance with Russia. The alternative to Western alliances is not an alliance with Russia, be it a military, economic or political one, but rather a non-aligned status. Simultaneously, region, language and identity remain important predictors of a pro-Western orientation, and in particular, support for NATO membership. Ukrainians who claim a European identity, speak Ukrainian and who live in the country's West and Centre and have a hardline approach to Donbas' occupied territories are much more likely to be NATO accession supporters. Furthermore, as Ukrainian public opinion on NATO and EU membership does not exist in a vacuum, this paper also reverses perspectives and discusses public attitudes within select NATO and EU member states towards Ukraine. Despite Ukrainians' increased readiness to join the alliance, key NATO member-states' publics are far from enthusiastic about it.

Setting the Context: Ukraine, NATO and the EU

The post-Euromaidan government in Kyiv has clearly adopted a pro-Western integration agenda: Ukraine signed the political part of the Ukraine-Europe Association Agreement on March 21, 2014 and the economic part on June 27, 2014. Moreover, on January 1,

2016 Ukraine joined the EU's Deep and Comprehensive Free Trade Area, with President Petro Poroshenko setting 2020 as a target for Ukraine to submit an EU membership application.

With respect to Euro-Atlantic integration, Ukraine had already applied for NATO's Membership Action Plan in 2008, but after Viktor Yanukovych's victory in the 2010 presidential elections the country resumed its previous policy of non-alignment and plans to join NATO were shelved. However, in the wake of Russia's aggressive military interference in Ukraine, the newly elected Ukrainian parliament renounced its country's non-aligned status in December of 2014.

Meanwhile, in September of 2016 Ukraine officially requested to join NATO's Enhanced Opportunities Program, which includes countries such as Australia, Finland, Georgia, Jordan and Sweden. And in February of 2017, after another flare-up of violence in the Donbas, Poroshenko announced that he intended to hold a national referendum concerning whether or not Ukraine should seek NATO membership. Since then, Ukrainian parliamentarians adopted legislation (on June 8, 2017) making NATO integration a foreign policy priority, with Poroshenko announcing in July 2017 that Ukraine would begin discussions with NATO concerning a membership action plan and implement reforms needed to allow it to meet membership criteria by 2020.

The Interplay of National Identity, Domestic Politics and International Relations

Commenting on Ukraine's post-communist transformation, Roman Szporluk emphasized as early as the 1990s the considerable degree to which foreign and domestic policies were intertwined: "[s]uccess or failure in managing Ukraine's major 'internal' problems today will be affected by the relations it establishes between itself and the world community" (1997, 113). In other words, Ukraine's orientation towards its neighbors and the decisions it makes regarding its international alignments directly affect how the country is managed. Building closer ties with either the West or

Russia and the other CIS states implies the acceptance of certain norms in domestic politics and public life. Consequently, foreign policy preferences have become a constitutive element of broader political, cultural and social dissent within Ukrainian society (Shulman 1998).

In this context, there seems to be a tension between the extent to which the Euromaidan and the Revolution of Dignity were about wanting to belong to Europe (which in practice meant signing the Association Agreement and striving to join the Union) and the extent to which protestors opposed a corrupt regime because they wanted to "live in a normal country." However, when EU membership is understood not as an end in and of itself, but as a means of ensuring democratic standards, the rule of law and economic stability, this tension appears moot.

Moreover, although NATO and EU memberships are not interdependent (meaning that joining one is not a prerequisite for joining the other), both nonetheless share a number of key membership criteria. In addition to demanding that prospective states meet its military criteria, NATO also expects them to have a market economy, stable democratic system and demonstrated commitment to the rule of law and human rights. Similarly, while EU accession is predicated upon meeting economic, cultural and (increasingly) political criteria, Central and Eastern European states have long regarded joining the Union a civilizational and strategic choice that would guarantee them security from Russia (Niżnik 2015). In other words, both EU and NATO memberships function as means of ensuring not only economic prosperity and democracy, but also security.

Consequently, foreign policy expectations are closely associated with national identification within Ukraine (Munro 2007). However, the rather simplistic view that Ukraine's internal divisions run along ethnic and linguistic lines has long been challenged (Barrington 2002; Fomina 2014; Gentile 2015). Michael Gentile instead refers to Ukraine's geopolitical identities: the pro-Western and pro-Russian/Soviet ones (2015). Geopolitical identity can be defined as "the sense of national self flagged by the country's leaders that informs its actions at the global scale" (Jansson 2007, 402). Gentile discusses partially irreconcilable geopolitical narratives that pertain to an understanding of the past, Ukraine's desired position in the world, relations with its neighbors and its values and symbols, all of which shape specific variants of Ukrainian national identity as being "'occupied' by geopolitics" (2015, 205). As he explains: "In essence, these identities become geopolitical, and the population internalizes them as such" (ibid.). Gentile also demonstrates that even in places believed to be traditionally pro-Russian, the situation is actually quite complex. His research in Luhansk in 2013, for instance, reveals the growing presence of pro-Western geopolitical identities (2015).

I find the term "geopolitical" useful in this discussion because it denotes the complex interplay between space, identity and visions of the past, present and future fairly well (including how these pertain to international relations and preferred alliances). However, I reject classical geopolitical research's deterministic approach. Instead, my perspective is informed by a critical geopolitics that examines identities' and spaces' social construction of the ways in which they are made meaningful with the help of various ideas, narratives and actors (O'Tuathail 1996; Agnew 1998).

Consequently, this chapter looks at how the Ukrainian public's geopolitical identity has changed in the aftermath of Crimea's annexation and the military conflict with Russia. It draws on survey data regarding support for NATO membership as an important indicator of Ukrainians' geopolitical orientation.

Generally, as Clemens reminds us, opinion poll data on foreign policy issues requires caution on the part of analysts. Two questions can be raised here: can public attitudes be accurately measured and do actually they matter? On the one hand, the quality of survey data may be questionable due to the issue's low salience and the respondents' low information levels. As Hans Rattinger noted: "a large amount of the volatility of public opinion on these matters is due to the pervasiveness of nonattitudes" (in Clemens 1992, 30) On the other, there is the question of the relationship between elite and mass public attitudes. In the case of complex foreign and security policy issues, it is elite attitudes that lead public opinion instead of the opposite. But in the case of NATO membership, the issue is rather straightforward and has been in the public domain for decades now. It has more to do with a civilizational choice and general geopolitical orientation, and does not require specific knowledge of security and military policies' intricacies.

The descriptive statistics utilized in this paper to illustrate the evolution of mass attitudes toward NATO and the EU — as well as possible Russian-led political, economic and military alliances — are drawn from opinion polls conducted in Ukraine between 2009 and 2017. The Ilko Kucheriv Democratic Initiatives Foundation (DIF) very kindly shared with me the dataset of their most recent (2017) poll on attitudes towards NATO, allowing me to conduct a more in-depth analysis. Nationwide polling of Ukraine's population was conducted by DIF in conjunction with the Kyiv-based Razumkov Center between June 9–13, 2017. In total, 2,018 respondents 18 years of age or older (with a margin of error of +/- 2.3%) were polled across Ukraine (Crimea and the occupied territories in Luhansk and Donetsk oblasts were excluded from the sample). In addition, this chapter also surveys differences in public opinion within select EU and NATO member states concerning how Ukrainian accession into these organizations is viewed.

Attitudes towards NATO Membership and Region, Language and Identity

The war in the Donbas has brought about a significant change in Ukrainians' perceptions of security and how to ensure it. A threefold leap in support for NATO membership took place immediately after the annexation of Crimea and the start of Russian military involvement in Ukraine. Since May 2014, NATO membership has been perceived as the best guarantor of Ukraine's security: more than 40% of Ukraine's population shares this view. In contrast, support for aligning with Russia has steeply declined, dropping from 31% in 2007 to just 6% in 2017. The idea of non-alignment has also declined in popularity, with around a quarter of the population currently believing that Ukraine should remain neutral and not join any military alliance (graph 1).

Graph 1. Support for Various Security Options in Ukraine

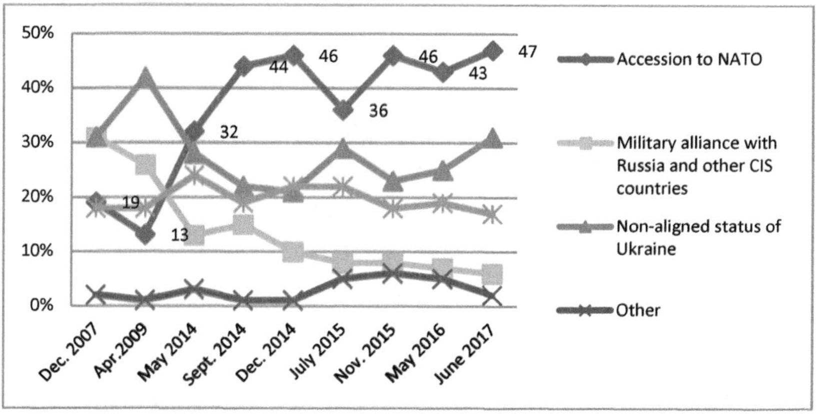

[Graph showing trends from Dec. 2007 to June 2017 for: Accession to NATO (reaching 32, 44, 46, 36, 46, 43, 47); Military alliance with Russia and other CIS countries; Non-aligned status of Ukraine (starting at 19, 13); Other]

Source: DIF's and Razumkov Center's 2017 dataset, author's own elaboration.

Nevertheless, when given more options regarding various types of alliances, Ukrainians have much more mixed opinions. Very few Ukrainians with a pro-Western orientation would opt for either only NATO membership (3%) or only EU membership (8%). Rather, they would opt for both (25%). However, a non-aligned status is also rather popular (21%), while a quarter supports the creation of a new regional union with other friendly states, but without Russia. Only 8% claim to support Ukraine's membership in a union where a major role is played by Russia (graph 2).

Graph 2. Support for Various Integration Models

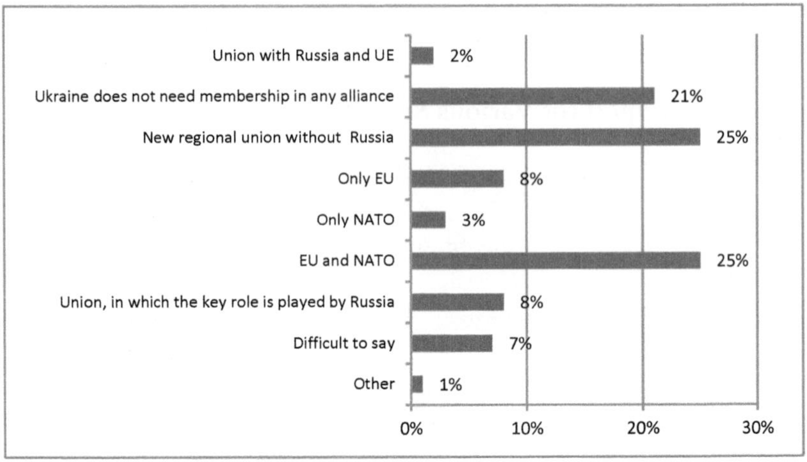

Option	%
Union with Russia and UE	2%
Ukraine does not need membership in any alliance	21%
New regional union without Russia	25%
Only EU	8%
Only NATO	3%
EU and NATO	25%
Union, in which the key role is played by Russia	8%
Difficult to say	7%
Other	1%

Source: Institute of World Policy (2017)

In other words, Ukrainian society is divided into those with a clear pro-Western orientation and those who are keen to look for other options. However, these options do not include alliances with Russia anymore.

The readiness to vote in a referendum on NATO membership among the Ukrainian public has not changed within the past five years; more than 60% of Ukrainians claimed in 2012 and claim now that they would take part in such a referendum (DIF 2017). Questioning Ukrainians as to how they would vote in a referendum on NATO membership gives us purely speculative results. Such a referendum is not yet on the political agenda, and pre-referendum lobbying might sway voters' opinions. However, potential voters' responses measured over time bolsters previous evidence regarding a diametric change in public opinion concerning support for Ukraine's geopolitical options. While in 2012 only 26% of the Ukrainian population ready to vote in a referendum claimed they would support NATO membership and 61% claimed they would vote against it, in 2017 70% claimed they would support NATO accession and only 26% claimed they would vote against it. Notably, the number of respondents who had difficulty in choosing between positions also diminished considerably (graph 3).

Graph 3. Percent Claiming They Would Vote for NATO Accession in Referendum *(as a percentage of those who declared they planned to vote in a referendum)*

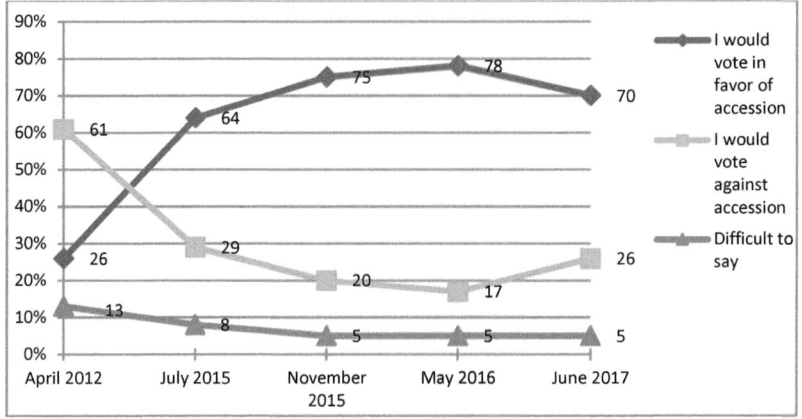

Source: DIF's and Razumkov Center's 2017 dataset, author's own elaboration.

The high level of reported support for NATO in a hypothetical referendum, when compared to only slightly more than 40% of the overall population supporting NATO, is attributable to the fact that supporters of trans-Atlantic military cooperation are more likely to claim they will take part in the referendum.

Considerable changes regarding attitudes towards NATO membership have also taken place in the regions that have traditionally been unsupportive of this option. Compared with the situation in 2012, support for NATO membership in the country's South and East has increased by 13 and 30 percentage points, respectively.

Table 1. Changing Perceptions of NATO by Regions, 2012-2017[1]

	2012	2017	Change
West	34%	81%	+47
Center	14%	68%	+54
South	7%	20%	+13
East	2%	32%	+30

Source: DIF 2017.

Populations in the East and South of Ukraine today remain divided over whether NATO poses a security threat or guarantee. But before the fighting in Donbas began, people from these two regions almost unanimously rejected the notion of Ukraine joining NATO (table 2).

Table 2. What does NATO mean for Ukraine?

	West	Center	South	East
A defense mechanism	63%	48%	19%	30%
A threat	4%	11%	19%	28%
Neither a defense mechanism nor a threat	22%	27%	25%	31%
Difficult to say	12%	14%	37%	11%

Source: DIF's and Razumkov Center's 2017 dataset, author's own elaboration.

In a similar vein, differences regarding European identity still depend on the region of residence. Rather predictably, people living in western Ukraine are most likely to claim they consider themselves European, whereas the population in the East of the country is less likely to do so. However, it is worth pointing out that these regional differences are not that significant: while 52% of people who live in the West macro-region claim to consider themselves European, 36% of the population in the South and 29% in the East consider themselves so. And a large share of populations in all regions claims they do not feel European (table 3).

---

[1] The "macroregions," as defined by DIF, are: Western: Volynska, Zakarpatska, Ivano-Frankivska, Lvivska, Rivnenska, Ternopilska and Chernivetska; Central: Kyiv city, Kyiv region, Vinnytska, Zhytomyrska, Kirovohradska, Khmelnytska, Poltavska, Sumska, Cherkaska and Chernihivska; Southern: Mykolaivska, Odessa and Khersonska; Eastern: Dnipropetrovska, Zaporizka, and Kharkivska and the parts of Donetsk and Luhansk regions controlled by Ukraine.

Table 3. Do you consider yourself European?

	Definitely yes	Rather yes	Rather no	Definitely no	Difficult to say	Total
West	18%	34%	28%	13%	8%	100%
Center	8%	28%	34%	24%	6%	100%
South	12%	24%	17%	32%	16%	100%
East	9%	20%	28%	36%	6%	100%
Total	11%	27%	29%	26%	8%	100%

Source: DIF's and Razumkov Center's 2017 dataset, author's own elaboration.

The relatively low percentage of people claiming to consider themselves European in the West and Center may come as a surprise. However, European identity is a complex phenomenon that involves cultural, economic and political dimensions. When answering this question, people may consider all or only some of them. Indeed, as answers to other questions demonstrate, the current economic and political situation in the country may prevent many people from claiming to be European.

Nevertheless, southern and eastern Ukraine still remain much more prone to Russia's influence. According to a 2015 study by the Kyiv International Institute of Sociology (KIIS), southern and eastern Ukraine are much more receptive to a propagandistic narrative that can be summarized in the following chain of arguments:

> *Euromaidan was organized by the United States together with Ukrainian nationalists → As a result, Ukrainian nationalists gained power and now threaten the Russian-speaking population of Ukraine → Crimea and the East of Ukraine have been exposed to danger → Crimea has been saved by its inclusion into Russia, and the East rose in rebellion and longs for autonomy and security → But the Ukrainian nationalists, who illegally seized power, are now waging war upon their own people.*

The effectiveness of the Russian propaganda index is based upon respondents' acceptance of Maidan conspiracy theories, negative attitudes towards the USA, support for Crimea's annexation and negative attitudes towards the Anti-terrorist Operation (ATO), trust towards Russian mass media and distrust of Ukrainian mass media. According to the Index results, Russian propaganda's lowest level of influence exists in Ukraine's western (score=12 on a 100 scale) and central (score=19) regions, while its influence is much higher in the southern (score=32) and eastern (score=48) regions. Respondents' language preferences also factored into how receptive they were to this propaganda. While the overall index score for Ukrainian speakers was only 12, it was 38 for Russian speakers. In other words, where people live and what language they speak remains a significant factor in their geo-political orientations, the latter at least partially reinforced by propagandistic messages in tune with these orientations (KIIS 2015).

Furthermore, irrespective of the region of residence, sharing a European identity as well as having ties to Europe, including willingness to travel to the EU, and the significance attached to lifting Schengen visa requirements, are good predictors of a person's support for NATO membership (table 4).

Table 4. European identity and support for NATO membership

		If you took part in a NATO referendum, how would you vote?	
		Vote for	Vote against
Are you planning to visit one of the Schengen states?	Definitely yes	79%	11%
	Rather yes	60%	22%
	Rather no	53%	30%
	Definitely no	32%	50%
How important is the introduction of a visa-free regime within the EU states for you?	Very important	78%	13%
	Rather important	66%	16%
	Of little importance	45%	34%
	Not important at all	28%	54%
Do you consider yourself European?	Definitely yes	67%	25%
	Rather yes	66%	21%
	Rather no	48%	32%
	Definitely no	29%	55%

Source: DIF's and Razumkov Center's 2017 dataset, author's own elaboration.

Those who identify themselves as European are more likely to vote "yes" in a NATO referendum. Similarly, those who value the possibility of closer association with the EU, including along an interpersonal dimension, are also strong supporters of NATO. Among those who state that they are definitely going to visit a Schengen state in the foreseeable future, 79% claim they would support NATO accession in a referendum. And 78% of those who want to abolish the visa barrier between the EU and Ukraine also express a pro-NATO accession position. While these are predictable results, consistent with common knowledge, they once again demonstrate that support for NATO among many is not just a matter of ensuring security but also a civilizational choice with a pro-Western orientation.

At the same time, maintaining close ties to Russia through visiting and receiving family and friends translates into less support for NATO membership (table 5).

Table 5. Ties to Russia and Support for NATO Membership

		If you took part in a NATO referendum, how would you vote?	
		Vote For	Vote Against
What is your attitude towards a possible visa regime with Russia?	Support	74%	15%
	Do not support	34%	47%
Do you have friends or family from Russia who have visited you in the past three years?	Yes	34%	44%
	No	50%	32%
Have you been to Russia in the past three years?	Yes	32%	48%
	No	50%	32%
Have your family or friends from Russia visited you in the last three years?	Yes	34%	44%
	No	50%	32%

Source: DIF's and Razumkov Center's 2017 dataset, author's own elaboration.

Research demonstrates that the language considered native and the language spoken in different social situations (including within the private sphere) may differ. Hence two questions regarding language were asked in the study: what is the respondent's native language and what language does the respondent speak at home? More detailed analysis shows that there are differences between groups which consistently identify with either the Ukrainian or Russian languages and their attitudes towards NATO membership: while 58% of respondents who claim Ukrainian as their native language and speak Ukrainian at home would vote for NATO membership, only 31% of respondents who claim Russian as their native language and speak Russian at home would support NATO membership (table 6). This may also apply to the cultural sphere. For example, proponents of quotas for Ukrainian language programs on television are much more likely to state that they would vote in favor of NATO membership (72% among strong supporters of quotas also support NATO accession) (table 6).

Table 6. Language Preferences and Support for NATO

	Would vote for	Would vote against	Difficult to say
RU native and RU at home	31%	50%	18%
UA native and RU at home	36%	48%	17%
RU native and UA at home (only 7 resp)	67%	17%	16%
UA native and UA at home	58%	24%	18%
Total	48%	33%	18%

Source: DIF's and Razumkov Center's 2017 dataset, author's own elaboration.

Table 7. Position on Conflict Resolution Policies in Donbas and Support for NATO Membership

		If you took part in a NATO referendum, how would you vote?	
		Vote For	Vote Against
Do you support the Ukrainian Council for National Security and Defense's blockade of trade with the "DNR" and "LNR"?	Fully support	75%	17%
	Rather support	60%	21%
In your opinion, should compromises be made with Russia and leaders of the self-proclaimed Donetsk and Luhansk republics in order to achieve peace?	Peace at any price; we need to make compromises with anybody about anything	27%	55%
	We should make some compromises for peace, but not with anyone and about anything	50%	33%
	Peace in Donbas can be achieved only by force- when one side wins	73%	15%
What should be done to achieve peace in Donbas?	Renew control over DNR and LNR by military force	74%	13%
	Stop financing the territories occupied by DNR and LNR	63%	27%
	Force Russia to stop meddling in the Donbas conflict (by strengthening international sanctions and imposing pressure on Russia in international structures)	63%	22%
	Amnesty for all who took part in military activities in Donbas	25%	60%
	Separation of the territories occupied by DNR and LNR from Ukraine	62%	25%

Generally, what should the policy towards uncontrolled territories be?	Officially recognize these territories as occupied and stop any trade, contacts, service provisions, payment of pensions, etc.	72%	17%
	Preserve economic blockade, but keep humanitarian contacts (movement of population, payment of pensions, water supply).	56%	26%
	Try to develop economic and humanitarian relations with uncontrolled territories as much as we can	23%	60%

Source: DIF's and Razumkov Center's 2017 dataset, author's own elaboration.

Support for NATO goes hand-in-hand with having a hardline stance on Donbas. Ukrainians who, when asked what the general policy towards the uncontrolled territories should be, would prefer to officially recognize these territories as occupied and to stop any trade, interpersonal contacts, service provisioning or payment of pensions are much more likely to support NATO membership: 72% in this group would vote "yes" in a referendum on accession while only 17% would vote "no" (table 7).

Rather predictably, those who believe in a military resolution to the conflict are also much more likely to vote "yes" in such a referendum, while only 27% of those who favor making far-reaching compromises would vote similarly (table 7). Clearly, NATO membership is seen as a way to firmly separate Ukraine from Russia and ensure its security. For some, this also implies a readiness to forsake Donbas in order to ensure stability in the rest of the country.

While differences between these regions are undeniable, important changes in public opinion regarding Ukraine's integration orientation and notions about the sources of security are noticeable among the more traditionally pro-Russian regions.

These changes are even more significant if we take into account the extent of Russian propaganda being disseminated there.

Reversing the Perspective: Support for Ukraine's Membership in the EU and NATO Among Current Member States

While Ukrainians have diametrically changed their attitudes towards NATO accession and are now willing to join the club, the club members are visibly less enthusiastic about such a step. The Pew Research Institute surveyed public opinion among several main NATO players: the USA, Canada, France, Germany, Italy and Poland. There are considerable differences evinced across these states. The most supportive are Canadians (65%), Americans (62%) and Poles (59%). In contrast, the majority of Germans (57%) and a plurality of Italians (46%) are against offering Ukraine membership in NATO, while only 36% of Germans and 35% of Italians favor it. Interestingly, considerable differences of opinion exist among older and younger generational cohorts. While in Europe it is the younger generations who are most supportive of Ukraine's membership in NATO, in the USA it is older ones (Simmons et al. 2015).

Graph 4. Support for Ukraine's Membership in NATO, 2015

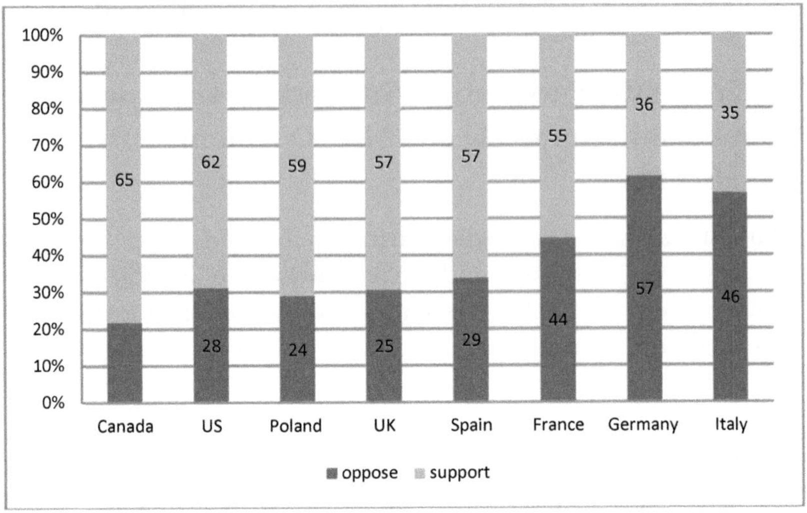

Country	Oppose	Support
Canada	22	65
US	28	62
Poland	24	59
UK	25	57
Spain	29	57
France	44	55
Germany	57	36
Italy	46	35

Source: Simmons et al. 2015.

Remarkably, while in several countries public opinion support regarding Ukraine's NATO membership has considerably decreased in the aftermath of the Russian military's incursion into Ukraine, the percentage of supporters in the United States, United Kingdom and Spain has increased by double digits. Publics in other countries have remained unmoved, including Poland (where support has been rather high for almost a decade), France, Italy and Germany (the latter having a soft spot for Russia and afraid to provoke it by becoming involved in a region perceived as Russia's backyard) (Simmons et al. 2015).

Surveyed publics in NATO member states are even less willing to send arms to Ukraine. The most supportive are Poles, but even among them only half (50%) are in favor of such an action. The strongest opponents of sending weaponry to Ukraine are found among Germans (77% opposed), Spaniards (66% opposed), and Italians (65% opposed). Americans, meanwhile, are divided on this issue, with 46% in favor and 43% against arming Ukraine (graph 5).

Graph 5. Support for Sending Arms to Ukraine, 2015

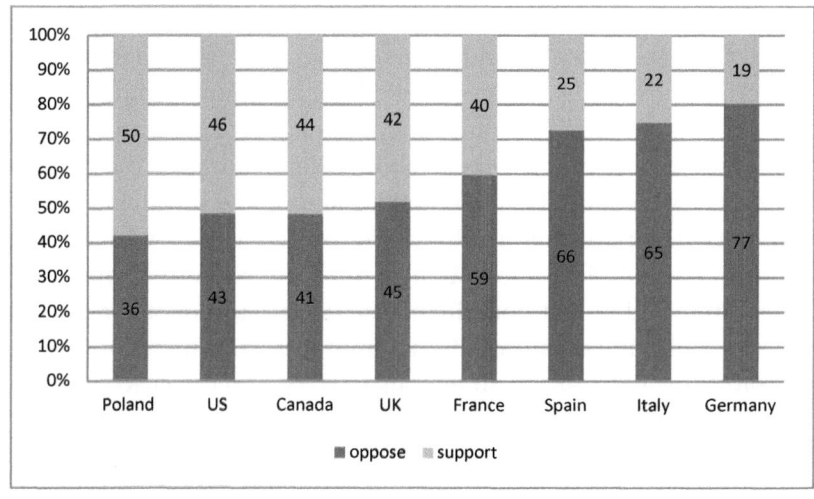

Source: Simmons et al., 2015.

The question of the Ukrainian public's support for NATO membership remains purely hypothetical now. As Andreas Umland, among others, reminds us, Ukrainians' hopes are not likely to be fulfilled anytime soon due to the West's new caution regarding Russia after its military interventions in Crimea, eastern Ukraine and Syria. As he puts it: "many people in Western Europe would be strictly against committing to a possible war with a country that has the capacity to eradicate the whole of humanity. Ukraine and Georgia will only have a chance to enter NATO once their confrontations with Russia are fully over, that is, when they won't need NATO's protection any more" (Umland 2016).

Conclusion

Russian aggression against Ukraine in the wake of the Euromaidan has made Ukrainians much more supportive not only of EU membership for their country, but also NATO membership (the latter has always been a much more controversial issue). These changes have taken place in all Ukraine's regions, both those which have traditionally been seen as pro-Western and those that have traditionally been considered more pro-Russian. If there was a referendum on whether or not Ukraine should join NATO right now, the "yes" vote would win. At the same time, identifiable regional differences in geopolitical orientation (connected to perceptions of identity, culture and language) continue to persist.

The research presented above demonstrates that while differences in geopolitical orientations among the Ukrainian public still persist, support for pro-Russian options (alliances with Russia) is very limited. The alternative to the pro-Western geopolitical orientation today is a non-alliance status or support for alliances with neighboring countries, but without Russia. While those living in traditionally pro-Russian regions have been more susceptible to pro-Russian propaganda, as previous research (KIIS 2015) has demonstrated, a clearly pro-Russian geopolitical orientation has also evaporated in these regions.

Moreover, the data analysis shows that the desire to separate from Russia, symbolically and physically (e.g., by introducing a visa regime), goes hand-in-hand with being supportive of NATO membership. Possessing a European identity makes one much more likely to support NATO membership. In other words, support for Ukraine joining NATO appears to be about both strategic and civilizational choices; it is not just about military security, but also about the country's future development trajectory and the values that will define it.

The way language fits into this equation supports the call for not treating the interplay between ethno-linguistic differences and foreign policy preferences in a deterministic way. Instead, it suggests the impact of personal choice. What appears to matter are not inherited linguistic identities (i.e., what people consider as their native language), but rather what language people choose to speak at home. Those who consider Ukrainian to be their native language, but speak Russian at home, are considerably less likely to support NATO than those who consider Russian to be their native language, but speak Ukrainian at home.

In this context it is particularly important to notice evolving regional dynamics in support of Ukraine's joining international alliances. Not only in the Center and the West, but also in the East and South, support for Russian-led economic, cultural, political and security unions have dropped considerably. At the same time, NATO membership, traditionally the most divisive and controversial topic, has become more widely accepted as a guarantee of Ukraine's security in the south and east.

NATO supporters are not only less willing to favor any compromises over the Donbas and more inclined to support military solutions to the conflict, they are also very angry and frustrated with their fellow Donbas nationals. In fact, they are ready to separate Donbas from Ukraine and sever all ties in order to ensure peace. Reintegrating Ukraine's population after the end of the war promises to be a huge domestic challenge. The old pro-Russian geopolitical orientation is not so easy to shed, particularly due to the difficult economic, social and political situations that are related to the ongoing military conflict, intensive propaganda, internal animosities between eastern and western regions, and mutual accusations of who is responsible for provoking the current crisis.

Needless to say, Ukrainians' responses on voting in a NATO referendum just reflect the current state of public opinion, which can still be swayed once a referendum is announced and both camps start campaigning. Therefore, a pro-NATO outcome cannot be taken for granted. It will only be the result of an information campaign that raises awareness of what security guarantees NATO can provide, what membership in the organization entails and what the path towards it is (particularly in the regions with a traditionally pro-Russian geopolitical orientation, which are also more exposed to Russian propaganda) (KIIS 2015).

Finally, we have seen that NATO member states' publics are divided on whether or not to support Ukraine's membership in these organizations. There is a great deal of skepticism here. Presumably one of the reasons for it concerns traditional geopolitical thinking — namely, assigning Ukraine a priori to Russia's sphere of influence and being fearful of retribution from Moscow's side.

References

Agnew, J.A. *Geopolitics: Re-visioning World Politics* (London: Routledge, 1998).

Barrington, L.W. (2002) Views of the 'Ethnic Other' in Ukraine. *Nationalism and Ethnic Politics* 8(2), 83–96.

Fomina, J. (2014) Language, Identity, Politics - the Myth of Two Ukraines Warsaw and Berlin: The Institute of Public Affairs and Bertelsmann Foundation.

Gentile, M. (2015) West oriented in the East-oriented Donbas: a political stratigraphy of geopolitical identity in Luhansk, Ukraine," *Post-Soviet Affairs*, 31:3 (2015): 201–223.

Jansson, D. (2007) The Haunting of the South: American Geopolitical Identity and the Burden of Southern History. *Geopolitics* 12(3), 400–425.

DIF (Ilko Kucheriv Democratic Initiatives Foundation) (2017) Public opinion of the population of Ukraine on NATO. Retrieved from: http://dif.org.ua/article/referendum-shchodo-vstupu-do-nato-buv-bi-vigraniy-prote-tse-pitannyadilit-ukrainu.

Institute of World Policy (2017) Retrieved from: https://drive.google.com/file/d/0B_mp0v6tWhA3Zi05OWFVT254Uzg/view.

Konieczna, J. (2001) *Polska-Ukraina. Wzajemny wizerunek*. Institute of Public Affairs: Warsaw.

KIIS (Kyiv International Institute of Sociology) (2017) The index of Russian propaganda effectiveness. Retrieved from: http://kiis.com.ua/?lang=ukr&cat=reports&id=510&page=1.

Clemens, C. (1992) Changing Public Perceptions of NATO. In Kirchner, E. and J. Sperling (eds.) *The Federal Republic of Germany and NATO: 40 Years After*. Palgrave Macmillan New York, 29–53.

Munro, N. (2007) Which Way Does Ukraine Face? Popular Orientations Toward Russia and Western Europe. *Problems of Post-Communism*. 54(6), 43–58.

Niżnik, J. (2015) Are There Positive Effects of Euroscepticism? In: Bârgăoanu, A. Radu L. and D. Varela (eds.) *United by or Against Euroscepticism? An Assessment of Public Attitudes towards Europe in the Context of the Crisis*. Newcastle upon Tyne, UK: Cambridge Scholars Publishing, 208–222.

O'Tuathail, G. (1996) *Critical Geopolitics: The Politics of Writing Global Space*. Minneapolis: University of Minnesota Press.

Simmons, K., Bruce S. and J. Poushter (2015) NATO Publics Blame Russia for Ukrainian Crisis, but Reluctant to Provide Military Aid. Pew Research Center. Retrieved from: http://www.pewglobal.org/2015/06/10/nato-publics-blame-russia-for-ukrainian-crisis-but-reluctant-to-provide-military-aid/.

Szporluk, R. (1997) Ukraine from an Imperial Periphery to a Sovereign State. In: Graubard, S.R. (ed.) *A New Europe for the Old.* New Brunswick and London: Transaction Publishers, 85–120.

Umland, A. (2016) Ukraine's Understandable But Senseless Hope for NATO Membership. Atlantic Council. Retrieved from: http://www.atlanticcouncil.org/blogs/ukrainealert/ukraine-s-understandable-but-senseless-hope-for-nato-membership.

Andrzej Szabaciuk

Demography and Migration as Determinants of Ukrainian Policy in the Context of State Security

The aim of this chapter is to analyze a number of determinants that have had, or may have, a significant impact on the character and shape of contemporary Ukraine's population policy in the context of state security. A drastically shrinking population, forced mass-migration from areas affected by armed conflict, and, above all, a new wave of economic emigration to the European Union are key challenges that Ukrainian authorities will have to face in the near future. The adequacy and effectiveness of the actions they take will have a huge influence on state security broadly understood, which is particularly important in the context of a prolonged conflict with Russia that threatens the stability and territorial integrity of the state. Ukraine's lack of an effective population policy may, in the long run, lead to a deepening of the crisis and further destabilize the region, which will have far-reaching consequences from the point of view of the European Union and the post-Cold War international system.

The Euromaidan, which unfolded between late 2013 and early 2014 in Ukraine, diametrically altered the geopolitical situation in Central and Eastern Europe. Deteriorating relations between Russia and Ukraine, the two largest countries in the region, threaten the further escalation of tensions and the outbreak of full-scale armed conflict. Meanwhile, the imposition of sanctions, together with a decline in foreign direct investment, the collapse of hydrocarbon commodity prices, and the downward spiral in ruble and hryvnia exchange rates against the US dollar have all added to destabilizing the economic situation in Central and Eastern Europe. As a result, the living conditions of millions of citizens of the post-Soviet states have drastically worsened: real wages have gone down, the cost of living has risen, unemployment has become a serious problem, and the level of societal security has declined.

Given this context, the plight of Ukraine today is extremely difficult. Moreover, the complicated geopolitical situation and prolonged economic crisis have diverted attention from other disturbing processes that may directly affect Ukraine's future. Namely, decision-makers in Kyiv are not able to stop the progressive depopulation of the state. Ukraine is facing a serious demographic crisis, resulting in its population declining from 51.7 to 42.8 million between 1991 and 2015 (Ukraine 2016, 23). Demographic processes are directly linked to Ukraine's growing socio-economic problems, but also its political problems, which not only result from the current poor state of the country's relations with the Russian Federation, but also Ukraine's dysfunctional political system. The weakness of the central government and a lack of resources have resulted in an inability to implement a population policy suitable to these new realities. Thus far, the new Ukrainian authorities have primarily focused on helping Internally Displaced Persons (IDPs) from eastern Ukraine and Crimea, and on halting the influx of immigrants from Russia (who, it is feared, will support the separatist forces and deepen the destabilization of the state).

In the meantime, the problems of negative population growth in Ukraine, low life expectancy, and various social pathologies linked to the difficult economic situation of the state did not disappear. The mass emigration of people out of Ukraine is also a great concern. However, the authorities in Kyiv do not see this latter issue in only a negative light; indeed, in the short term, temporary economic emigration provides a partial solution to some of Ukraine's pressing social problems. Nevertheless, if radical political and economic reforms that can result in significant improvements in the living conditions of ordinary Ukrainians are not enacted, this may fundamentally change the nature of the current emigration situation, gradually transforming it into a permanent emigration. In the context of these considerations, it is worth emphasizing that at present Kyiv does not have any real means of stopping or even reducing this outflow of Ukrainians from the country for economic reasons. All in all, the problems of our eastern neighbor are reminiscent of the challenges the Polish state faced over the last two decades. Working out an adequate return program for emigrants in the workforce can have a significant impact on the broader development of the country in the coming decades.

The aim of this chapter is to analyze a number of determinants that have had, or may have, a significant impact on the character and shape of contemporary Ukraine's population policy in the context of state security. Below, I will consider the adequacy and effectiveness of this policy and its potential short-term and long-term consequences for Ukraine and its neighbors.

1. Demographic and Socio-Economic Determinants of Ukrainian Population Policy

An analysis of Ukraine's population policy cannot be undertaken without considering its economic, political, historical, geographic and cultural determinants. Specifically, the Soviet heritage has had a significant impact on all of these, and it continues to shape migration streams in the post-communist region. Consequently, it is decisive for analyzing the factors that today affect the security of an independent Ukraine in its contemporary, multi-faceted conflict with the Russian Federation.

Table 1. Population of Ukraine (in thousands)

1990	51,838.5
1995	51,728.4
2000	49,429.8
2005	47,280.8
2010	45,962.9
2013	45,553.0
2014	45,426.2
2015	42,928.9
2016	42,760.5

Source: *Derzhavna sluzhba statystyky Ukraïny*, (accessed September 13, 2016).

Socio-economic factors are generally key to an individual's decision to emigrate. After the collapse of the Soviet Union, practically all countries in the region faced a severe economic downturn, which was a consequence of, among other things, chaotic economic reforms. Hyperinflation, falling real household incomes, the massive bankruptcies of state-owned enterprises, and rampant privatization were common. Structural unemployment, along with a growing informal economy controlled by organized crime, was also frequently evinced. Since the breakup of the Soviet Union, the Ukrainian economy has been plunged into a prolonged downturn, suffering a 22.93% contraction of its GDP in 1994 alone. It was only in 2000 that, for the first time in years, Ukraine finally recorded GDP growth, albeit at a minimal level (Bajor 2013, 103–105).

This complex socio-economic situation continues to negatively affect the demographic situation of the state. Ukraine has been unable to curb its deepening demographic problems for years. Unhealthy lifestyles, including high rates of alcohol and drug addiction and low levels of healthcare, conspire to shorten the average life expectancy of Ukrainians, especially men. On average, men live 67.1 years, women 76.9 years—which puts Ukraine in 149th place among 224 countries (CIA 2016). Very low birthrates also pose a serious challenge for Ukrainian authorities. At present, there are 1.54 live births per woman of childbearing age (where 2.1 live births is considered replacement level), placing Ukraine in 192nd place among 224 countries (CIA 2016).

Low fertility is not only a consequence of the lack of employment stabilization among the population of Ukraine, but is also linked to a number of additional social problems, including familial. The number of divorces in Ukraine is relatively high; for example, in 2011 there were on average 2.8 divorces per 1000 people (Marriages 2011; Perelli-Harris 2008, 1172), whereas in the European Union in 2015 it usually did not exceed 2.5 (in Poland the commensurate number is 1.8; meanwhile, in Denmark [which has the highest rate of divorces among the EU member states] the figure reaches 3.4) (Meridge 2016).

The low birth rate is also a consequence of the abortion culture in a number of post-Soviet states. It is worth stressing that by 1988, the number of abortions in Ukraine was 1.5 times greater than live births. It was only in 2000 that live births finally exceeded the number of abortions. Even so, in 2007 the official abortion rate was 0.8 per 1000 women of childbearing age, with evidence suggesting that many of the procedures are performed in private abortion clinics, so the abortion rate may actually be closer to 1.6 (Perelli-Harris 2008, 1160–1161).

Table 2. Natural Population Growth in Ukraine

Year	Births	Deaths	Balance
1989	690,981	600,590	90,391
1990	657,202	629,602	27,600
1991	630,813	669,960	-39,147
1992	596,785	697,110	-100,325
1993	557,467	741,662	-184,195
1994	521,545	764,669	-243,124
1995	492,861	792,587	-299,726
1996	467,211	776,717	-309,506
1997	442,581	754,151	-311,570
1998	419,238	719,954	-300,716
1999	389,208	739,170	-349,962
2000	385,126	758,082	-372,956
2001	376,478	745,952	-369,474
2002	390,688	754,911	-364,223
2003	408,589	765,408	-356,819
2004	427,259	761,261	-334,002
2005	426,086	781,961	-355,875
2006	460,368	758,092	-297,724
2007	472,657	762,877	-290,220
2008	510,589	754,460	-243,871
2009	512,525	706,739	-194,214
2010	497,689	698,235	-200,546
2011	502,595	664,588	-161,993
2012	520,705	663,139	-142,434
2013	503,657	662,368	-158,711

Source: *Demohrafichnyĭ shchorichnyk «Naselenniā Ukraïny» 2013*. Kyïv: Derzhavna Sluzhba Statystyky Ukraïny 2014, s. 63.

The prolonged post-Soviet economic downturn was also accompanied by other, frequently overwhelming, social problems that have likewise affected the demographic situation of the state. Lack of work and life prospects fostered the spread of pathological behavior. Like in Russia, alcoholism, drug addiction and prostitution are all serious problems in Ukraine. In particular, the widespread popularity of hard drugs, coupled with a lack of access to sterilized syringes and a low awareness of the dangers of infection, all make for a rapidly increasing number of people in Ukraine infected with HIV. While we do not know exactly how many people are affected by this problem, according to UNAIDS estimates, in 2015 there were 190 to 250 thousand infected individuals, most residing in southeastern Ukraine (*Harmonizovanyĭ* 2014). However, the actual number of those infected may be much larger.

Ukraine's difficult economic situation began to improve gradually after 2000, which in some ways was connected with improvements in the economic situation of the Russian Federation, one of Ukraine's main trading partners. Still, in 2006 about 60% of the population of Ukraine lived below the poverty line; and although this figure dropped by 30% in the wake of the 2008 financial crisis (Rettinger 2011, 56), as a consequence of the escalation of the Ukrainian-Russian conflict in 2014 (and the accompanying severe economic downturn and the collapse of the exchange rate of the hryvnia against the US dollar), the proportion of people living below the poverty threshold reached the level of the 1990s and now stands at more than 80% of country population (Za chertoĭ 2015).

There is no doubt that this dramatic economic situation is an important factor contributing to the mass exodus of citizens from Ukraine. The apparent lack of economic recovery and the slow pace of reform will all be conducive to keeping this trend going for the foreseeable future. This brings a number of threats from the point of view of state social security, primarily due to the scale of the phenomenon. The UN Population Division predicts that by 2050 the total population of Ukraine will continue to decline to below 34 million (Twigg et al. 2014). Demographic decline threatens the stability of Ukraine's statehood and may, in the future, hamper the implementation of ambitious economic reforms, which are particularly needed given the prolonged conflict between Russia and Ukraine.

2. Ukraine in the Context of Migration Processes

Difficult political and socio-economic circumstances have a significant impact on the decision to choose the direction of labor migration. Migration systems, however, also shape historical, geographical and cultural conditions. There is a long tradition in the lands of present-day Ukraine of labor migration to the East. This was typical for the Tsarist period, but on an even greater scale we can observe it in the Soviet era. At that time, central infrastructure projects, the collectivization of agriculture or forced resettlement favored frequent changes in the place of residence. Often, with voluntary migration, there was hope for an improvement in living conditions (Fedyuk et al. 2016, 2).

After the disintegration of the Soviet Union, these trends continued and the largest streams of economic immigrants went from Ukraine to the Russian Federation. This process was particularly noticeable after the year 2000 (i.e., once Russia began to gradually emerge from its own economic downturn due to significant increases in energy resource prices, hydrocarbons being one of the main sources of federal budget revenue). The improvement in Russia's economic situation brought about the recovery of demand for unskilled labor from abroad, these migrants preferentially drawn, for political as well as practical reasons, from the inhabitants of the post-Soviet space (Konończuk 2012, 9–13). In this regard, the visa-free regime maintained by the Kremlin made it simple for Ukrainians to travel eastward. Meanwhile, the Central European countries gradually became harder for Ukrainians to emigrate to, as they began to impose visa regimes in order to synchronize national laws with those of the European Union (Szulecka 2016, 51–54).

In addition, historical conditions have facilitated the social and cultural integration of Ukrainians into Russia society. In particular, many of the people living in the eastern regions of Ukraine speak Russian, while others speak *surzhyk*, a colloquial variant of the Ukrainian language with significant Russian influences (Kościółek 2012, 454–455). Moreover, many of them have family or friends in Russia, which simplifies the creation of migration networks and makes it much easier to complete various formalities, such as registering accommodations. Informal networks are also extremely useful in legalizing employment or penetrating the informal economy (Szabaciuk 2014, 94–95).

But while this form of social capital simplifies tasks such as finding employment abroad, it also poses serious challenges back home at a time when the Russian Federation is pursuing aggressive policies towards Ukraine and other Eastern European countries like Moldova, Georgia and Belarus. Moreover, the Russian Federation's approach to Russian-speaking people after the Russian-Georgian war of 2008, along with its annexation of Crimea and destabilization in the Donbas, poses a serious security challenge not only for states in the region, but also for the global security system (Laruelle 2015, 90–95).

For almost two decades, the Russian Federation was the most popular destination for economic migrants from Ukraine. However, quantifying the precise scale of this phenomenon is extremely difficult, as the vast majority of Eastern European economic migrants to Russia found employment in the informal economy. Despite their best efforts, even the Russian authorities do not have accurate statistics regarding this trend. In 2010, they estimated that between 200 and 300 thousand Ukrainians lived in the Russian Federation. However, unofficial estimates suggest that the number may be anywhere from 800 thousand to 3 million (Fedyuk et al. 2016, 6).

Today, however, Ukrainians have real opportunities to diversify where they migrate. Particularly given the current geopolitical situation, more and more Ukrainians are opting to emigrate to the West. These migration streams are stimulated by the significant number of Ukrainians living in vibrant diasporas within the United States (about 1 million), Canada (1.25 million), Israel (260,000), and in individual European Union countries (Fedyuk et al. 2016, 3–7). According to Eurostat data, in 2015 citizens of Ukraine comprised the largest category of people outside the European Union who received their first EU residence permit. In total, in 2015 2.6 million EU residence permits were granted, 499,992 of which were received by Ukrainians—and of these, 86% were issued by Polish authorities. The most common cause for applying for temporary residence is employment (75.2%), education (6.1%), and family reasons (5.9%) (*Residence* 2016). But Eurostat data is based on 2015 statistics; in 2016 the number of Ukrainian economic migrants to Poland increased sharply. According to data from the Polish Ministry of Family, Labor and Social Policy, in 2016 there were 1.26 million employers who submitted statements to the Labor Offices concerning their willingness to hire Ukrainians,[1] while in 2015 only 762,700 such statements were registered (*Cudzoziemcy* 2015–2017). Even if we consider that Eurostat data may not be fully reliable and the number of registered statements concerning the willingness of Polish employers to hire a Ukrainian workforce does not always match the real volumes of migration flows from Ukraine, the trend seems clear.

Poland is obviously not the only country receiving economic migrants from Ukraine. It is estimated that around 200 thousand Ukrainians live in the Federal Republic of Germany. Meanwhile, Italy hosts some 226 thousand people of Ukrainian origin, the Czech Republic 100 thousand, Spain 85 thousand, Portugal 41 thousand, and Greece 17 thousand. Of course, these figures are likely underestimated because it is difficult to accurately assess the scale of employment of Ukrainians in the informal economy (Fedyuk et al. 2016, 134–197).

The importance of this economic migration, from the point of view of Ukraine's economy, is confirmed by World Bank data. Over the past 20 years, the share of cash transfers from abroad has increased sharply. While in 2000 it constituted 0.1% of GDP, in 2015 it reached 6.35%. Overall, in 2015 cash transfers amounted to 6 billion USD, which puts Ukraine in first place relative to nominal money transfers in the post-Soviet area. Transfers to Tajikistan,

---

[1] A simplified procedure for employing migrant workers from 6 post-soviet states (Ukraine, Belarus, Russia, Moldova, Georgia and from 2014 also Armenia) was introduced by the Polish government in 2006. It allows Polish employers to hire temporary economic migrants from those countries without the need to obtain a full work permit for a period of up to 180 days a year.

Uzbekistan and Moldova are much smaller (3.1 billion USD, 2.6 billion USD and 1.7 billion USD, respectively), but they also comprise a higher share of GDP (in Tajikistan: 36.6%, in Moldova: 26.2%, and in Uzbekistan 9.3%) (World Bank 2017).

Money transfers, made by emigrants to their families in the home country, are an important factor contributing to the decline in poverty. Family's financial surpluses are often used to purchase housing, invest in agricultural equipment, or develop small domestic businesses. These transfers also function to build social capital while working abroad, which can then be utilized upon the migrants' return to Ukraine.

Ukrainian authorities should take into account the migration processes currently observed in Eastern Europe and be aware of the positive and negative consequences of growing emigration. The increasing importance of labor migration to the West, especially in the short-term, may be a significant factor in helping to free Ukraine from Russia's sphere of influence and may help accelerate the process of reforming, modernizing and democratizing the Ukrainian state. However, much will depend on whether Ukraine's new leaders will create conditions favorable for the return of these economic emigrants and whether they will be able to manage the social capital this societal group is able to offer.

3. Political Factors Governing Ukrainian Population Policy: The Conflict with the Russian Federation

Apart from historical, geographical, cultural, socio-economic and demographic determinants, political factors also have a significant impact on Ukrainian population policy. There are two aspects to these: first, how Ukrainian authorities interact with citizens (this aspect of population policy is currently in the conceptualization stage); and second, how other states relate to Ukraine and its population. In the last decade, the most liberal approach concerning economic immigrants from Ukraine was exhibited by Poland and the Russian Federation, but Russia latter changed its migration law after the escalation of the Ukrainian-Russian conflict. This new migration policy is strictly connected with the Russian Federation's strategy in the post-Soviet area, which Moscow treats as an exclusive zone of Russian influence.

Attempts to reconstruct the Kremlin's neo-imperial position in the post-Soviet space have been pursued with varying intensity since the collapse of the USSR. However, the presidency of Vladimir Putin provided the impetus for intensifying efforts aimed at reintegrating the region under Russia's aegis. The Russian Federation has been attempting to strengthen its influence skillfully, utilizing a combination of hard and soft power. The approach consists of a well-thought-out and coordinated policy, which is intended to deepen the political and economic dependence of regional states on the Kremlin, carried out across four main arenas: political, military, economic and socio-cultural (Szeptycki 2013). Russian migration policy is one of the elements of this strategy.

The merging of Russia's migration policy with its foreign policy has been visible since 2007, when Russia's President approved a new vision of its migration policy which entailed reducing the influx of cheap labor from the Commonwealth of Independent States (CIS) and launching a program to encourage the return of so-called "Russian-speaking compatriots" living in the post-Soviet space (*Kontseptsiia* 2017).

In the first version of this return program, approved in 2007, participants were not free to choose their place of residence — they were distributed among selected federal subjects affected by depopulation and internal migration, meaning many were slated to be settled in the Asian part of Russia. As a result, in 2007–2009, only 16 thousand people decided to take advantage of this program. However, in the new iteration of this program, approved by Presidential Decree on September 14, 2012, most of the previous restrictions were abolished and the number of regions participating in the program was increased, which contributed to a significant growth in the number of applicants. In total, between 2011–2015 more than 410 thousand people participated in the return program. The largest group consisted of Russian-speaking exiles from Ukraine (*Monitoring* 2016).

In addition to this program, there were also measures undertaken aimed at regulating immigration flows into Russia. Starting in 2010, authorities have capped the number of invitations issued to foreign workers across Russia's federal subjects (this covers only unskilled labor, and not highly qualified migrants). The authorities followed the same principles as in the original return of compatriots program. The largest allowances were established for the Far East Federal District, the smallest for the most attractive districts in the European part of Russia (Szabaciuk 2014, 95–97).

Migrant work permissions were complemented by a patent system, also introduced in 2010. Patents were not limited by quotas, but immigrants had to pay for them and could work only as domestic help or in agriculture. In 2011, as many as 44% of patents were issued to the Central Federal District, of which over half belonged to the Moscow region (Szabaciuk 2014, 96–97).

However, the system of patents and work permits proved to be ineffective, as most migrants from the post-Soviet area could easily overcome the rules and join the informal economy, so the Russian authorities decided to modify it. The most severe restrictions were introduced on January 1, 2014. The new policy specified that CIS citizens could legally reside on the territory of the Russian Federation for only 90 days within a 180-day period. Before then, the practice had been that CIS residents in Russia without a worker visa had to leave the territory of the Federation once every three months for at least one day. As of January 1, 2015, the patent system no longer fulfilled the function of supplementing the work permit system and was extended to all professions. The Russian authorities have effectively forced immigrants from countries not covered by the visa-regime to buy patents without the option of applying for work permits, which are limited by quotas and reserved for citizens of visa-regime covered countries. These people had to not only pay for the patent, but also pass a test proving knowledge of Russian language, history and law, in addition to paying for the requisite medical examinations (Szabaciuk 2016a, 205–206).

These new regulations have dramatically increased the costs borne by economic migrants from the CIS and limited their opportunities for employment in the shadow economy. Patent prices are set by the individual federal units, taking into account the level of interest in work at a particular job site. For example, in 2016 in the Moscow region, the cost for a monthly patent was 4542 rubles, four times higher than the year before. The cost in the Leningrad region for the same period was 3 thousand rubles. The highest cost of patents was in the Yamalo-Nenets Autonomous Okrug (7412.5 rubles), the lowest in the North Caucasus republics, where prices did not exceed 1900 rubles (Szabaciuk 2016a, 206). Moreover, this modification of immigration regulations was accompanied by more frequent controls on the legality of employment.

The reform of Russia's immigration policy coincided with the foundation of the Eurasian Economic Union (EEU). Citizens of EEU member states are allowed to work in Russia without applying for work permits or patents—nor are they required to take exams to prove their knowledge of the Russian language or Russia's history and laws (*Skol'ko* 2017). We can therefore assume that the new immigration policy of the Russian Federation is an attempt to limit access to the Russian labor market for countries that did not choose to join the EEU, particularly Ukraine and some Central Asian states.

Even more problematic, from the point of view of Ukraine's population policy, was the annexation of Crimea and the armed conflict in the Donetsk and Luhansk regions, which forced tens of thousands of people to leave their homes in search of a safe haven. Some of these people decided to go abroad, mostly to Russia. Others sought refuge in areas controlled by the Ukrainian army. As a result, the new Ukrainian authorities have not only had to spend significant financial resources to resist the aggression of pro-Russian separatists, but also to help shelter Ukrainians fleeing the war.

In total, more than 1.7 million internally displaced persons (IDP) are officially registered in Ukraine. However, many of them registered only to get support from the Ukrainian authorities, and to have their pensions deposited in Ukrainian banks—a requirement introduced by President Petro Poroshenko in November 2014. Following verification by the Interdepartmental Coordinating Staff in the first half of 2016, the number of internally displaced persons eligible for state aid has been reduced to 1.27 million (Szabaciuk 2016b, 66–73).

The economic crisis caused by Russia's aggression against Ukraine has made the new Ukrainian authorities unable to provide adequate support to Ukrainians fleeing the war. Lack of funding currently makes it impossible to implement programs to assist with social integration, provide psychological support, or foster professional development. Without financial help from abroad, the situation of IDPs in Ukraine will not change significantly. This opinion is confirmed by field research. The vast majority of forced migrants do not see any opportunities in the near future to improve their situation, so that is why some of them consider emigration (Szabaciuk 2016b, 72–74).

Another important factor encouraging emigration is Ukraine's domestic political situation. Ukraine's political system, for a long time suspended somewhere between authoritarianism and liberal democracy, is slowly starting to move into the direction of Western Europe. However, the initial rapid phase of economic reforms has now slowed, and societal enthusiasm for more reforms is declining (indeed, Ukrainian society is increasingly expressing its dissatisfaction with the current state of affairs). In spite of numerous declarations and promises on the part of the government, corruption, nepotism, and bureaucratic incompetence have not been eliminated. Many of Ukraine's public policies, in particular its completely ineffective and under-financed social policy, leave a lot to be desired (Stępniewski 2016, 57–73). Without significant support from abroad, especially the European Union, Ukraine alone will not be able to cope with the challenges facing it, which will probably generate new waves of economic emigrants and negatively affect the social integration of internally displaced persons.

Conclusion

The violent escalation of the Russian-Ukrainian conflict, the annexation of Crimea and the outbreak of bloody separatism in the Donbas have all worsened the already complicated socio-political situation of Ukraine. Currently, the biggest challenge facing Ukrainian authorities is the country's progressively deteriorating demographic crisis, which has already resulted in a 20% fall in Ukraine's population over the course of the past two decades. It will be impossible to stop this process without radical systemic and economic reforms, well-financed social policies and improvements in health-care provisioning. Consequently, the effectiveness of the implementation of the pro-European reform package will largely depend on improving the effectiveness of Ukraine's population policy. If successful, this will significantly increase the standard of living of ordinary citizens, which will translate into an increase in the level of internal security in Ukraine. Conversely, without these important changes, the ability of the state to resist the multi-faceted aggression of Russia will not increase.

In this context, it is crucial to utilize the positive aspects of migration processes. The mass emigration of Ukrainians, which is to a large extent temporary or circular, may have a positive impact on Ukrainian society as remittances reduce poverty. Appropriately exploited, it can foster economic development and improve the innovation and competitiveness of the Ukrainian economy. Consequently, Ukrainian authorities should make greater use of the social and cultural capital associated with this new wave of migration to the West (including mass educational migration to Poland).

The Ukrainian crisis has contributed to a greater consolidation of Ukrainian society and has radically altered the direction of the migration streams. This alteration is a consequence of the considerable economic downturn in Russia after 2014, the collapse of the ruble's exchange rate, and the new restrictive migration policy of the Russian Federation. Currently, the most popular emigration destination for Ukrainians is Poland, both among inhabitants of Western and Eastern Ukraine. This mass influx of Ukrainians into Poland is primarily a consequence of Poland's liberal migration policy towards some Eastern European states. A simplified procedure for legalizing employment based on employers' declarations of willingness to employ persons from Ukraine, Belarus, Georgia, Moldova, Armenia, and the Russian Federation was introduced in

2006 by an ordinance from the Ministry of Labor and Social Policy that modified previous legislation dating from April 20, 2004. However, this provision can be rescinded at any time. And presently, we do not see other European Union countries exhibiting the political will to liberalize their labor markets and open them up to Ukrainian economic immigrants. Consequently, deteriorating Polish-Ukrainian relations, which are primarily a consequence of disputes over the historical policies of both states, may in the future make it more difficult for Ukrainians to take up work in the European Union.

Another great challenge facing Ukrainian authorities is the integration of internally displaced persons who left their homes after the annexation of Crimea and during the bloody fighting in the Donbas. The success of these activities is crucial for maintaining the unity of the Ukrainian state. In this regard, an effective and well-thought-out program of social inclusion could contribute to reducing the cultural distance between Ukraine's eastern and western territories. In developing an IDP integration program, Ukraine should draw conclusions from the failures of other states that found themselves in similar situations. It is important to not duplicate the errors of Georgia, where more than 250 thousand internally displaced persons from Abkhazia and South Ossetia still reside in temporary camps created for their needs in the 1990s, after the first Georgian — Abkhazian and Georgian — South Ossetian conflict. It is therefore necessary to quickly settle the housing problem and issues of employment.

It is also important to improve access to education, medical services, and for the state to provide essential food and medicines. The resources allocated for this purpose by the Ukrainian authorities should be treated as an investment in the stability and development of the state. Similarly, European countries should address this problem, as an independent and growing Ukraine will also help create a safer Europe.

The specificity of Russian aggression towards Ukraine reinforces the belief that the security of the Ukrainian state rests not only in protecting it against military aggression. It is no secret that the Kremlin wants to take advantage of the divisions evident in

Ukrainian society by playing off Ukraine's Russian- and Ukrainian-speaking populations. Actively counteracting this policy, ensuring stable demographic and economic growth, and skillfully managing migration are now broadly part of Ukraine's state security, and it is critical to recognize this.

References

Bajor, P. (2013). Sytuacja gospodarcza i uwarunkowania surowcowo-infrastrukturalne niepodległej Ukrainy. *Nowa Ukraina*, No. 13.

CIA World Factbook 2016 (2016). Retrieved from https://www.cia.gov/library/publications/resources/the-world-factbook/geos/up.html

Cudzoziemcy pracujący w Polsce – statystyki (2015–2017). Data of Ministry of Family, Labor and Social Policy. Retrieved from https://www.mpips.gov.pl/analizy-i-raporty/cudzoziemcy-pracujacy-w-polsce-statystyki

Demohrafichnyĭ shchorichnyk «Naselennia̅ Ukraïny» 2013 (2014). Kyïv: Derzẖavna Sluzẖba Statystyky Ukraïny.

Fedyuk, O., Kindler, M. (2016). Migration of Ukrainians to the European Union: Background and Key Issues. In O. Fedyuk, M. Kindler (Eds), *Ukrainian Migration to the European Union Lessons from Migration Studies*, Warsaw: Springer Open.

Harmonizovanyĭ zvit Ukraïny pro dosia̅hnutyĭ prohres u zdiĭsnenni natsional'nykh zakhodiv u vidpovid' na epidemiiu̅ SNIDY (GARPR Ukraine). Zvitnyĭ period: sichen' 2012 r. – hruden' 2014 (2014). Kyïv.

Kończuk, W. (2012). Najlepszy sojusznik Rosji. Kondycja i perspektywy rosyjskiego sektora naftowego, *Prace OSW*, No. 39.

Kontseptsii̅a̅ demograficheskoĭ politiki Rossiĭskoĭ Federatsii na period do 2025 goda (2007). *Demoscope Weekly*, 9.10.2007. Retrieved from http://demoscope.ru/weekly/knigi/koncepciya/koncepciya25.html

Kościółek, J. (2012). Język ukraiński wobec wyzwań współczesnej sytuacji społeczno-politycznej na Ukrainie. *Przegląd Wschodnioeuropejski*, No. 3.

Laruelle, M. (2015). Russia as a "Divided Nation" from Compatriots to Crimea: A Contribution to the Discussion on Nationalism and Foreign Policy. *Problems of Post-Communism*, Vol. 62, No. 2.

Marriage and divorce statistics. Eurostat (2016). Retrieved from http://ec.europa.eu/eurostat/statisticsexplained/index.php/File:C

rude_divorce_rate,_selected_years,_1960-2015_(per_1_000_persons). png

Marriages and crude marriage rates, by urban/rural residence: 2007 – 2011 (2011). United Nations Statistical Division. Retrieved from https://unstats.un.org/unsd/demographic/products/dyb/dyb2011/Table23.pdf

Monitoring gosudarstvennoĭ programmy po okazaniiū sodeĭstviiā dobrovol'nomu pereseleniiū v Rossiĭskuiū Federatsiiū sootechestvennikov, prozhivaiūshchikh za rubezhom. Glavnoe Upravlenie po voprosam migratsii MVD (2016). Retrieved from http://гувм.мвд.рф

Perelli-Harris, B. (2008). Ukraine: On the border between old and new in uncertain times. *Demographic Research*, No. 19(29).

Residence permits for non-EU citizens EU Member States issued a record number of 2.6 million first residence permits in 2015. Main beneficiaries from Ukraine and the United States, Eurostat, 211/2016 (2016). Retrieved from http://ec.europa.eu/eurostat/documents/2995521/7715617/3-27102016-BP-EN.pdf/ca706fa0-14fc-4b71-a2e2-46b2b933f8f8

Rettinger, R. (2011). Wpływ kryzysu gospodarczego na sytuację demograficzną Ukrainy. *Prace Komisji Geografii Przemysłu*, No. 18.

Skol'ko stoit razreshenie na rabotu v Rossii dliā trudovykh migrantov (2017). Retrieved from http://customsforum.ru

Stępniewski, T. (2016). Ukraine Crisis and European Union's Eastern Partnership Revisited. *Annales UMCS. Sectio K: Politologia*, No. 2.

Szabaciuk, A. (2014). Wybrane problemy polityki imigracyjnej Federacji Rosyjskiej. *Rocznik Nauk Społecznych KUL*, Vol. 42, No. 3.

Szabaciuk, A. (2016a). Wpływ kryzysu migracyjnego na procesy migracyjne na obszarze poradzieckim. *Rocznik Instytutu Europy Środkowo-Wschodniej*, No. 5.

Szabaciuk, A. (2016b). Zapomniane ofiary wojny. Osoby wewnętrznie przesiedlone (IDP) na Ukrainie. *Studia Europejskie*, No. 3.

Szeptycki, A. (2013). Ukraina wobec Rosji. Studium zależności. Warszawa: Warsaw University Publishing.

Szulecka, M. (2016). Regulating Movement of the Very Mobile: Selected Legal and Policy Aspects of Ukrainian Migration to EU Countries. In O. Fedyuk, M. Kindler (Eds), *Ukrainian Migration to the European Union Lessons from Migration Studies*, Warsaw: Springer Open.

Twigg, J., Wayne Merry, E. (2014). Ukraine's Real Crisis: A Demographics and Health Time Bomb. *The National Interest*, December 15, 2014.

Retrieved from http://nationalinterest.org/feature/ukraines-real-crisis-demographics-health-time-bomb-11851

Ukraine in figures 2015. Statistical Publication (2016). Kyiv: State Statistics Services Publication.

World Bank Data (2017). Retrieved from https://data.worldbank.org

Za chertoĭ bednosti v Ukraine zhivet bolee 80% naseleniia̅ – deputat (2015), UNIAN.

Notes on Contributors

Joanna Fomina, Ph.D., is an assistant professor at the Institute of Philosophy and Sociology of the Polish Academy of Sciences in Warsaw, Poland, and a member of the European Studies Unit. Areas of professional interest include the EU's Eastern policy, migration and migrant integration policies in the EU, and Euroscepticism and populism.
E-mail address: jfomina@ifispan.waw.pl

Jussi P. Laine, Doctor of Social Sciences, is an assistant professor of multidisciplinary border studies at the Karelian Institute of the University of Eastern Finland and holds the title of Docent of Human Geography from the University of Oulu, Finland. He is Vice President of the Association for Borderlands Studies and currently also serves on the Steering Committee of the International Geographical Union's Commission on Political Geography.
E-mail address: jussi.laine@uef.fi

Yuriy Matsiyevsky is an associate professor of political science and the head of the Center for Political Research at the National University of Ostroh Academy (Ukraine). He received his doctoral degree in political science from Lviv University in 1996 and his habilitation from the Ivan Kuras Institute of Political and Ethnic Studies at the National Academy of Sciences of Ukraine in 2016. Previously he studied at the Graduate School for Social Research in Warsaw, Poland. Since 1999 he has taught at National University of Ostroh Academy. Areas of expertise include: Ukraine, democratization, informal institutions, and comparative politics.
E-mail address: yuriym2000@yahoo.com

George Soroka received his Ph.D. in Political Science from Harvard University in 2014. He has lived and studied throughout the post-Soviet region, most recently in Kyiv. His research interests include the post-communist politics of history, the rise of right-wing political parties in Europe, Russian foreign policy, the role of

religion in politics, and comparative democratization. Currently, he is Lecturer on Government and Assistant Director of Undergraduate Studies in the Government Department at Harvard University.
E-mail address: soroka@fas.harvard.edu

Tomasz Stępniewski, Doctor Habilitatus (Polish Academy of Sciences, Warsaw, Poland), is an associate professor and holder of the Eastern Studies Chair at the Institute of Political Science and International Affairs, Faculty of Social Sciences, the John Paul II Catholic University of Lublin. Areas of expertise: the EU's eastern policy, European security, international relations in the CIS (Commonwealth of Independent States), and Russia's policy toward Eastern Europe.
E-mail address: tomasz.stepniewski5@gmail.com

Andrzej Szabaciuk, Ph.D., is a political scientist and historian who graduated from the European Collegium of Polish and Ukrainian Universities in Lublin. He currently serves as an assistant professor in the Institute of Political Science and International Affairs at the John Paul II Catholic University of Lublin. Research interests include Eastern European issues in a broad sense, encompassing: migration, the religious and ethnic policies of post-Soviet states, and the situation of national and religious minorities in the former Eastern bloc.
E-mail address: aszabaciuk@gmail.com

Yuval Weber, Ph.D., is a Global Fellow at the Woodrow Wilson Center and is the inaugural Kennan Institute Fellow at the Daniel Morgan Graduate School, where he is on leave from the Faculty of World Economy and International Affairs at the National Research University - Higher School of Economics (Moscow, Russia). He is a Center Associate at the Davis Center for Russian and Eurasian Studies at Harvard University, and previously served as a Visiting Assistant Professor in the Department on Government at Harvard University.
E-mail address: yuvalweber@gmail.com

SOVIET AND POST-SOVIET POLITICS AND SOCIETY
Edited by Dr. Andreas Umland | ISSN 1614-3515

1   Андреас Умланд (ред.) | Воплощение Европейской конвенции по правам человека в России. Философские, юридические и эмпирические исследования | ISBN 3-89821-387-0

2   Christian Wipperfürth | Russland – ein vertrauenswürdiger Partner? Grundlagen, Hintergründe und Praxis gegenwärtiger russischer Außenpolitik | Mit einem Vorwort von Heinz Timmermann | ISBN 3-89821-401-X

3   Manja Hussner | Die Übernahme internationalen Rechts in die russische und deutsche Rechtsordnung. Eine vergleichende Analyse zur Völkerrechtsfreundlichkeit der Verfassungen der Russländischen Föderation und der Bundesrepublik Deutschland | Mit einem Vorwort von Rainer Arnold | ISBN 3-89821-438-9

4   Matthew Tejada | Bulgaria's Democratic Consolidation and the Kozloduy Nuclear Power Plant (KNPP). The Unattainability of Closure | With a foreword by Richard J. Crampton | ISBN 3-89821-439-7

5   Марк Григорьевич Меерович | Квадратные метры, определяющие сознание. Государственная жилищная политика в СССР. 1921 – 1941 гг | ISBN 3-89821-474-5

6   Andrei P. Tsygankov, Pavel A. Tsygankov (eds.) | New Directions in Russian International Studies | ISBN 3-89821-422-2

7   Марк Григорьевич Меерович | Как власть народ к труду приучала. Жилище в СССР – средство управления людьми. 1917 – 1941 гг. | С предисловием Елены Осокиной | ISBN 3-89821-495-8

8   David J. Galbreath | Nation-Building and Minority Politics in Post-Socialist States. Interests, Influence and Identities in Estonia and Latvia | With a foreword by David J. Smith | ISBN 3-89821-467-2

9   Алексей Юрьевич Безугольный | Народы Кавказа в Вооруженных силах СССР в годы Великой Отечественной войны 1941-1945 гг. | С предисловием Николая Бугая | ISBN 3-89821-475-3

10 Вячеслав Лихачев и Владимир Прибыловский (ред.) | Русское Национальное Единство, 1990-2000. В 2-х томах | ISBN 3-89821-523-7

11 Николай Бугай (ред.) | Народы стран Балтии в условиях сталинизма (1940-е – 1950-е годы). Документированная история | ISBN 3-89821-525-3

12 Ingmar Bredies (Hrsg.) | Zur Anatomie der Orange Revolution in der Ukraine. Wechsel des Elitenregimes oder Triumph des Parlamentarismus? | ISBN 3-89821-524-5

13 Anastasia V. Mitrofanova | The Politicization of Russian Orthodoxy. Actors and Ideas | With a foreword by William C. Gay | ISBN 3-89821-481-8

14 Nathan D. Larson | Alexander Solzhenitsyn and the Russo-Jewish Question | ISBN 3-89821-483-4

15 Guido Houben | Kulturpolitik und Ethnizität. Staatliche Kunstförderung im Russland der neunziger Jahre | Mit einem Vorwort von Gert Weisskirchen | ISBN 3-89821-542-3

16 Leonid Luks | Der russische „Sonderweg"? Aufsätze zur neuesten Geschichte Russlands im europäischen Kontext | ISBN 3-89821-496-6

17 Евгений Мороз | История «Мёртвой воды» – от страшной сказки к большой политике. Политическое неоязычество в постсоветской России | ISBN 3-89821-551-2

18 Александр Верховский и Галина Кожевникова (ред.) | Этническая и религиозная интолерантность в российских СМИ. Результаты мониторинга 2001-2004 гг. | ISBN 3-89821-569-5

19 Christian Ganzer | Sowjetisches Erbe und ukrainische Nation. Das Museum der Geschichte des Zaporoger Kosakentums auf der Insel Chortycja | Mit einem Vorwort von Frank Golczewski | ISBN 3-89821-504-0

20 Эльза-Баир Гучинова | Помнить нельзя забыть. Антропология депортационной травмы калмыков | С предисловием Кэролайн Хамфри | ISBN 3-89821-506-7

21 Юлия Лидерман | Мотивы «проверки» и «испытания» в постсоветской культуре. Советское прошлое в российском кинематографе 1990-х годов | С предисловием Евгения Марголита | ISBN 3-89821-511-3

22 Tanya Lokshina, Ray Thomas, Mary Mayer (eds.) | The Imposition of a Fake Political Settlement in the Northern Caucasus. The 2003 Chechen Presidential Election | ISBN 3-89821-436-2

23 Timothy McCajor Hall, Rosie Read (eds.) | Changes in the Heart of Europe. Recent Ethnographies of Czechs, Slovaks, Roma, and Sorbs | With an afterword by Zdeněk Salzmann | ISBN 3-89821-606-3

24 *Christian Autengruber* | Die politischen Parteien in Bulgarien und Rumänien. Eine vergleichende Analyse seit Beginn der 90er Jahre | Mit einem Vorwort von Dorothée de Nève | ISBN 3-89821-476-1

25 *Annette Freyberg-Inan with Radu Cristescu* | The Ghosts in Our Classrooms, or: John Dewey Meets Ceauşescu. The Promise and the Failures of Civic Education in Romania | ISBN 3-89821-416-8

26 *John B. Dunlop* | The 2002 Dubrovka and 2004 Beslan Hostage Crises. A Critique of Russian Counter-Terrorism | With a foreword by Donald N. Jensen | ISBN 3-89821-608-X

27 *Peter Koller* | Das touristische Potenzial von Kam"janec'–Podil's'kyj. Eine fremdenverkehrsgeographische Untersuchung der Zukunftsperspektiven und Maßnahmenplanung zur Destinationsentwicklung des „ukrainischen Rothenburg" | Mit einem Vorwort von Kristiane Klemm | ISBN 3-89821-640-3

28 *Françoise Daucé, Elisabeth Sieca-Kozlowski (eds.)* | Dedovshchina in the Post-Soviet Military. Hazing of Russian Army Conscripts in a Comparative Perspective | With a foreword by Dale Herspring | ISBN 3-89821-616-0

29 *Florian Strasser* | Zivilgesellschaftliche Einflüsse auf die Orange Revolution. Die gewaltlose Massenbewegung und die ukrainische Wahlkrise 2004 | Mit einem Vorwort von Egbert Jahn | ISBN 3-89821-648-9

30 *Rebecca S. Katz* | The Georgian Regime Crisis of 2003-2004. A Case Study in Post-Soviet Media Representation of Politics, Crime and Corruption | ISBN 3-89821-413-3

31 *Vladimir Kantor* | Willkür oder Freiheit. Beiträge zur russischen Geschichtsphilosophie | Ediert von Dagmar Herrmann sowie mit einem Vorwort versehen von Leonid Luks | ISBN 3-89821-589-X

32 *Laura A. Victoir* | The Russian Land Estate Today. A Case Study of Cultural Politics in Post-Soviet Russia | With a foreword by Priscilla Roosevelt | ISBN 3-89821-426-5

33 *Ivan Katchanovski* | Cleft Countries. Regional Political Divisions and Cultures in Post-Soviet Ukraine and Moldova| With a foreword by Francis Fukuyama | ISBN 3-89821-558-X

34 *Florian Mühlfried* | Postsowjetische Feiern. Das Georgische Bankett im Wandel | Mit einem Vorwort von Kevin Tuite | ISBN 3-89821-601-2

35 *Roger Griffin, Werner Loh, Andreas Umland (eds.)* | Fascism Past and Present, West and East. An International Debate on Concepts and Cases in the Comparative Study of the Extreme Right | With an afterword by Walter Laqueur | ISBN 3-89821-674-8

36 *Sebastian Schlegel* | Der „Weiße Archipel". Sowjetische Atomstädte 1945-1991 | Mit einem Geleitwort von Thomas Bohn | ISBN 3-89821-679-9

37 *Vyacheslav Likhachev* | Political Anti-Semitism in Post-Soviet Russia. Actors and Ideas in 1991-2003 | Edited and translated from Russian by Eugene Veklerov | ISBN 3-89821-529-6

38 *Josette Baer (ed.)* | Preparing Liberty in Central Europe. Political Texts from the Spring of Nations 1848 to the Spring of Prague 1968 | With a foreword by Zdeněk V. David | ISBN 3-89821-546-6

39 *Михаил Лукьянов* | Российский консерватизм и реформа, 1907-1914 | С предисловием Марка Д. Стейнберга | ISBN 3-89821-503-2

40 *Nicola Melloni* | Market Without Economy. The 1998 Russian Financial Crisis | With a foreword by Eiji Furukawa | ISBN 3-89821-407-9

41 *Dmitrij Chmelnizki* | Die Architektur Stalins | Bd. 1: Studien zu Ideologie und Stil | Bd. 2: Bilddokumentation | Mit einem Vorwort von Bruno Flierl | ISBN 3-89821-515-6

42 *Katja Yafimava* | Post-Soviet Russian-Belarussian Relationships. The Role of Gas Transit Pipelines | With a foreword by Jonathan P. Stern | ISBN 3-89821-655-1

43 *Boris Chavkin* | Verflechtungen der deutschen und russischen Zeitgeschichte. Aufsätze und Archivfunde zu den Beziehungen Deutschlands und der Sowjetunion von 1917 bis 1991 | Ediert von Markus Edlinger sowie mit einem Vorwort versehen von Leonid Luks | ISBN 3-89821-756-0

44 *Anastasija Grynenko in Zusammenarbeit mit Claudia Dathe* | Die Terminologie des Gerichtswesens der Ukraine und Deutschlands im Vergleich. Eine übersetzungswissenschaftliche Analyse juristischer Fachbegriffe im Deutschen, Ukrainischen und Russischen | Mit einem Vorwort von Ulrich Hartmann | ISBN 3-89821-691-8

45 *Anton Burkov* | The Impact of the European Convention on Human Rights on Russian Law. Legislation and Application in 1996-2006 | With a foreword by Françoise Hampson | ISBN 978-3-89821-639-5

46 *Stina Torjesen, Indra Overland (eds.)* | International Election Observers in Post-Soviet Azerbaijan. Geopolitical Pawns or Agents of Change? | ISBN 978-3-89821-743-9

47 *Taras Kuzio* | Ukraine – Crimea – Russia. Triangle of Conflict | ISBN 978-3-89821-761-3

48 *Claudia Šabić* | "Ich erinnere mich nicht, aber L'viv!" Zur Funktion kultureller Faktoren für die Institutionalisierung und Entwicklung einer ukrainischen Region | Mit einem Vorwort von Melanie Tatur | ISBN 978-3-89821-752-1

49 *Marlies Bilz* | Tatarstan in der Transformation | Nationaler Diskurs und Politische Praxis 1988-1994 | Mit einem Vorwort von Frank Golczewski | ISBN 978-3-89821-722-4

50 *Марлен Ларюэль (ред.)* | Современные интерпретации русского национализма | ISBN 978-3-89821-795-8

51 *Sonja Schüler* | Die ethnische Dimension der Armut. Roma im postsozialistischen Rumänien | Mit einem Vorwort von Anton Sterbling | ISBN 978-3-89821-778-7

52 *Галина Кожевникова* | Радикальный национализм в России и противодействие ему. Сборник докладов Центра «Сова» за 2004-2007 гг. | С предисловием Александра Верховского | ISBN 978-3-89821-721-7

53 *Галина Кожевникова и Владимир Прибыловский* | Российская власть в биографиях I. Высшие должностные лица РФ в 2004 г. | ISBN 978-3-89821-796-5

54 *Галина Кожевникова и Владимир Прибыловский* | Российская власть в биографиях II. Члены Правительства РФ в 2004 г. | ISBN 978-3-89821-797-2

55 *Галина Кожевникова и Владимир Прибыловский* | Российская власть в биографиях III. Руководители федеральных служб и агентств РФ в 2004 г. | ISBN 978-3-89821-798-9

56 *Ileana Petroniu* | Privatisierung in Transformationsökonomien. Determinanten der Restrukturierungs-Bereitschaft am Beispiel Polens, Rumäniens und der Ukraine | Mit einem Vorwort von Rainer W. Schäfer | ISBN 978-3-89821-790-3

57 *Christian Wipperfürth* | Russland und seine GUS-Nachbarn. Hintergründe, aktuelle Entwicklungen und Konflikte in einer ressourcenreichen Region| ISBN 978-3-89821-801-6

58 *Togzhan Kassenova* | From Antagonism to Partnership. The Uneasy Path of the U.S.-Russian Cooperative Threat Reduction | With a foreword by Christoph Bluth | ISBN 978-3-89821-707-1

59 *Alexander Höllwerth* | Das sakrale eurasische Imperium des Aleksandr Dugin. Eine Diskursanalyse zum postsowjetischen russischen Rechtsextremismus | Mit einem Vorwort von Dirk Uffelmann | ISBN 978-3-89821-813-9

60 *Олег Рябов* | «Россия-Матушка». Национализм, гендер и война в России XX века | С предисловием Елены Гощило | ISBN 978-3-89821-487-2

61 *Ivan Maistrenko* | Borot'bism. A Chapter in the History of the Ukrainian Revolution | With a new introduction by Chris Ford | Translated by George S. N. Luckyj with the assistance of Ivan L. Rudnytsky | ISBN 978-3-89821-697-5

62 *Maryna Romanets* | Anamorphosic Texts and Reconfigured Visions. Improvised Traditions in Contemporary Ukrainian and Irish Literature | ISBN 978-3-89821-576-3

63 *Paul D'Anieri and Taras Kuzio (eds.)* | Aspects of the Orange Revolution I. Democratization and Elections in Post-Communist Ukraine | ISBN 978-3-89821-698-2

64 *Bohdan Harasymiw in collaboration with Oleh S. Ilnytzkyj (eds.)* | Aspects of the Orange Revolution II. Information and Manipulation Strategies in the 2004 Ukrainian Presidential Elections | ISBN 978-3-89821-699-9

65 *Ingmar Bredies, Andreas Umland and Valentin Yakushik (eds.)* | Aspects of the Orange Revolution III. The Context and Dynamics of the 2004 Ukrainian Presidential Elections | ISBN 978-3-89821-803-0

66 *Ingmar Bredies, Andreas Umland and Valentin Yakushik (eds.)* | Aspects of the Orange Revolution IV. Foreign Assistance and Civic Action in the 2004 Ukrainian Presidential Elections | ISBN 978-3-89821-808-5

67 *Ingmar Bredies, Andreas Umland and Valentin Yakushik (eds.)* | Aspects of the Orange Revolution V. Institutional Observation Reports on the 2004 Ukrainian Presidential Elections | ISBN 978-3-89821-809-2

68 *Taras Kuzio (ed.)* | Aspects of the Orange Revolution VI. Post-Communist Democratic Revolutions in Comparative Perspective | ISBN 978-3-89821-820-7

69 *Tim Bohse* | Autoritarismus statt Selbstverwaltung. Die Transformation der kommunalen Politik in der Stadt Kaliningrad 1990-2005 | Mit einem Geleitwort von Stefan Troebst | ISBN 978-3-89821-782-8

70 *David Rupp* | Die Rußländische Föderation und die russischsprachige Minderheit in Lettland. Eine Fallstudie zur Anwaltspolitik Moskaus gegenüber den russophonen Minderheiten im „Nahen Ausland" von 1991 bis 2002 | Mit einem Vorwort von Helmut Wagner | ISBN 978-3-89821-778-1

71 *Taras Kuzio* | Theoretical and Comparative Perspectives on Nationalism. New Directions in Cross-Cultural and Post-Communist Studies | With a foreword by Paul Robert Magocsi | ISBN 978-3-89821-815-3

72 *Christine Teichmann* | Die Hochschultransformation im heutigen Osteuropa. Kontinuität und Wandel bei der Entwicklung des postkommunistischen Universitätswesens | Mit einem Vorwort von Oskar Anweiler | ISBN 978-3-89821-842-9

73 *Julia Kusznir* | Der politische Einfluss von Wirtschaftseliten in russischen Regionen. Eine Analyse am Beispiel der Erdöl- und Erdgasindustrie, 1992-2005 | Mit einem Vorwort von Wolfgang Eichwede | ISBN 978-3-89821-821-4

74 *Alena Vysotskaya* | Russland, Belarus und die EU-Osterweiterung. Zur Minderheitenfrage und zum Problem der Freizügigkeit des Personenverkehrs | Mit einem Vorwort von Katijn Malfliet | ISBN 978-3-89821-822-1

75 *Heiko Pleines (Hrsg.)* | Corporate Governance in post-sozialistischen Volkswirtschaften | ISBN 978-3-89821-766-8

76 *Stefan Ihrig* | Wer sind die Moldawier? Rumänismus versus Moldowanismus in Historiographie und Schulbüchern der Republik Moldova, 1991-2006 | Mit einem Vorwort von Holm Sundhaussen | ISBN 978-3-89821-466-7

77 *Galina Kozhevnikova in collaboration with Alexander Verkhovsky and Eugene Veklerov* | Ultra-Nationalism and Hate Crimes in Contemporary Russia. The 2004-2006 Annual Reports of Moscow's SOVA Center | With a foreword by Stephen D. Shenfield | ISBN 978-3-89821-868-9

78 *Florian Küchler* | The Role of the European Union in Moldova's Transnistria Conflict | With a foreword by Christopher Hill | ISBN 978-3-89821-850-4

79 *Bernd Rechel* | The Long Way Back to Europe. Minority Protection in Bulgaria | With a foreword by Richard Crampton | ISBN 978-3-89821-863-4

80 *Peter W. Rodgers* | Nation, Region and History in Post-Communist Transitions. Identity Politics in Ukraine, 1991-2006 | With a foreword by Vera Tolz | ISBN 978-3-89821-903-7

81 *Stephanie Solywoda* | The Life and Work of Semen L. Frank. A Study of Russian Religious Philosophy | With a foreword by Philip Walters | ISBN 978-3-89821-457-5

82 *Vera Sokolova* | Cultural Politics of Ethnicity. Discourses on Roma in Communist Czechoslovakia | ISBN 978-3-89821-864-1

83 *Natalya Shevchik Ketenci* | Kazakhstani Enterprises in Transition. The Role of Historical Regional Development in Kazakhstan's Post-Soviet Economic Transformation | ISBN 978-3-89821-831-3

84 *Martin Malek, Anna Schor-Tschudnowskaja (Hrsg.)* | Europa im Tschetschenienkrieg. Zwischen politischer Ohnmacht und Gleichgültigkeit | Mit einem Vorwort von Lipchan Basajewa | ISBN 978-3-89821-676-0

85 *Stefan Meister* | Das postsowjetische Universitätswesen zwischen nationalem und internationalem Wandel. Die Entwicklung der regionalen Hochschule in Russland als Gradmesser der Systemtransformation | Mit einem Vorwort von Joan DeBardeleben | ISBN 978-3-89821-891-7

86 *Konstantin Sheiko in collaboration with Stephen Brown* | Nationalist Imaginings of the Russian Past. Anatolii Fomenko and the Rise of Alternative History in Post-Communist Russia | With a foreword by Donald Ostrowski | ISBN 978-3-89821-915-0

87 *Sabine Jenni* | Wie stark ist das „Einige Russland"? Zur Parteibindung der Eliten und zum Wahlerfolg der Machtpartei im Dezember 2007 | Mit einem Vorwort von Klaus Armingeon | ISBN 978-3-89821-961-7

88 *Thomas Borén* | Meeting-Places of Transformation. Urban Identity, Spatial Representations and Local Politics in Post-Soviet St Petersburg | ISBN 978-3-89821-739-2

89 *Aygul Ashirova* | Stalinismus und Stalin-Kult in Zentralasien. Turkmenistan 1924-1953 | Mit einem Vorwort von Leonid Luks | ISBN 978-3-89821-987-7

90 *Leonid Luks* | Freiheit oder imperiale Größe? Essays zu einem russischen Dilemma | ISBN 978-3-8382-0011-8

91 *Christopher Gilley* | The 'Change of Signposts' in the Ukrainian Emigration. A Contribution to the History of Sovietophilism in the 1920s | With a foreword by Frank Golczewski | ISBN 978-3-89821-965-5

92 *Philipp Casula, Jeronim Perovic (eds.)* | Identities and Politics During the Putin Presidency. The Discursive Foundations of Russia's Stability | With a foreword by Heiko Haumann | ISBN 978-3-8382-0015-6

93 *Marcel Viëtor* | Europa und die Frage nach seinen Grenzen im Osten. Zur Konstruktion ‚europäischer Identität' in Geschichte und Gegenwart | Mit einem Vorwort von Albrecht Lehmann | ISBN 978-3-8382-0045-3

94 *Ben Hellman, Andrei Rogachevskii* | Filming the Unfilmable. Casper Wrede's 'One Day in the Life of Ivan Denisovich' | Second, Revised and Expanded Edition | ISBN 978-3-8382-0044-6

95 *Eva Fuchslocher* | Vaterland, Sprache, Glaube. Orthodoxie und Nationenbildung am Beispiel Georgiens | Mit einem Vorwort von Christina von Braun | ISBN 978-3-89821-884-9

96 *Vladimir Kantor* | Das Westlertum und der Weg Russlands. Zur Entwicklung der russischen Literatur und Philosophie | Ediert von Dagmar Herrmann | Mit einem Beitrag von Nikolaus Lobkowicz | ISBN 978-3-8382-0102-3

97 *Kamran Musayev* | Die postsowjetische Transformation im Baltikum und Südkaukasus. Eine vergleichende Untersuchung der politischen Entwicklung Lettlands und Aserbaidschans 1985-2009 | Mit einem Vorwort von Leonid Luks | Ediert von Sandro Henschel | ISBN 978-3-8382-0103-0

98 *Tatiana Zhurzhenko* | Borderlands into Bordered Lands. Geopolitics of Identity in Post-Soviet Ukraine | With a foreword by Dieter Segert | ISBN 978-3-8382-0042-2

99 *Кирилл Галушко, Лидия Смола (ред.)* | Пределы падения – варианты украинского будущего. Аналитико-прогностические исследования | ISBN 978-3-8382-0148-1

100 *Michael Minkenberg (ed.)* | Historical Legacies and the Radical Right in Post-Cold War Central and Eastern Europe | With an afterword by Sabrina P. Ramet | ISBN 978-3-8382-0124-5

101 *David-Emil Wickström* | Rocking St. Petersburg. Transcultural Flows and Identity Politics in the St. Petersburg Popular Music Scene | With a foreword by Yngvar B. Steinholt | Second, Revised and Expanded Edition | ISBN 978-3-8382-0100-9

102 *Eva Zabka* | Eine neue „Zeit der Wirren"? Der spät- und postsowjetische Systemwandel 1985-2000 im Spiegel russischer gesellschaftspolitischer Diskurse | Mit einem Vorwort von Margareta Mommsen | ISBN 978-3-8382-0161-0

103 *Ulrike Ziemer* | Ethnic Belonging, Gender and Cultural Practices. Youth Identitites in Contemporary Russia | With a foreword by Anoop Nayak | ISBN 978-3-8382-0152-8

104 *Ksenia Chepikova* | ‚Einiges Russland' - eine zweite KPdSU? Aspekte der Identitätskonstruktion einer postsowjetischen „Partei der Macht" | Mit einem Vorwort von Torsten Oppelland | ISBN 978-3-8382-0311-9

105 *Леонид Люкс* | Западничество или евразийство? Демократия или идеократия? Сборник статей об исторических дилеммах России | С предисловием Владимира Кантора | ISBN 978-3-8382-0211-2

106 *Anna Dost* | Das russische Verfassungsrecht auf dem Weg zum Föderalismus und zurück. Zum Konflikt von Rechtsnormen und -wirklichkeit in der Russländischen Föderation von 1991 bis 2009 | Mit einem Vorwort von Alexander Blankenagel | ISBN 978-3-8382-0292-1

107 *Philipp Herzog* | Sozialistische Völkerfreundschaft, nationaler Widerstand oder harmloser Zeitvertreib? Zur politischen Funktion der Volkskunst im sowjetischen Estland | Mit einem Vorwort von Andreas Kappeler | ISBN 978-3-8382-0216-7

108 *Marlène Laruelle (ed.)* | Russian Nationalism, Foreign Policy, and Identity Debates in Putin's Russia. New Ideological Patterns after the Orange Revolution | ISBN 978-3-8382-0325-6

109 *Michail Logvinov* | Russlands Kampf gegen den internationalen Terrorismus. Eine kritische Bestandsaufnahme des Bekämpfungsansatzes | Mit einem Geleitwort von Hans-Henning Schröder und einem Vorwort von Eckhard Jesse | ISBN 978-3-8382-0329-4

110 *John B. Dunlop* | The Moscow Bombings of September 1999. Examinations of Russian Terrorist Attacks at the Onset of Vladimir Putin's Rule | Second, Revised and Expanded Edition | ISBN 978-3-8382-0388-1

111 *Андрей А. Ковалёв* | Свидетельство из-за кулис российской политики I. Можно ли делать добро из зла? (Воспоминания и размышления о последних советских и первых послесоветских годах) | With a foreword by Peter Reddaway | ISBN 978-3-8382-0302-7

112 *Андрей А. Ковалёв* | Свидетельство из-за кулис российской политики II. Угроза для себя и окружающих (Наблюдения и предостережения относительно происходящего после 2000 г.) | ISBN 978-3-8382-0303-4

113 *Bernd Kappenberg* | Zeichen setzen für Europa. Der Gebrauch europäischer lateinischer Sonderzeichen in der deutschen Öffentlichkeit | Mit einem Vorwort von Peter Schlobinski | ISBN 978-3-89821-749-1

114 *Ivo Mijnssen* | The Quest for an Ideal Youth in Putin's Russia I. Back to Our Future! History, Modernity, and Patriotism according to Nashi, 2005-2013 | With a foreword by Jeronim Perović | Second, Revised and Expanded Edition | ISBN 978-3-8382-0368-3

115 *Jussi Lassila* | The Quest for an Ideal Youth in Putin's Russia II. The Search for Distinctive Conformism in the Political Communication of Nashi, 2005-2009 | With a foreword by Kirill Postoutenko | Second, Revised and Expanded Edition | ISBN 978-3-8382-0415-4

116 *Valerio Trabandt* | Neue Nachbarn, gute Nachbarschaft? Die EU als internationaler Akteur am Beispiel ihrer Demokratieförderung in Belarus und der Ukraine 2004-2009 | Mit einem Vorwort von Jutta Joachim | ISBN 978-3-8382-0437-6

117 *Fabian Pfeiffer* | Estlands Außen- und Sicherheitspolitik I. Der estnische Atlantizismus nach der wiedererlangten Unabhängigkeit 1991-2004 | Mit einem Vorwort von Helmut Hubel | ISBN 978-3-8382-0127-6

118 *Jana Podßuweit* | Estlands Außen- und Sicherheitspolitik II. Handlungsoptionen eines Kleinstaates im Rahmen seiner EU-Mitgliedschaft (2004-2008) | Mit einem Vorwort von Helmut Hubel | ISBN 978-3-8382-0440-6

119 *Karin Pointner* | Estlands Außen- und Sicherheitspolitik III. Eine gedächtnispolitische Analyse estnischer Entwicklungskooperation 2006-2010 | Mit einem Vorwort von Karin Liebhart | ISBN 978-3-8382-0435-2

120 *Ruslana Vovk* | Die Offenheit der ukrainischen Verfassung für das Völkerrecht und die europäische Integration | Mit einem Vorwort von Alexander Blankenagel | ISBN 978-3-8382-0481-9

121 *Mykhaylo Banakh* | Die Relevanz der Zivilgesellschaft bei den postkommunistischen Transformationsprozessen in mittel- und osteuropäischen Ländern. Das Beispiel der spät- und postsowjetischen Ukraine 1986-2009 | Mit einem Vorwort von Gerhard Simon | ISBN 978-3-8382-0499-4

122 *Michael Moser* | Language Policy and the Discourse on Languages in Ukraine under President Viktor Yanukovych (25 February 2010–28 October 2012) | ISBN 978-3-8382-0497-0 (Paperback edition) | ISBN 978-3-8382-0507-6 (Hardcover edition)

123 *Nicole Krome* | Russischer Netzwerkkapitalismus Restrukturierungsprozesse in der Russischen Föderation am Beispiel des Luftfahrtunternehmens "Aviastar" | Mit einem Vorwort von Petra Stykow | ISBN 978-3-8382-0534-2

124 *David R. Marples* | 'Our Glorious Past'. Lukashenka's Belarus and the Great Patriotic War | ISBN 978-3-8382-0574-8 (Paperback edition) | ISBN 978-3-8382-0675-2 (Hardcover edition)

125 *Ulf Walther* | Russlands "neuer Adel". Die Macht des Geheimdienstes von Gorbatschow bis Putin | Mit einem Vorwort von Hans-Georg Wieck | ISBN 978-3-8382-0584-7

126 *Simon Geissbühler (Hrsg.)* | Kiew – Revolution 3.0. Der Euromaidan 2013/14 und die Zukunftsperspektiven der Ukraine | ISBN 978-3-8382-0581-6 (Paperback edition) | ISBN 978-3-8382-0681-3 (Hardcover edition)

127 *Andrey Makarychev* | Russia and the EU in a Multipolar World. Discourses, Identities, Norms | With a foreword by Klaus Segbers | ISBN 978-3-8382-0629-5

128 *Roland Scharff* | Kasachstan als postsowjetischer Wohlfahrtsstaat. Die Transformation des sozialen Schutzsystems | Mit einem Vorwort von Joachim Ahrens | ISBN 978-3-8382-0622-6

129 *Katja Grupp* | Bild Lücke Deutschland. Kaliningrader Studierende sprechen über Deutschland | Mit einem Vorwort von Martin Schulz | ISBN 978-3-8382-0552-6

130 *Konstantin Sheiko, Stephen Brown* | History as Therapy. Alternative History and Nationalist Imaginings in Russia, 1991-2014 | ISBN 978-3-8382-0665-3

131 *Elisa Kriza* | Alexander Solzhenitsyn: Cold War Icon, Gulag Author, Russian Nationalist? A Study of the Western Reception of his Literary Writings, Historical Interpretations, and Political Ideas | With a foreword by Andrei Rogatchevski | ISBN 978-3-8382-0589-2 (Paperback edition) | ISBN 978-3-8382-0690-5 (Hardcover edition)

132 *Serghei Golunov* | The Elephant in the Room. Corruption and Cheating in Russian Universities | ISBN 978-3-8382-0570-0

133 *Manja Hussner, Rainer Arnold (Hgg.)* | Verfassungsgerichtsbarkeit in Zentralasien I. Sammlung von Verfassungstexten | ISBN 978-3-8382-0595-3

134 *Nikolay Mitrokhin* | Die "Russische Partei". Die Bewegung der russischen Nationalisten in der UdSSR 1953-1985 | Aus dem Russischen übertragen von einem Übersetzerteam unter der Leitung von Larisa Schippel | ISBN 978-3-8382-0024-8

135 *Manja Hussner, Rainer Arnold (Hgg.)* | Verfassungsgerichtsbarkeit in Zentralasien II. Sammlung von Verfassungstexten | ISBN 978-3-8382-0597-7

136 *Manfred Zeller* | Das sowjetische Fieber. Fußballfans im poststalinistischen Vielvölkerreich | Mit einem Vorwort von Nikolaus Katzer | ISBN 978-3-8382-0757-5

137 *Kristin Schreiter* | Stellung und Entwicklungspotential zivilgesellschaftlicher Gruppen in Russland. Menschenrechtsorganisationen im Vergleich | ISBN 978-3-8382-0673-8

138 *David R. Marples, Frederick V. Mills (eds.)* | Ukraine's Euromaidan. Analyses of a Civil Revolution | ISBN 978-3-8382-0660-8

139 *Bernd Kappenberg* | Setting Signs for Europe. Why Diacritics Matter for European Integration | With a foreword by Peter Schlobinski | ISBN 978-3-8382-0663-9

140 *René Lenz* | Internationalisierung, Kooperation und Transfer. Externe bildungspolitische Akteure in der Russischen Föderation | Mit einem Vorwort von Frank Ettrich | ISBN 978-3-8382-0751-3

141 *Juri Plusnin, Yana Zausaeva, Natalia Zhidkevich, Artemy Pozanenko* | Wandering Workers. Mores, Behavior, Way of Life, and Political Status of Domestic Russian Labor Migrants | Translated by Julia Kazantseva | ISBN 978-3-8382-0653-0

142 *David J. Smith (eds.)* | Latvia – A Work in Progress? 100 Years of State- and Nation-Building | ISBN 978-3-8382-0648-6

143 *Инна Чувычкина (ред.)* | Экспортные нефте- и газопроводы на постсоветском пространстве. Анализ трубопроводной политики в свете теории международных отношений | ISBN 978-3-8382-0822-0

144 *Johann Zajaczkowski* | Russland – eine pragmatische Großmacht? Eine rollentheoretische Untersuchung russischer Außenpolitik am Beispiel der Zusammenarbeit mit den USA nach 9/11 und des Georgienkrieges von 2008 | Mit einem Vorwort von Siegfried Schieder | ISBN 978-3-8382-0837-4

145 *Boris Popivanov* | Changing Images of the Left in Bulgaria. The Challenge of Post-Communism in the Early 21st Century | ISBN 978-3-8382-0667-7

146 *Lenka Krátká* | A History of the Czechoslovak Ocean Shipping Company 1948-1989. How a Small, Landlocked Country Ran Maritime Business During the Cold War | ISBN 978-3-8382-0666-0

147 *Alexander Sergunin* | Explaining Russian Foreign Policy Behavior. Theory and Practice | ISBN 978-3-8382-0752-0

148 *Darya Malyutina* | Migrant Friendships in a Super-Diverse City. Russian-Speakers and their Social Relationships in London in the 21st Century | With a foreword by Claire Dwyer | ISBN 978-3-8382-0652-3

149 *Alexander Sergunin, Valery Konyshev* | Russia in the Arctic. Hard or Soft Power? | ISBN 978-3-8382-0753-7

150 *John J. Maresca* | Helsinki Revisited. A Key U.S. Negotiator's Memoirs on the Development of the CSCE into the OSCE | With a foreword by Hafiz Pashayev | ISBN 978-3-8382-0852-7

151 *Jardar Østbø* | The New Third Rome. Readings of a Russian Nationalist Myth | With a foreword by Pål Kolstø | ISBN 978-3-8382-0870-1

152 *Simon Kordonsky* | Socio-Economic Foundations of the Russian Post-Soviet Regime. The Resource-Based Economy and Estate-Based Social Structure of Contemporary Russia | With a foreword by Svetlana Barsukova | ISBN 978-3-8382-0775-9

153 *Duncan Leitch* | Assisting Reform in Post-Communist Ukraine 2000–2012. The Illusions of Donors and the Disillusion of Beneficiaries | With a foreword by Kataryna Wolczuk | ISBN 978-3-8382-0844-2

154 *Abel Polese* | Limits of a Post-Soviet State. How Informality Replaces, Renegotiates, and Reshapes Governance in Contemporary Ukraine | With a foreword by Colin Williams | ISBN 978-3-8382-0845-9

155 *Mikhail Suslov (ed.)* | Digital Orthodoxy in the Post-Soviet World. The Russian Orthodox Church and Web 2.0 | With a foreword by Father Cyril Hovorun | ISBN 978-3-8382-0871-8

156 *Leonid Luks* | Zwei „Sonderwege"? Russisch-deutsche Parallelen und Kontraste (1917-2014). Vergleichende Essays | ISBN 978-3-8382-0823-7

157 *Vladimir V. Karacharovskiy, Ovsey I. Shkaratan, Gordey A. Yastrebov* | Towards a New Russian Work Culture. Can Western Companies and Expatriates Change Russian Society? | With a foreword by Elena N. Danilova | Translated by Julia Kazantseva | ISBN 978-3-8382-0902-9

158 *Edmund Griffiths* | Aleksandr Prokhanov and Post-Soviet Esotericism | ISBN 978-3-8382-0903-6

159 *Timm Beichelt, Susann Worschech (eds.)* | Transnational Ukraine? Networks and Ties that Influence(d) Contemporary Ukraine | ISBN 978-3-8382-0944-9

160 *Mieste Hotopp-Riecke* | Die Tataren der Krim zwischen Assimilation und Selbstbehauptung. Der Aufbau des krimtatarischen Bildungswesens nach Deportation und Heimkehr (1990-2005) | Mit einem Vorwort von Swetlana Czerwonnaja | ISBN 978-3-89821-940-2

161 *Olga Bertelsen (ed.)* | Revolution and War in Contemporary Ukraine. The Challenge of Change | ISBN 978-3-8382-1016-2

162 *Natalya Ryabinska* | Ukraine's Post-Communist Mass Media. Between Capture and Commercialization | With a foreword by Marta Dyczok | ISBN 978-3-8382-1011-5

163 *Alexandra Cotofana, James M. Nyce (eds.)* | Religion and Magic in Socialist and Post-Socialist Contexts. Historic and Ethnographic Case Studies of Orthodoxy, Heterodoxy, and Alternative Spirituality | With a foreword by Patrick L. Michelson | ISBN 978-3-8382-0989-0

164 *Nozima Akhrarkhodjaeva* | The Instrumentalisation of Mass Media in Electoral Authoritarian Regimes. Evidence from Russia's Presidential Election Campaigns of 2000 and 2008 | ISBN 978-3-8382-1013-1

165 *Yulia Krasheninnikova* | Informal Healthcare in Contemporary Russia. Sociographic Essays on the Post-Soviet Infrastructure for Alternative Healing Practices | ISBN 978-3-8382-0970-8

166 *Peter Kaiser* | Das Schachbrett der Macht. Die Handlungsspielräume eines sowjetischen Funktionärs unter Stalin am Beispiel des Generalsekretärs des Komsomol Aleksandr Kosarev (1929-1938) | Mit einem Vorwort von Dietmar Neutatz | ISBN 978-3-8382-1052-0

167 *Oksana Kim* | The Effects and Implications of Kazakhstan's Adoption of International Financial Reporting Standards. A Resource Dependence Perspective | With a foreword by Svetlana Vlady | ISBN 978-3-8382-0987-6

168 *Anna Sanina* | Patriotic Education in Contemporary Russia. Sociological Studies in the Making of the Post-Soviet Citizen | With a foreword by Anna Oldfield | ISBN 978-3-8382-0993-7

169 *Rudolf Wolters* | Spezialist in Sibirien Faksimile der 1933 erschienenen ersten Ausgabe | Mit einem Vorwort von Dmitrij Chmelnizki | ISBN 978-3-8382-0515-1

170 *Michal Vít, Magdalena M. Baran (eds.)* | Transregional versus National Perspectives on Contemporary Central European History. Studies on the Building of Nation-States and Their Cooperation in the 20th and 21st Century | With a foreword by Petr Vágner | ISBN 978-3-8382-1015-5

171 *Philip Gamaghelyan* | Conflict Resolution Beyond the International Relations Paradigm. Evolving Designs as a Transformative Practice in Nagorno-Karabakh and Syria | With a foreword by Susan Allen | ISBN 978-3-8382-1057-5

172 *Maria Shagina* | Joining a Prestigious Club. Cooperation with Europarties and Its Impact on Party Development in Georgia, Moldova, and Ukraine 2004–2015 | With a foreword by Kataryna Wolczuk | ISBN 978-3-8382-1084-1

173 *Alexandra Cotofana, James M. Nyce (eds.)* | Religion and Magic in Socialist and Post-Socialist Contexts II. Baltic, Eastern European, and Post-USSR Case Studies | With a foreword by Anita Stasulane | ISBN 978-3-8382-0990-6

174 *Barbara Kunz* | Kind Words, Cruise Missiles, and Everything in Between. The Use of Power Resources in U.S. Policies towards Poland, Ukraine, and Belarus 1989–2008 | With a foreword by William Hill | ISBN 978-3-8382-1065-0

175 *Eduard Klein* | Bildungskorruption in Russland und der Ukraine. Eine komparative Analyse der Performanz staatlicher Antikorruptionsmaßnahmen im Hochschulsektor am Beispiel universitärer Aufnahmeprüfungen | Mit einem Vorwort von Heiko Pleines | ISBN 978-3-8382-0995-1

176 *Markus Soldner* | Politischer Kapitalismus im postsowjetischen Russland. Die politische, wirtschaftliche und mediale Transformation in den 1990er Jahren | Mit einem Vorwort von Wolfgang Ismayr | ISBN 978-3-8382-1222-7

177 *Anton Oleinik* | Building Ukraine from Within. A Sociological, Institutional, and Economic Analysis of a Nation-State in the Making | ISBN 978-3-8382-1150-3

178 *Peter Rollberg, Marlene Laruelle (eds.)* | Mass Media in the Post-Soviet World. Market Forces, State Actors, and Political Manipulation in the Informational Environment after Communism | ISBN 978-3-8382-1116-9

179 *Mikhail Minakov* | Development and Dystopia Studies in Post-Soviet Ukraine and Eastern Europe | With a foreword by Alexander Etkind | ISBN 978-3-8382-1112-1

180 *Aijan Sharshenova* | The European Union's Democracy Promotion in Central Asia A Study of Political Interests, Influence, and Development in Kazakhstan and Kyrgyzstan in 2007–2013 | With a foreword by Gordon Crawford | ISBN 978-3-8382-1151-0

181 *Andrey Makarychev, Alexandra Yatsyk (eds.)* | Boris Nemtsov and Russian Politics. Power and Resistance | With a foreword by Zhanna Nemtsova | ISBN 978-3-8382-1122-0

182 *Sophie Falsini* | The Euromaidan's Effect on Civil Society. Why and How Ukrainian Social Capital Increased after the Revolution of Dignity | With a foreword by Susann Worschech | ISBN 978-3-8382-1131-2

183 *Andreas Umland (ed.)* | Ukraine's Decentralization Challenges and Implications of the Local Governance Reform after the Euromaidan Revolution | ISBN 978-3-8382-1162-6

184 *Leonid Luks* | A Fateful Triangle. Essays on Contemporary Russian, German and Polish History | ISBN 978-3-8382-1143-5

185 *John B. Dunlop* | The February 2015 Assassination of Boris Nemtsov and the Flawed Trial of his Alleged Killers. An Exploration of Russia's "Crime of the 21st Century" | ISBN 978-3-8382-1188-6

186 *Vasile Rotaru* | Russia, the EU, and the Eastern Partnership. Building Bridges or Digging Trenches? | ISBN 978-3-8382-1134-3

187 *Marina Lebedeva* | Russian Studies of International Relations. From the Soviet Past to the Post-Cold-War Present | With a foreword by Andrei P. Tsygankov | ISBN 978-3-8382-0851-0

188 *Tomasz Stępniewski, George Soroka (eds.)* | Ukraine after Maidan. Revisiting Domestic and Regional Security | ISBN 978-3-8382-1075-9

189 *Petar Cholakov* | Ethnic Entrepreneurs Unmasked. Political Institutions and Ethnic Conflicts in Contemporary Bulgaria | ISBN 978-3-8382-1189-3

190 *A. Salem, G. Hazeldine, D. Morgan (eds.)* | Higher Education in Post-Communist States. Comparative and Sociological Perspectives | ISBN 978-3-8382-1183-1

191 *Igor Torbakov* | After Empire. Nationalist Imagination and Symbolic Politics in Russia and Eurasia in the Twentieth and Twenty-First Century | With a foreword by Serhii Plokhy | ISBN 978-3-8382-1217-3

192 *Aleksandr Burakovskiy* | Jewish-Ukrainian Relations in Late and Post-Soviet Ukraine. Articles, Lectures and Essays from 1986 to 2016 | ISBN 978-3-8382-1210-4

193 *Natalia Shapovalova, Olga Burlyuk (eds.)* | Civil Society in Post-Euromaidan Ukraine. From Revolution to Consolidation | With a foreword by Richard Youngs | ISBN 978-3-8382-1216-6

194 *Franz Preissler* | Positionsverteidigung, Imperialismus oder Irredentismus? Russland und die „Russischsprachigen", 1991–2015 | ISBN 978-3-8382-1262-3

195 *Marian Madeła* | Der Reformprozess in der Ukraine 2014-2017. Eine Fallstudie zur Reform der öffentlichen Verwaltung | Mit einem Vorwort von Martin Malek | ISBN 978-3-8382-1266-1

196 *Anke Giesen* | „Wie kann denn der Sieger ein Verbrecher sein?" Eine diskursanalytische Untersuchung der russlandweiten Debatte über Konzept und Verstaatlichungsprozess der Lagergedenkstätte „Perm'-36" im Ural | ISBN 978-3-8382-1284-5

197 *Alla Leukavets* | The Integration Policies of Belarus and Ukraine vis-à-vis the EU and Russia. A Comparative Case Study Through the Lenses of a Two-Level Games Approach | ISBN 978-3-8382-1247-0

198 *Oksana Kim* | The Development and Challenges of Russian Corporate Governance I. The Roles and Functions of Boards of Directors | With a foreword by Sheila M. Puffer | ISBN 978-3-8382-1287-6

199 *Thomas D. Grant* | International Law and the Post-Soviet Space I. Essays on Chechnya and the Baltic States | With a foreword by Stephen M. Schwebel | ISBN 978-3-8382-1279-1

200 *Thomas D. Grant* | International Law and the Post-Soviet Space II. Essays on Ukraine, Intervention, and Non-Proliferation | With a foreword by Stephen M. Schwebel | ISBN 978-3-8382-1280-7

201 *Slavomir Michalek, Michal Stefansky* | The Age of Fear. The Cold War and Its Influence on Czechoslovakia 1945–1968 | ISBN 978-3-8382-1285-2

202 *Iulia-Sabina Joja* | Romania's Strategic Culture 1990–2014. Continuity and Change in a Post-Communist Country's Evolution of National Interests and Security Policies | With a foreword by Heiko Biehl | ISBN 978-3-8382-1286-9

203 *Andrei Rogatchevski, Yngvar B. Steinholt, Arve Hansen, David-Emil Wickström* | War of Songs. Popular Music and Recent Russia-Ukraine Relations | With a foreword by Artemy Troitsky | ISBN 978-3-8382-1173-2

204 *Maria Lipman (ed.)* | Russian Voices on Post-Crimea Russia. An Almanac of Counterpoint Essays from 2015–2018 | ISBN 978-3-8382-1251-7

205 *Ksenia Maksimovtsova* | Language Conflicts in Contemporary Estonia, Latvia, and Ukraine. A Comparative Exploration of Discourses in Post-Soviet Russian-Language Digital Media | With a foreword by Ammon Cheskin | ISBN 978-3-8382-1282-1

ibidem.eu